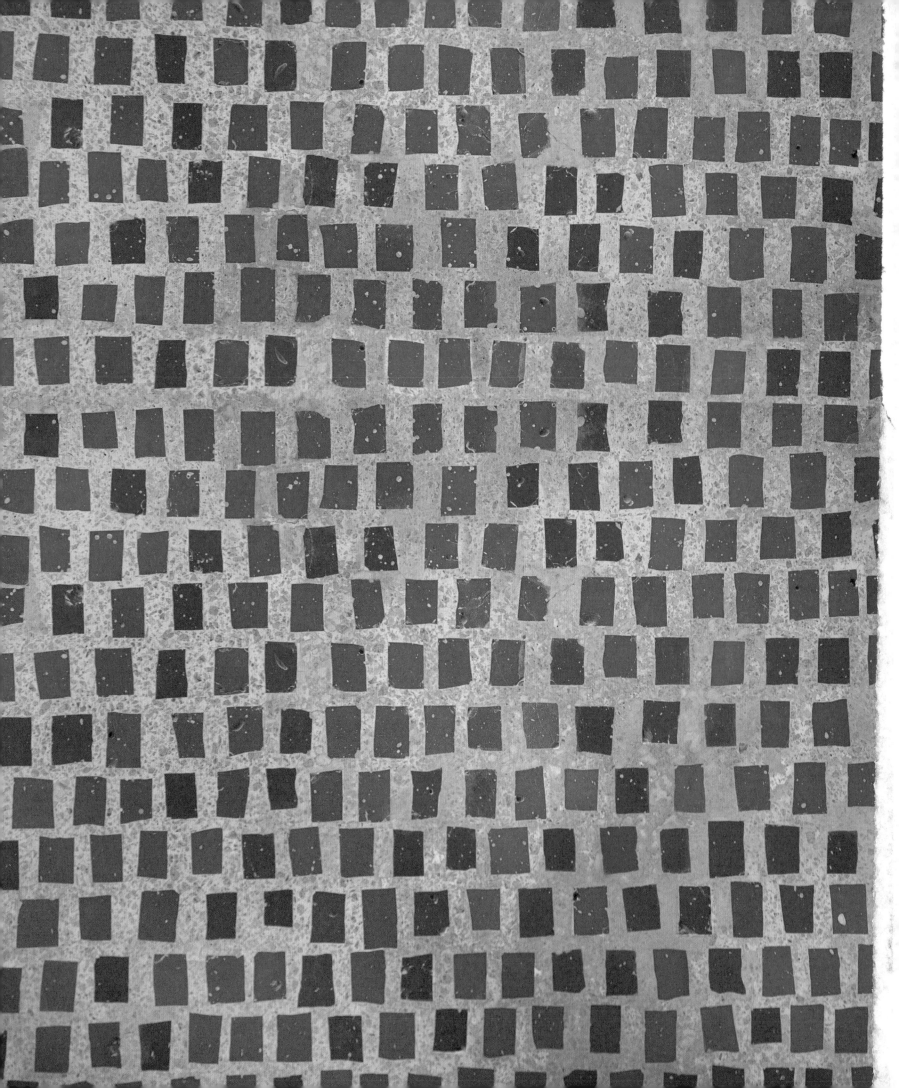

Key Interiors Since 1900

Graeme Brooker

Published in 2013
by Laurence King Publishing Ltd
361–373 City Road
London EC1V 1LR
Tel +44 20 7841 6900
Fax +44 20 7841 6910
E enquiries@laurenceking.com
www.laurenceking.com

A catalogue record for this book is available from the British Library

ISBN 978 178067 268 7
Designed by The Urban Ant Ltd
Original design concept by Jason Godfrey
Project managed by Henrietta Heald
Picture research by Sophia Gibb
Printed in China

Key Interiors Since 1900

Graeme Brooker

Laurence King Publishing

Contents

Chapter 4: Display

Chapter 5: Leisure

Chapter 6: Culture

Introduction
A particular history

History is one of a series of discourses about the world. These discourses do not create the world but they do appropriate it and give it all the meaning it has.[1]

This book outlines a history of modern interior architecture and design, told through a selection of spaces designed since 1900, each created autonomously within the envelope of an existing building. Whilst the architectural container or context is acknowledged in every case, the interiors have all been created in a historically and stylistically independent manner. These interiors thus constitute what might be considered 'exemplary' forms of interior space. In other words, the creation of interior space through

reuse – independently of, as opposed to simultaneously with, the envelope in which they are contained – most clearly highlights the archetypal forms of interior architecture and design.

The history of interior architecture and design is often outlined in parallel with the development of architecture. But the process of creating an interior is quite different from the process of making architecture, a procedure where 'new build' is the primary form of spatial expression. The creation of an interior is generally based on an understanding of, and a working in conjunction with, existing spaces and buildings. Whether the existing component of this process is a real building, or merely the outline of a project drawn

on a screen or a page, the given space
will often provide the impetus for the
design and hence the creation of the
interior space. Therefore the history
of interior architecture and design
cannot adequately be articulated by a
history of architecture – the enclosure
within which it is contained.

This approach excludes many buildings
that house what may be considered
'classic' examples of modern spaces,
including interiors that have been
used to delineate the discourse of the
broader history of the built environment.
However, the general history of the
built environment and its associated
canon is already well covered. The
hope is that this approach will allow the
history of interior space to be viewed

as a distinct entity, independent of
the established norms of other built
environment histories – particularly
architecture – and enable the discipline
of the design of interior space in
existing buildings to develop its own
spatial and historical discourse.

It is widely acknowledged that
the design of the interior is a
multidisciplinary and diverse practice.
It is a process that is undertaken by
many built environment specialists,
ranging from designers and architects
to installation artists, decorators and
conservationists. It is a field of study
that is primarily engaged with the
creation of a range of environments
that articulate a multiplicity of
spatial functions and identities.

The understanding of inside space
can involve a broad and expansive
enquiry – one that touches upon
a wide range of spatial subjects,
including buildings, the environment,
human occupation, scenography,
performative environments and issues
concerning materiality and the body. It
might involve pragmatic issues, such
as fabrication, or it might concern
more esoteric circumstances, such
as the psychological or atmospheric
conditions of inside space. Whatever
form or function an interior manifests,
and whatever qualities it communicates,
the end product is always the result of
a diverse and assorted range of spatial
processes and practices.

Reusing buildings

*Broadly speaking, for the interior
designer, there will be two approaches:
the first is the integrated, where the
interior is indivisible from the structure
and where pattern, form, texture and
lighting are part of the architecture,
and qualities of permanence and
monumentality are sought. The
second, which may be termed the
'Superimposed', is where the interior is
required to be more flexible and easily
modified or even transformed without
mutilating the architecture in which it is
temporarily contained.*[2]

The reuse of existing buildings to create
interior space allows the designer to
select and choose how to construct and
form space via the information derived
from the existing environment. As Hugh
Casson suggested in his influential
1968 book on interiors, *Inscape*, this
may manifest itself in two ways: as an
integrated interior, where old and new
are difficult to separate, or as one
where the interior is pronounced,
creating a distinctive layer inside the
extant space. Whichever method or
approach is taken, it is clear that the
existing and the new share a close
relationship, and both respond in some
way to each other's qualities.

The other distinguishing feature of
an interior is its close connection
to inhabitation and occupation. The
interior is often cited as the barometer
of the culture and life of its inhabitants.
As Bourdieu states:

*The interior marks the perspective
of the subject, his relationship to
himself and to the world.*[3]

Interior space encloses the daily
routines of human life. Different
spaces will invoke different responses,
depending on their function and
organization, their history and
atmosphere, and their environmental
and material conditions. At the centre of
this activity is the 'room' – an enclosure
of space within which occupancy, in
its myriad forms, takes place. In the
chapters of this book, 'occupancy'
is used to describe use rather than
function. This is in order to suggest
the looser, more ambiguous form of
inhabitation reflected by the adaptation
of existing buildings for new use.

The precise qualities of functionalism
– which is a central principle of
Modernism – generally prevent any
spatial ambiguities, as indicated by

the aphorism 'form follows function'.
When buildings are reused, however,
function becomes a highly flexible
element of the design process.
The new form will follow the new
occupation rather than the previous
function, albeit possibly influenced
by the old form of the building.
So the reuse of buildings is more
correctly described through patterns
of occupation. Rodolfo Machado
clearly states this when talking about
functionalism and form in his seminal
essay 'Old Buildings as Palimpsest':

*Another element that can increase
the potential for criticism [in
remodelling] is the notion of 'type'
in architecture. Through it one can
easily conceive of a remodelling
activity that deals with the notion
of type transformation. This could
be the most critical function
remodelling could offer, considering
the antithesis toward the notion
of type in the premise of the
modern movement.*[4]

Left Lehrer Architects' own office, housed in a huge open-plan warehouse in Silverlake, Los Angeles, USA.

Below The reception of the Una Hotel Vittoria in Florence, Italy, by Fabio Novembre. The entrance area is dominated by a loop of mosaic tiles that flow through the reception to form the desk.

The interior canon

In contrast to history's linear composition, canons can be composed of diverse juxtapositions, where seemingly diverse types, different time frames and cultures can be brought together as a singular concept.[5]

The development of a canon, a list of key moments in history, will always be contentious. The outlines of the discipline of interior space are ambiguous and fluid, a position that arguably requires a nimble and dexterous approach, but which also allows the subject to be constantly redefined – in my view, a positive attribute. The evolution of the interior as a discipline with its own theoretical

underpinning and histories must be mapped out in order to reinforce the perception of this as a substantial discipline in its own right.

Interior architecture, design and decoration are subjects that are quite often perceived as intellectually lightweight. The teaching and understanding of interiors have generally had to rely on spatial, sociological and even literary theory and supposition, using ideas that never really quite fit. This has, in turn, created the lack of a philosophical 'identity', distinct from other built environment disciplines. The result has been a paucity of serious publications underpinning the

independent history and theory of the subject.

The prominence of the interior on television and in the media, in the form of cosmetic makeover shows, however misrepresentative of the discipline, suggests an appetite for its understanding and consumption. At this point in time, in the UK, the USA and around the world, the discipline has attained a unique status, allowing critical assessment through both existing and new sets of parameters. I hope that this book will not only contribute to a much-needed body of knowledge in this sphere, but also add to these changes and outline a history of the discipline at this critical juncture.

About this book

As mentioned above, this book is organized around forms of 'occupation'. The ambiguity inherent in the description of the six spatial types that constitute the chapters of this book hopefully makes explicit the loose fit of interior and building envelope. The six forms of occupation are: Home, Work, Shop, Display, Leisure and Culture. Each chapter includes an introductory contextual essay that explores ideas and earlier developments in each particular category. This is then followed by a series of historical and contemporary exemplary interiors, which are analysed in more depth. Each case study is contextualized by location, immediate environment and exterior or architectural envelope. It is then examined in depth by establishing its relationship and position within the existing building, its planning and organization of rooms, its form and structure, detail and furnishing, atmosphere, colour and materiality. This information is arranged under the headings of Context, Concept, Organization and Detail – four key stages in the process of making interior space. Formal drawings, such as plans and sections, alongside diagrams, sketches and photographs support the case studies throughout.

1 Keith Jenkins, *Re-thinking History*, Routledge, 1991, p.5

2 Hugh Casson, *Inscape*, Architectural Press, 1968, p.17

3 Pierre Bourdieu, *Distinction: A Social Critique of the Judgement of Taste*, translated by Richard Nice, Harvard University Press, 1984, p.128

4 Rodolfo Machado, 'Old Buildings as Palimpsest', *Progressive Architecture*, November 1976, p.49

5 Suzie Attiwill, 'What's in a Canon?', in Edward Hollis et al. (editors), *Thinking Inside the Box: A Reader in Interiors for the 21st Century*, Middlesex University Press, 2007, p.65

Left The kitchen area of Allan Wexler's Crate House, an experimental house that is divided into the essential elements required for a living space.

There is no way of isolating living experience from spatial experience.[1]

The home, more than any other interior space, offers a clear indication of the constant and changing nature of patterns of social activity. Domestic space is a personal reflection of its inhabitants – a sign of their values and aspirations, a record of their character, culture and lifestyle. Therefore adapting a building in order to *house* its new inhabitants always places an emphasis upon the relationship and connections between both the lived experience of the space and its new occupation.

Domestic space often comprises a series of rooms that perform various domestic functions, such as cooking, eating, sleeping, relaxing and washing. The home will also enclose more esoteric entities such as memories, collections of objects and sentimental items – matter that has been solidified by the rituals of everyday life until it represents a person not only to themselves but also to other people. Therefore, when adapting a building to make a home, the composite of meanings, from the past, present and the future, form a complex weave of

material and immaterial conditions. These are circumstances and situations that the designer can select and edit as required. As Doris Salcedo suggested in the above quotation, both spatial and living experiences are entwined to such an extent that there is no way of unpicking or separating them. The making of a home in an existing building always involves the amalgamation and manipulation of both lived and about-to-be-lived experiences.

The developed surface

The interior emerged in addition to constructional, ornamental and surface definitions of inside space that were architectural. The interior was articulated through decoration, the literal covering of the inside of an architectural 'shell' with the soft 'stuff' of furnishing.[2]

The history of the home, created from reusing existing buildings, is a narrative that consists of the relationships between the past, present and future. The family house created by Sir John Soane between 1792 and 1823 epitomizes this narrative. Soane remodelled three adjoining London townhouses in Lincoln's Inn Fields

to create his family home. A striking feature of the interior of the house was the placement of objects that Soane had collected on his travels – a habit that from 1811 grew into an obsession, fuelled by the refusal of his sons to follow him into the profession of architecture.

What began as an understandable aspiration for an heir soured into an obsessive dream.[3]

Traditional collectables such as prints and paintings were accumulated and displayed in the house, alongside objects as diverse as death masks, casts and even a tomb (the sarcophagus of King Seti of Egypt, which was placed in the basement). Each object was carefully positioned in the interior. The density of these clustered objects embodied the obsessive and compulsive nature of Soane, the fervent collector.

In Soane's house the connection between the past, lived experience and the present was contained in this collection. The casts, statues and reliquary souvenirs that were attached to the walls and surfaces

CHAPTER 1 # Home

Right Looking east across the collection of objects in the dome area of the Soane Museum. A bust of Soane by Sir Francis Leggatt Chantrey is placed at the centre of the balustrade.

of the building formed a lining of the architectural envelope and created a skin that was independent of the existing shell and one that reflected the past back to the occupants. Soane's house exemplifies the close connection between lived and spatial experience. It also embodies the notion of the domestic interior as essentially a surface condition, a lining of an existing building shell – a condition that is, as Charles Rice suggested above, one of the defining characteristics of the nature of interior space.

Modernism and the home

The beginning of the twentieth century was dominated by the reformative zeal of Modernism, which concerned itself, amongst other things, with the function of domestic space – culminating with the infamous claim by Le Corbusier that the house was a machine, and one that was to be lived in.[4] The use of the machine analogy and the generally prevalent precise qualities of functionalism that it embodied eschewed any ambiguities in spatial form. Functionalism, a central principle of Modernism, was characterized by a rigid orthodoxy, one that was a decisive factor when designing and constructing a building. Its aphorism 'form follows function' suggested a rigid and inflexible bond between space and its use.

When buildings are adapted to accept new forms of occupation, determinant functionalist tendencies are considerably weakened. Although function might have initially shaped the building that is to be reused, its adaptation for a new use supersedes its original function. The old use can be considered redundant. Function is a flexible aspect of the design process in reuse. When the building envelope is adapted to contain a new form of occupation, new form does not follow the previous function. Instead new form will follow new occupation, possibly influenced by the old form of the building. The reuse of buildings is more correctly described through patterns or rituals of occupation. Therefore the determinant functionalist ideals of

Above left The Frankfurt Kitchen by Margarete Schütte-Lihotzky.

Above The Pao for the Nomad Woman, an installation in a department store exploring new ways of living in the city.

Below House of the Future, an experimental home shown at the Ideal Home Exhibition of 1956 predicting what domestic space might be like in the 1980s.

Modernism do not make sense when the function of a building changes through reoccupation and a new use.

This is not to say that Modernism was not important in the history of reusing buildings. The machine aesthetic of Functionalism may find expression in the history of domestic interiors in the reuse of buildings through technological innovations. New developments of servicing technologies, such as heating and plumbing, lighting and structure, as well as research into new arrangements of space led to many new innovations and experiments in the home. The Frankfurt Kitchen was installed in 10,000 homes in post-World War I Germany in order to modernize its social housing programme. The first fitted kitchen, designed by Margarete Schütte-Lihotzky in 1926–7, radically changed domestic space, with a room for cooking and preparing food that contained built-in cupboards, integrated appliances and even a foldaway ironing board. All were precisely worked out in order to create an efficient

and effortless space, one that drew inspiration from American social reformer Christine Frederick's research into space efficiency.

Throughout the twentieth century the house was often used as a speculative device, a predictor of the future and a leitmotif of change. In the *Daily Mail*-sponsored Ideal Home Exhibition in London in 1956, the British designers Alison and Peter Smithson designed and constructed a one-bedroom house with a garden inside the main hall of the exhibition space. The futuristic house was set in 1980, was constructed from ply and clad in moulded plastic, with built-in appliances serviced by invisible plumbing and under-floor heating.

The Smithsons' design imagined a future of endless raw materials yet their forward thinking included a silver foil roof to repel the rays of an overbearing sun and a direct link to a local nuclear power station, one that provided a constant source of energy to the house. Mobile furniture included a kitchen that

could be moved to wherever it was needed and a bed that was sunk into the floor when not in use.

The proposition that the home can act as a symbol of the future has also manifested in projected ideas of how cities change and influence patterns of occupation and the daily rituals of urban life. The 'Pao for the Nomad Woman' was an installation in the Seibu department store in Shibuya, Tokyo, designed in 1985 by Toyo Ito. Ito suggested that:

> Those who live in cities today are no longer able to create their own living cycle solely around their house. Instead, their life is made up like a collage of superficial but diverse experiences.[5]

The tent was erected on the shop floor of the department store and was intended to represent the dwelling required for a young, female citizen of the city. This woman ate out every day and night, socialized in the city, relaxed in the theatre and the cinema,

and washed and exercised in the gym and health club. Her wardrobe was either the dry cleaner or the locker at the health club where she started and finished her day. As Ito explained:

> The nomad woman of Tokyo plays her performance not in the secluded, privately owned house, but everywhere in the city. For her, restaurants, boutiques and all the urban installations can be a stage on which she 'lives', like an actress under the spotlight.[6]

Ito suggested that the Pao was the appropriate form of dwelling space as it represented the fast-changing pace of the modern city. The temporary shelter could be adapted to accommodate any future additions that this new urban condition may have required. Ordinary elements of a domestic space, such as kitchen, bathroom and lounge were no longer needed since the nomad woman ate and socialized outside the home. All she required was a bed to sleep in.

Readymade domestic space

It is no longer a matter of starting with a 'blank slate' or creating meaning on the basis of virgin material but of finding a means of insertion into the innumerable flows of production.[7]

If the early twentieth century can be characterized by Modernism and the orthodoxies of Functionalism, then recycling, reuse and the idea of the readymade distinguish the late twentieth and early twenty-first centuries. Recycling, sustainability and reuse in general is a compelling narrative that views the world as a limited resource. This is manifest in the reuse of buildings and objects in order to contain new uses as opposed to demolition and new-build. The reuse of existing buildings implies a strategy that is akin to the appropriation of 'found' objects. Much like the restitution of found fragments, the notion of reusing what is already extant can involve the import of unusual strategies and objects with which to realize a project. The design of a home can thus be made distinct by the choice and selection of unusual sites and objects. This chimes with current concerns in cultural production, where the reuse of the existing has been likened, by commentators such as Nicolas Bourriaud, to the processes of post-production in film-making.

The term 'readymade' was coined by Marcel Duchamp:

> *At another time – wanting to expose the basic antimony between art and readymades – I imagined a 'reciprocal readymade': use a Rembrandt as an ironing board.*[8]

Readymades share characteristics with the adaptation and changing of extant buildings. Gordon Matta-Clark treated found buildings as experiments – he could 'undo' them and in turn communicate hidden or previously unseen relationships and connections between space and people. In some respects his work was about exploring the dialect between interior and exterior and transforming buildings so that they no longer read as straightforward polarities in this conversation. He stated:

> *The determining factor is the degree to which my intervention can transform the structure into an act of communication. I see the work as a special stage in perpetual metamorphosis, a model for people's constant action on space as much as the space that surrounds them.*[9]

His most significant work on existing buildings took place on houses and, in particular, the exploration of the spaces in and between the interior and exterior.

In 'Splitting', a house in Englewood, New Jersey, the house was opened with a single cut down the middle of the building. This cut was accentuated by the removal of one side of the masonry pedestal that the building sat on. The 'split' was formed by the tilt of the house, a gap that expanded at the top of the building to a foot wide. Some visitors felt nervous in the house due to its instability, whilst others enjoyed the risk of 'crossing the divide' as they ascended the interior of the building.

Other types of 'readymades' can be seen in the work of designers who utilize 'off-the-peg' objects to realize a project. LOT-EK completed the reuse of the fourth floor of a former New York car park, turning it into an apartment and installing a petrol tank (appropriated from the back of a lorry) to create the bedrooms and bathrooms. The container bulkheads, installed inside the tank to control the movement of the liquid when in transit, matched the size of a mattress, and, when placed vertically in the space, had enough height for a two-storey shower room and toilet. Hydraulically operated openings relieved the claustrophobic potential of the interior of the capsule.

The choice of unusual objects and buildings, and found or readymade spaces and elements, which are then converted into homes forms a narrative superseding the rigid orthodoxy that constitutes a tight and fixed bind between form and function. The history of unusual and often spectacularly reused buildings illustrates a desire to live in spaces that are highly personal. There is an alternative to demolition for all forms of building that is sustainable and provides unusual and distinct places for people to inhabit. Redundant churches, warehouses, power and generating stations, remnants of water towers, grain silos, wartime bunkers, public houses, farm buildings, theatres, bank buildings and shops are being retained and imaginatively adapted in order to accommodate new ways of living. This chapter includes a series of case studies that examine the reuse of buildings to form houses that all offer new ways of occupying domestic space. Each one explores the connections between the past and the present, and the lived and spatial experiences of a space, in order to redefine what new forms of living in existing buildings can mean.

1 Doris Salcedo, cited in Carlos Basualdo, *Doris Salcedo*, Phaidon Press, 2000, p.17

2 Charles Rice, *The Emergence of the Interior*, Routledge, 2007, p.3

3 Susan Feinberg, 'The Genesis of Sir John Soane's Museum Idea', *Journal of the Society of Architectural Historians*, vol. 43, 1984, p.225

4 Le Corbusier, *Vers une architecture*, first published in 1923 as a series of articles in *L'Esprit Nouveau*. Reissued by Dover Publications, 1985, p.227

5 Toyo Ito, 'The Pao for a Nomad Woman', *Japan Architecture*, July 1986, p.44

6 *Ibid.*

7 Nicolas Bourriaud, *Postproduction. Culture as Screenplay: How Art Reprograms the World*, Lukas and Sternberg, 2010, p.13

8 Marcel Duchamp, 'Apropos of Readymades' (1961 MoMA lecture), cited in David Evans, *Appropriation*, Whitechapel Gallery/MIT Press, 2009, p.40

9 Gordon Matta-Clark, 'The Greene Street Years' in *Gordon Matta-Clark* (exhibition catalogue), IVAM Centre, 1993, p.361

Left In an apartment designed by LOT-EK, the bedrooms and bathrooms are located in two petrol tanks, one placed vertically in the loft and the other fixed horizontally across the space.

PROJECT   **Maison de Verre**

DESIGNERS   Pierre Chareau, Bernard Bijvoet (assistant) and Louis Dalbert (metalwork)

LOCATION   Paris, France

DATE   1928–31

Above The large double-height salon of the Maison de Verre.

Left The glass façade glows at night when seen from the courtyard entrance.

Context

The Maison de Verre (House of Glass) was built in an unpretentious courtyard site in a traditional, quiet, leafy street on Paris's Left Bank. It was built to house Dr Jean Dalsace and his family. It was also designed to accommodate the doctor's gynaecology practice. The original building was a four-storey eighteenth-century townhouse that Dalsace purchased with the intention of demolishing it completely.

Concept

The light circulates freely through this block, the first floor of which is devoted to medicine, the second floor to social life and the third to night-time privacy.[1]

Chareau understood the Dalsace family well enough to realize that the balance between public and private spaces, working and socializing, was sometimes quite fluid. This house was therefore conceived as a bespoke interior, a carefully measured space that was designed to fit the exact requirements of its inhabitants. This manifested itself in two ways: the direct and easy spatial connections between work and domestic space and the central location of the 'salon', the main entertaining space of the house.

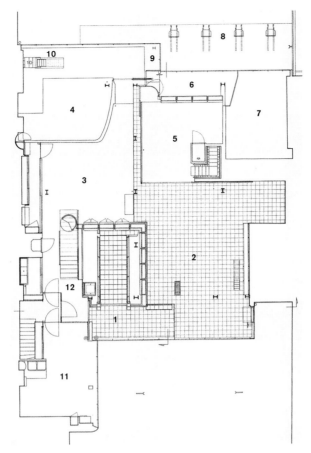

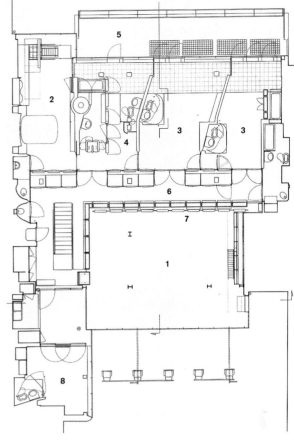

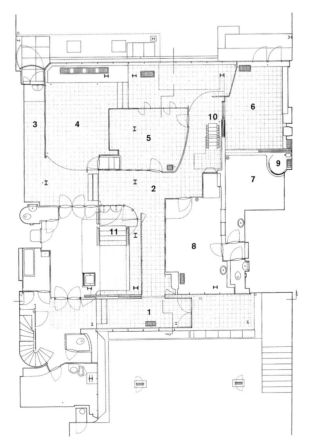

Left Ground-floor plan.
1 Entrance lobby
2 Main corridor
3 Passage leading to garden
4 Waiting room
5 Reception
6 Doctor's consulting room
7 Examination room
8 Surgery
9 Changing room
10 Stairs to study
11 Main stairs to salon

Above First-floor plan.
1 Landing
2 Main salon
3 Dining room
4 Sitting room
5 Study
6/7 Voids
8 Lights
9 Conservatory
10 Retractable stairs to master bedroom
11 Kitchen
12 Stairs to mezzanine

Above left Second-floor plan.
1 Void over salon
2 Master bedroom
3 Bedroom
4 Master bathroom
5 Terrace
6 Corridor/gallery
7 Storage units/balustrade
8 Maid's quarters

The original four-storey house was enclosed on all sides by party walls of varying heights. It had a forecourt and a garden to the rear. The Dalsaces had intended to demolish the whole building, but because of a tenant who refused to move from her top-floor apartment, Chareau had to devise a new strategy with which to realize the house. He demolished the lower two floors of the house and retained the top two storeys of the building, along with its existing access staircase. The upper floors were then supported on new slender steel columns. The volume that resulted from this demolition was big enough to allow three new floors to be inserted into the existing space.

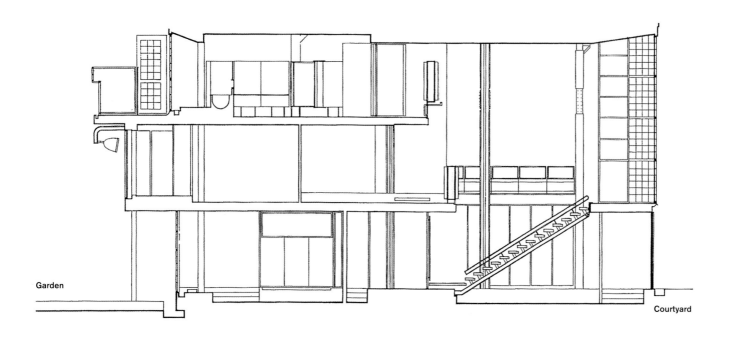

Garden

Courtyard

Left The construction of the house under the retained existing building ensured that the compact three floors of the garden side of the building could be counterpointed by the light and airy double-height salon on the courtyard side.

Above Cupboards with a pale-ash-veneer backing are positioned on the second-floor mezzanine balcony in order to facilitate storage and to screen the sleeping quarters from view.

Above The full-height glass-brick wall floods the main salon with natural light. This dramatic and elegant room was used as the main living space as well as for the purpose of entertaining.

Organization

The house was planned to contain the doctor's practice, combined with a family home, supported by a maid's quarters. The practice was located on the ground floor, the first floor was the living space and the second floor was the private sleeping quarters.

A narrow service wing of three floors was built into the forecourt as an extension to the house and this contained the kitchen, workroom and a maid's quarters. The front and back of the new house were sheathed in a new translucent glass-brick screen wall, which was cantilevered clear of the new structure to create a free façade. This opaque skin created an insular space that allowed natural light to flood into the interior but did not let the view out.

Above The new structural frame made of bolted and riveted black-and-orange steel columns supported the floor and walls of both the new and existing houses.

Top Openings in the glass wall were on the garden side of the house. Ground-floor windows were opened inwards with a winding wheel situated lower down on the steel frame.

The doctor's practice on the ground floor comprised a reception and waiting room, consulting and examination room, and a small space for surgery. A stair near the consulting room led up to a first-floor small study, or office, on the garden side of the house, connecting the lower-floor clinic with the living level and allowing the doctor to move effortlessly between the two.

The main living quarters on the first floor included a dining room and a large double-height salon, adjacent to the courtyard. Throughout the 1930s the house hosted gatherings of intellectuals, poets and musicians, and this double-height room was treated like a performance space, where recitals and social gatherings ensured that the family were at the epicentre of Parisian bourgeois life.

A balcony room on first-floor level projected into the garden. This was Annie Dalsace's boudoir. A small retractable ladder afforded the occupant direct access to the upper-level master bedroom.
The second-floor mezzanine level contained the bedrooms and bathrooms of the private family area. The master bedroom and the children's rooms all had their own bathrooms. Every room opened on to a large terrace that overlooked the garden.

The interior walls of the house were non-load-bearing and were organized independently of the steel columns of the building, freeing them from any structural responsibilities. Chareau was therefore free to shape the rooms and walls of the interior in any way that he saw fit.

Above The doctor's practice situated on the ground floor. The rubber flooring throughout reinforced its clinical qualities.

Above right The main staircase leading up to the first floor. Toughened-glass panels can be pulled across the lower level in order to separate the house from the practice.

Right Dr Dalsace's consulting room on the ground floor with a view to the garden.

Opposite, above One of the children's rooms, with en-suite bathroom.

Opposite, below The shower and bath unit of the master bathroom. The flexible nature of the room is exemplified by movable walls and multi-purpose storage units.

Detail

The Maison de Verre has established a significant position in design history based upon the groundbreaking use of a particular material. The house became known as 'The Transparent House' because of the glass-brick exterior envelope wall. Chareau also used the commission to perfect new prototypes of furniture and mechanical components. The house is often described as a 'machine for living in', and was considered comparable to the Villa Savoye, another seminal early-twentieth-century Modernist house.

The spatial identity of both the house and the practice was developed from a similar palette of materials. Dr Dalsace's practice ensured that a clinical and functional materiality was adopted throughout much of the building. Rubber flooring was used throughout the ground floor and also the living quarters of the house. The multiplicity of washbasins and showers in the bedrooms suggested a dedicated approach to cleanliness. Carefully considered, easily cleanable materials such as steel and ceramic tiles completed the palette of materials. This functional language was only relaxed in the more intimate areas of the house, such as the boudoir, where carpet was utilized, and in the bedrooms, where timber and tiles were used on the floors.

Chareau chose materials and details that were often derived from industrial practices and techniques. Mobile library ladders, sliding doors, bookcases and stairs were constructed using Louis Dalbert's considerable expertise in steel fabrication. Moving clerestory shutters, sliding partitions and rotating screen walls were executed with industrial precision. All moving components, such as the mobile perforated steel screens used to shield the more private aspects of the bathrooms, were balanced on rollers and could thus be moved quietly and effortlessly.

The only openings in the glass façade were located on the garden side of the house, where Chareau used railway carriage windows, made of

vertically sliding plate glass. Ventilation shutters, operated by turning a huge steel wheel, were positioned in the salon, and allowed fresh air into the main room. Throughout the house, mechanical services, such as cabling and ventilation, were hidden discreetly in separate vertical tubes. Polished lacquered vents set into the floors of the rooms were the only visible signs of the presence of the channelled air.

The Maison de Verre was recognized as a functionalist masterpiece and an important building in the development of the Modern movement. In the history of building reuse it is an exemplar of the unique fusion between function and occupant.

1 Dr Dalsace, quoted in Rene Herbst, *Un inventeur l'architecte*, Pierre Chareau, 1954, Paris, pp.7–8; cited in Kenneth Frampton, *Pierre Chareau – Architect and Craftsman*, Thames and Hudson, 1985, p.239

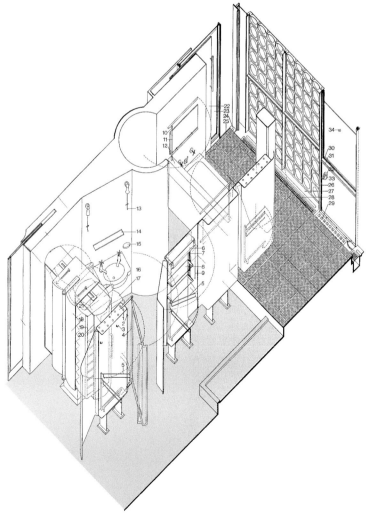

Beistegui Apartment

PROJECT

DESIGNERS
Le Corbusier;
décor and furniture
by Carlos de Beistegui
and Emilio Terry

LOCATION
Paris, France

DATE
1929–31

Above The garden 'room' of the apartment with its high walls that edited views of the city.

Left The apartment was built on top of an apartment block on the Champs Elysées.

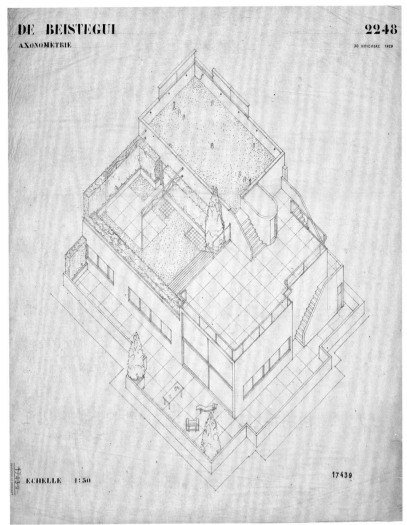

Above left A sketch of the room, showing the intended relationship with the city.

Above An axonometric drawing of the apartment.

Context

This rooftop penthouse was constructed on top of an undistinguished nineteenth-century apartment block on the prestigious Champs-Élysées in Paris. It was built for the wealthy client Carlos (Charles) de Bestegui. The penthouse was not intended to be a full-time residence for Beistegui but simply a house for parties and social events.

Concept

This is, indeed, a Surrealist conception of interior decoration. How otherwise should we explain the fact that an eighteenth-century portrait in oils, that one would normally expect to find hanging in the principal room of a flat, is exhibited on the concrete wall of the roof garden.[1]

In the well-documented complete works of Le Corbusier, the Beistegui apartment is afforded a very small footnote, yet this project was one of the architect's most intriguing and paradoxical works. De Beistegui was a collector of art and antiques and was known for his lavish parties, often hosting the cream of 1930s Parisian high society. Le Corbusier was acquainted with this same circle of people and was introduced to de Beistegui at one of his parties by his friend René Drouin, the French interior designer.

Le Corbusier was commissioned to design the penthouse and he conceived the apartment as a viewing space, a frame for the temporal occupation of the Parisian bourgeoisie. He imagined the occupants using the interior as a viewing device, both for watching themselves and for looking at the city in which it was located. The paradoxical nature of this Surrealist space – its uninhabited domestic interior, its temporal and stage-set quality, and the designer's play on looking, and of framing the city in various ways – has meant that it is often regarded as one of Le Corbusier's idiosyncratic follies. Yet it is precisely for these reasons that it can be considered an important exemplar of interior architecture and design, and the reuse of existing space.

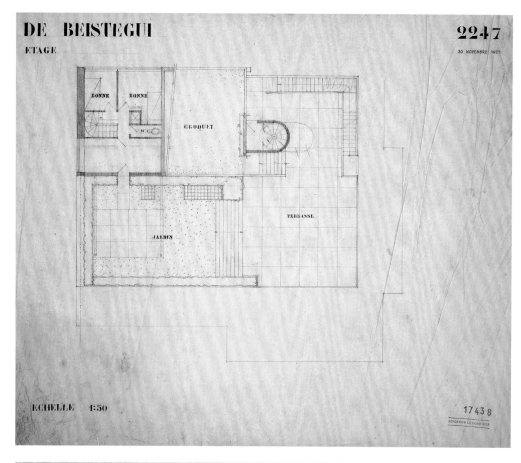

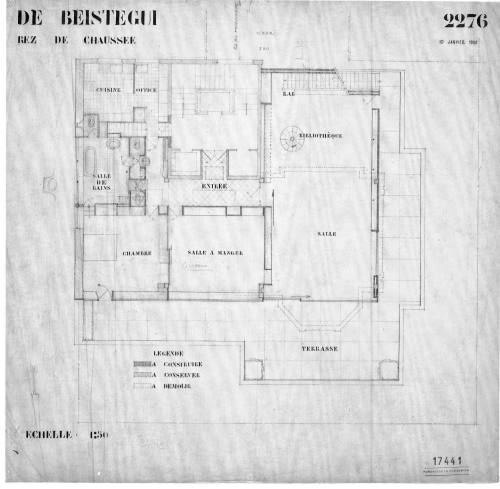

Organization

Built just a few years after his most famous building, the iconic Villa Savoye, Le Corbusier broke with convention and produced a playful, witty and ironic remodelling of the rooftop space. The penthouse consisted of a simple, white, two-storey box on the roof of an ornate yet relatively undistinguished Parisian building. The penthouse was entered on the lowest floor, at building roof level, where the kitchen, bathroom, bedroom, dining space, lounge and library were placed – an arrangement that suggested some semblance of the functions of a normal house. The upper floor of the apartment contained another bathroom, two bedrooms and the roof terrace.

The routine planning of the interior was enhanced by the carefully choreographed views from the interior towards the city. The entrance to the interior was via a narrow hall that was alleviated only by a series of inset rooftop glass panels. These created a view up to the roof terrace and the sky, and also lit the access space. The main salon contained a picture window with views across the city. A delicate spiral stair (so delicate that it failed during construction and had to be rebuilt) led to the garden and to the upper terrace.

Right The spiral staircase in the main room of the salon.

Far right Floor-to-ceiling sliding glass doors allowed light into the main salon and gave a view out of the room. The neatly trimmed hedges edging the roof garden were electronically configured so that, at the press of a button, they could be moved to reveal city landmarks.

Below right The stepped terraced garden. Glass panels are set into the floor, allowing light into the lower-level corridor.

Bottom right The periscope on the roof adjacent to the stairs leading up to the outdoor walled garden room.

Detail

Whilst unprepossessing in plan, the apartment was designed to become an 'event'. Le Corbusier configured the interior to be playful, and at the flick of a switch the space would transform and open up to the city. Electronically activated walls and doors altered the shape of the rooms as they moved across the floor. The chandelier could be retracted into the ceiling, allowing films to be projected on to the wall. On the roof terrace outside, the neatly trimmed hedges edging the parapet of the rooftop could be activated to move to one side of the window and allow framed views of famous Parisian landmarks such as the Eiffel Tower and the Arc de Triomphe.

The upper-level terrace was the most surreal of spaces. Instead of luxuriating in what would have been the best view across the city, Le Corbusier surrounded the garden with a wall, 1.5 metres (5 feet) high, thus editing out the lower half of the city. The unsettling quality of the garden was accentuated by the addition of an ornate fireplace, an element usually found inside an apartment; the exterior terrace garden was treated like an interior room, albeit one with no roof. Later images of this 'room' show de Beistegui and Terry's

extravagant decorative style, with chairs, an ornate sideboard and a grand mirror placed above the fireplace.

Despite its rooftop location, the interior was designed to feel integral to the city in which it was placed. As if to reaffirm this point, a small cabin on the roof terrace, accessed at the top of the spiral stair, contained a periscope through which to view Paris. In this apartment Le Corbusier, de Beistegui and Terry succeeded in creating an interior that was a place built for people to see from and to be seen in.

1 Alexander Watt, 'Fantasy on the Roofs of Paris', *Architectural Review*, 1936, p.156

PROJECT	**Casa Devalle**
DESIGNER	Carlo Mollino
LOCATION	Turin, Italy
DATE	1939–40

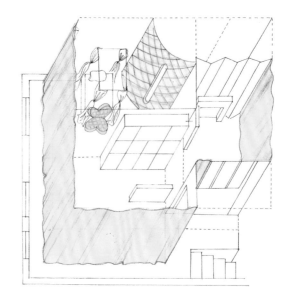

Above The mirrored butterfly wall of the gallery, enclosing the bedroom behind it, reflected in the wall of the entrance hall.

Left The interior was treated as though it were a sumptuous and enigmatic piece of scenography. These illusory qualities were heightened by theatrical elements such as curtains, mirrors and exaggerated upholstery.

Context

Carlo Mollino designed this apartment in a nineteenth-century Turin housing block for his friend, the architect Giorgio Devalle.

Concept

Carlo Mollino's work was closely related to his extraordinary life and character. The son of a leading engineer, Mollino practised architecture and interior and furniture design alongside other passions, such as flying, car racing and skiing. In 1953, after his father's death, he sought refuge in designing and racing cars, and took up stunt flying, only occasionally returning to design.

Mollino's zeal for speed and danger was matched by his obsession with the female form – a passion that was realized through his designs for furniture, buildings and fashion – and photography.

This obsession with speed and the streamlined appearance of cars, planes and the human figure gave Mollino a connection with the Italian Futurists. Yet he also embraced the irrational and florid style of Art Nouveau, an aesthetic that chimed with his decadent and esoteric predilections. Mollino's non-conformist impulses were a reaction to his

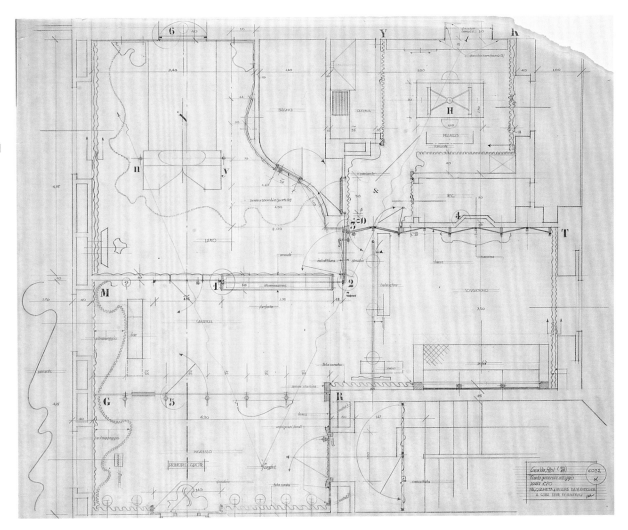

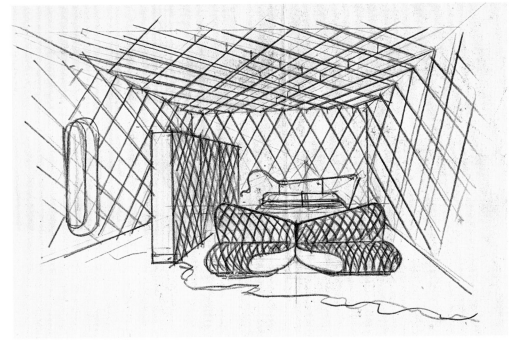

Above A rough sketch plan showing the layout of the small apartment. The entrance from the communal stair is at the bottom right of the drawing. The bedroom is located in the top left.

Left An early concept sketch of the bedroom with its opulent furniture.

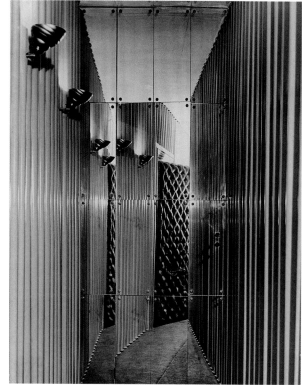

Left The mirrored walls of the apartment exaggerated the illusion of depth within the small space. Up-lighter lamps are set into the walls.

Far left The door into the bedroom, set behind the butterfly wall.

Below While lying in bed, Devalle was still able to see the entrance-hall door through a glass wall above the upholstered wardrobe doors.

Below left The cabin-style door to the bathroom was set into the upholstered walls of the bedroom.

was deliberate – Mollino often viewed his buildings and interiors as a series of picture frames or views, sequences that were exemplified by the photographic essays he would make of them. A photographic enlargement of a fictitious landscape was set into the wall of the study and framed by golden columns. This exaggerated the illusion of depth. Each room was a sumptuously atmospheric concoction, endlessly reflected to infinity in the apartment's mirrored walls.

Detail

Green-lit period mirror bed headboard, shaped and tempered. Divan forming the end of the bed in green velvet buttoned in light-blue green. Floor covered in light topaz-coloured wool. To the left a double full wall curtain, one ivory white, transparent, and one of heavy dark red velvet. Wall and ceiling padding in light violet shot-silk: on the surface of the ceiling, limited by the frame, the padding is replaced by plaster painted very pale rose white, veined with light blue so that the bed, isolated by the closed mosquito net, has the ceiling as a window in open contrast with the 'enclosure' of the padding and suggesting unlimited space-serenity.[1]

Organization

The apartment for Devalle combined all of Mollino's interests and united them in an enigmatic, complex and theatrical interior. Yet underneath these esoteric impulses the relatively small 70-square-metre (750-square-foot) space was organized in a rigorous and pragmatic fashion. Mirrored walls, faceted black-glass screens and sumptuously upholstered surfaces

reinforced the organic, sinuous, dynamic curves of the interior. The entrance was via the communal stair of the apartment block that led into the hall of the flat. This led to a gallery that flowed into a study. From the study the occupant could either enter the kitchen and dining space, or retire to the bedroom. This promenade through the interior

controlling father's influence and to the language of Fascism and Communism prevalent in Italy at that time.

Casa Devalle was conceived as an organic and surreal entity, one that combined aeronautical engineering with biomorphic imagery. It was a stage-set interior, one that acted as a backdrop for the life of its occupant.

The decadent, almost fetishistic preoccupation with materials and surfaces ensured that the interior of the Devalle house was an intense and theatrical experience. Mollino either designed or selected every last detail, utilizing his interest in aeronautical engineering and his craftsman's knowledge of structure and materials. These included the mirrored wall of the gallery, which was made from tempered glass and raw crystals and contained a showcase of butterflies, and a glass and black opaline display case, which was supported by thin brass struts and braced with slender steel rods. Mollino devised a system of up-lighters to illuminate the apartment, comprised of brushed-steel tubes with brass reflectors. He also designed many one-off pieces of furniture, including chairs in bent iron finished with extravagant velvet upholstery. The engineered quality of the furniture was counterpointed by sumptuous textures. A quilted silver satin settee was set into the wall in front of the fictitious framed landscape. Leaded bronze door handles, in the shape of hands, opened the mirrored doors. A large screen of glossy black opal contained a mirror reflecting the 'Trinacria' (the Devalle family crest). This supported a tempered glass shelf on which an unusual brass clock was framed.

At the centre of the apartment was the bedroom. The bed dominated this room, with a headboard in black opal and a customized bedspread. The end of the bed was the location for an aqua-green velvet couch in the shape of an exaggerated pair of lips, a nod to Molino's friend Salvador Dalí and the bachelor pad that he had designed. The door to the en-suite bathroom was set into the curved quilted wall and was constructed to look like the cabin door of an aeroplane or ocean liner.

The atmosphere of the space was composed with the use of exotic and semi-precious materials. Glass was reflective, clear, frosted or opal. Walls and ceilings were quilted. Doors were mirrored and set into reflective walls. Curtains, drapes and rugs were heavy dense velvet and covered walls as well as furniture. All of these details combined to create an interior that was both opulent and nocturnal.

---

1 Reproduced from a handwritten note by Mollino on the reverse of a photograph for publication. Fulvio Ferrari and Napoleone Ferrari, *The Furniture of Carlo Mollino*, Phaidon, 2006, p.190

Top left The couch at the foot of the bed was reminiscent of an oversized pair of lips.

Top right A clock for the Devalle apartment supported by the Trinacria, taken from the Devalle coat of arms.

Above A fictitious landscape image was set into the wall of the study and framed by golden columns.

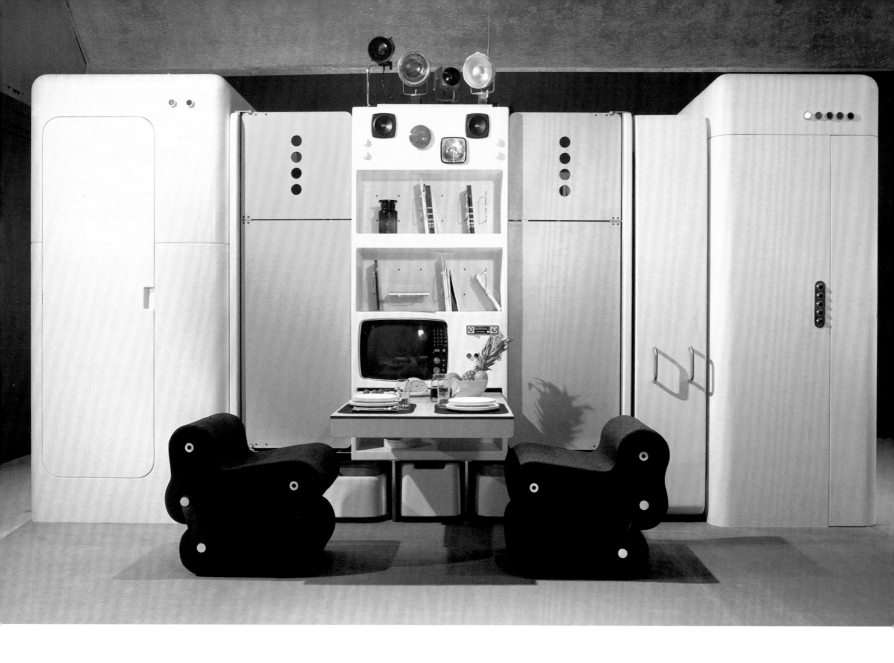

Total Furnishing Unit

PROJECT

DESIGNERS Joe Colombo, with collaboration from Ignazia Favata

LOCATION New York, NY, USA

DATE Designed 1971, exhibited 1972

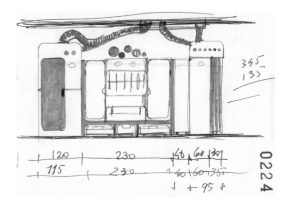

Above The Total Furnishing Unit set up and ready for dinner.

Left A concept sketch showing how the unit could be hooked up to services such as water and power.

Context

The 'Total Furnishing Unit' installation was displayed as part of the 1972 'Italy: The New Domestic Landscape' exhibition hosted by the Museum of Modern Art in New York.

Concept

The Italian designer Joe Colombo designed the 'Total Furnishing Unit' shortly before his death in 1971. Throughout the latter part of the twentieth century, post-war Italian architecture and design had become increasingly influential. This was not only due to the high quality of objects produced, as Italian manufacturing increased in size and productivity, but also the ability of the Italian designers to question social and cultural norms when designing objects and spaces.

Over 150 objects from the preceding decade in Italian design were selected to be shown at the MoMA exhibition, and 12 designers were commissioned to produce 'environments' with an accompanying statement articulating their position on the future of domestic space. These environments were to be considered as prototype housing that could be constructed by the building industry. Colombo's response to the brief was to conceive of a future habitat model that could be mass produced and achieve maximum compactness with a high level of flexibility. Colombo considered that the relationship between a unit, the city, green spaces and the occupants ensured that the unit could be a dynamic entity, and one that was in a constant state of transformation.

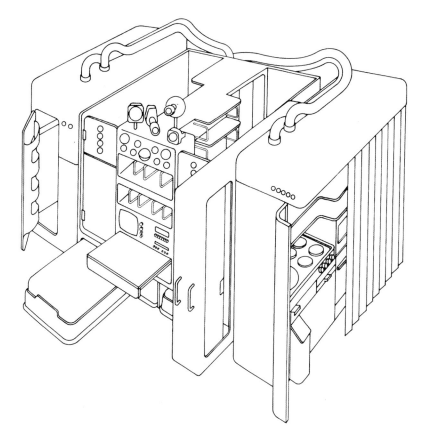

Left Axonometric sketch of the unit with all the doors open.

Left The kitchen section at one end of the unit.

Organization

Whilst built to be a model of future dwelling, and placed within a museum space, the Total Furnishing Unit was prescient in that it foresaw the differing needs of occupants in areas of high urban density. Colombo distilled the fundamental requirements of a family into a one-storey block measuring 4.8 metres (15 feet 8 inches) square, with a height of 3.6 metres (11 feet 10 inches) – approximately 23 square metres (248 square feet) in total. The module was designed to be placed in a space of approximately double that size and then hooked up to services such as water and electricity.

The main module contained the essential living requirements condensed into a series of cells, which Colombo named kitchen, cupboard, bed, bathroom and privacy. Each cell could be separated from the block and spread across the room that the unit inhabited and they could be used in different combinations. For example, the cupboard could be extended from the block to form a wall separating the kitchen from the bed unit, and so on. The bathroom and kitchen units were mono-functional in that they served no other purpose than that for which they were originally intended. The privacy or living area was multi-functional and was designed for sleeping, eating, reading, working and receiving guests. Depending on the time of day or night, and the requirements of the occupants, the blocks of the unit – the elements of furniture – could be slid out from the main module and deployed within the main space.

Detail

All the objects needed in a house should be integrated with the usable spaces; hence they no longer ought to be called furnishings but 'equipment'.[1]

Colombo insisted that the design accommodated the requirements of present and future living. He designed the unit to explore the fundamental requirements of function and was less interested in the superfluous elements of style, taste and prestige. The brief requested that the designers consider new methods of utilizing Italian manufacturing along with synthetic materials and fibres. Colombo specified that each module be constructed in a simple fashion with a lightweight timber carcass and a tough, hard-wearing melamine plastic cladding.

The module could be configured in a variety of arrangements, all utilizing the key components in different

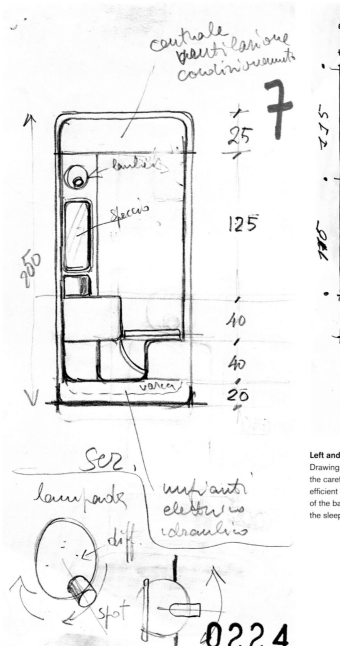

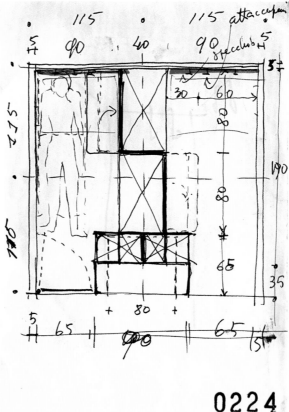

Left and above
Drawings depicting the careful and most efficient workings of the bathroom and the sleeping quarters.

ways. However, the bathroom always remained sealed inside its own unit, affording privacy to the occupant, whatever the configuration. Requirements for services such as water, electricity and waste disposal were all described in the brief as being 'assumed to be satisfied outside of the spatial boundaries of the environment' (in other words, the module could be hooked up to these services wherever it was constructed).

The kitchen was housed in another module and contained its own micro-environment of cooking, storing and preparing food. Both kitchen and bathroom elements were carefully detailed, with integrated sinks and taps, and with a built-in oven and fridge in the kitchen and a toilet in the bathroom. The main living space was positioned between the two polarities of eating and washing. Beds could be extruded from underneath the module and either configured as a lounge, organized around the built-in television, or placed next to the extended table for dining. The beds could then be configured later for sleeping.

1 Joe Colombo, quoted in Mateo Kries and Alexander Von Vegesack (editors), *Joe Colombo – Inventing the Future* (catalogue of the Milan 2005 exhibition), Vitra Design Museum, p.17

Left The kitchen.

Below left Beds are extruded from the lower level of the unit to make the lounge and some of the sleeping spaces. Wardrobes can be pulled out to enclose the space and make it more private.

PROJECT **Callender School Renovation**

DESIGNER George Ranalli

LOCATION Newport, USA

DATE 1979–81

Above The triple-height main living room of the owner's apartment.

Left The nineteenth-century Italianate schoolhouse.

Context

The host building was a listed historic landmark school, which had first opened in 1862. It was located in one of the oldest sections of Newport, Rhode Island. Six townhouse units were created, one of which was for the owners of the building, Mr and Mrs Boggs.

Concept

The reuse of an existing building to create a home is not just restricted to single-family dwellings. This project explores the notion of reworking extant space in order to create a high-density, multi-occupancy dwelling. Six new houses were intricately and carefully inserted into this two-storey building, utilizing the large basement and generous attic to form a jigsaw of interlocking habitats. Although strictly apartments, the use of the term 'house' is in recognition of the conceptual device that Ranalli employed in his realization of this project. Each dwelling was designed to act as though part of a city; a collective of houses forming a society of occupants. Each occupant has their own needs and requirements yet each shares public and private spaces with the responsibilities and civilities that that brings.

The existing building itself was an integral part of the city. Originally the local schoolhouse, it had been unoccupied since 1974. The exterior of the historic building was cleaned and restored. The cornicing, mouldings and detail of the interior were, where necessary, reinstated. The existing hallway and stairs of the old school were cleaned, repaired and retained in order to preserve some of the atmosphere of the old school building, as were the old classroom doors, which were reused as the entrances to each new house. The exterior and communal spaces of the building spoke of the institutional feel of the foreboding nineteenth-century Italianate schoolhouse, whilst the interiors of the dwellings were carefully designed and planned in order to provide new, unique and inviting domestic spaces.

Organization

The repair and preservation of the fabric of the building created a backdrop against which the new elements of the houses could then be inserted. The existing building was constructed in two sections, a process that resulted in a thick internal wall running north to south with an east–west cross-wall chimney breast running up through the floors of the building. This layout informed how the essential form of the building might be retained and the six new houses could be organized within it.

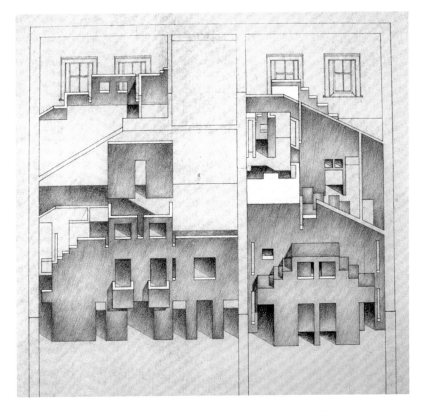

Above Axonometric sketch looking at the north side of the building.

Below Section cut through the south of the building. The owner's triple-height apartment is at the top left of the building.

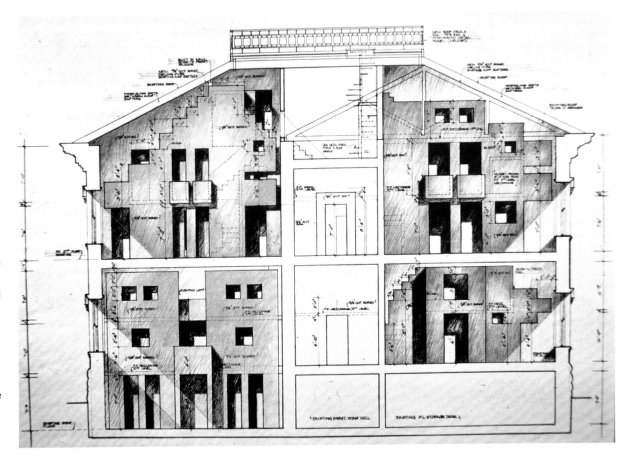

Below Plan of building before remodelling. Note the north–south internal wall and east–west cross wall and chimney breast.

Middle First-floor plan (left) and second-floor plan.

Bottom Basement plan (left) and ground-floor plan.

Four of the houses have a triple-height living space; the other two have a double-height space. The first three houses are accessed directly on the lower floor from the communal hall. The first house on the west side is a triplex. Entered on the first level, the triple-height main living space is situated in the basement. Kitchen, bathrooms, bedrooms and study, linked by a stair, are all organized behind the tall, notched 'city wall'. Both the slightly smaller second and third houses on this floor are duplex, with double-height living rooms that utilize the generous heights of the old classrooms with the use of mezzanines. The existing solid cross-wall divides duplexes two and three. The basement below these houses is used for services.

The three remaining houses occupy the upper floors of the schoolhouse and are accessed on the upper floor. The owner's triple-aspect house occupies the entire upper west side of the schoolhouse and utilizes all three floors, including the attic. Occupants enter on the first floor and into the centre of the house, where a core of kitchen, bathrooms, study and bedrooms are stacked on top of each other. The owners were afforded two 'city wall' façades: a living room 'screen' on the south side of the house and a dining room 'wall' on the north. Both are 'serviced' by the kitchen and bathroom 'core'. The master bedroom is on the second level and the library is at the top, in the eaves of the attic.

The other two houses of the building are smaller than the owner's house but are both triple-height spaces and were built into the second floor and the attic of the building.

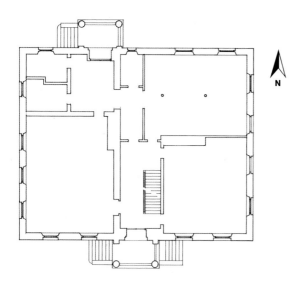

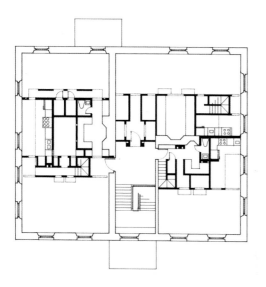

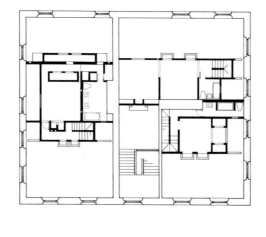

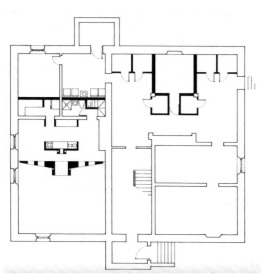

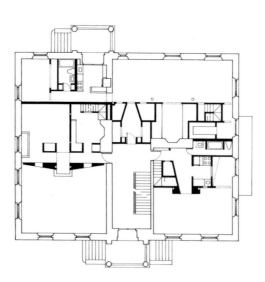

Above Model showing section through south façade (top) and north façade (bottom).

Detail

*The mock façades are collections
of walls, windows and doorways,
rooflines and columns – architectural
elements that are seen constantly,
yet which seem to take on a new
and symbolic importance here.
For these elements within the
Callender school serve much more
than a functional purpose; they
are ruminations on the nature of
architecture's inner workings,
studies in symmetry, openness
and enclosure.*[1]

The six houses are all linked by a
common theme; the response to the
elegant heights and proportions of the
extant interiors of the building. They are
also connected by the desire to unite
the dwellings with a similar yet nuanced
language to accommodate the different
inhabitants. This strategy resulted
in a set of interior 'façades' inserted
into each apartment. They divide the
private and public functions of the
spaces and aesthetically aggrandize
the living space of each home. In each
of the units Ranalli developed a spatial
sequence which was unique and
dramatized the relationship between
the smaller intimate rooms and the
larger 'public' spaces. This collective
assembly of façades, grouped around
the central hall of the old school, forms
a symbolic city around the community
of inhabitants, each with its own
mixture of private and public spaces.

1 Paul Goldberger, 'Callender School', *Architectural
Digest*, December 1981, p.63

Above right The
notched walls of
the apartments are
designed to be
read as façades of
buildings inside their
own interior cities.

Above far right The
institutional atmosphere
of the communal
hallway contrasts with
the colourful interior
walls of the apartments.
The old school doors
are reused for the front
doors to the 'houses'.

Right The triple-height
apartment on the west
side of the building that
starts in the basement
and is entered at
ground-floor level.

PROJECT	**Penthouse at 23 Beekman Place**
DESIGNERS	Paul Rudolph, Donald Luckenbill (project architect) and Vincent J. DeSimone (structural engineer)
LOCATION	New York, NY, USA
DATE	1977–88

Above The view towards the East River from the third-level dining area.

Left The apartment on top of the Neo-Georgian housing block in upper Manhattan.

Context

This four-storey rooftop addition was designed for the architect himself, Paul Rudolph. The host building was a five-storey Neo-Georgian upper Manhattan townhouse, which had been remodelled in the 1930s. Rudolph rented an apartment on the fourth floor in 1965 and in 1976 purchased the whole building for $300,000. In 1977 he started work on the conversion of the first four floors into apartments and the construction of his own penthouse – work that was ongoing due to his constant reappraisal of his personal living space, and not 'officially' finished until 1988.

Concept

Often, when a home is designed by its inhabitant, the house becomes a project for experimentation, a process that then influences ideas and proposals for new commissions. This method leaves the house in a constant state of flux as its occupant tests new configurations and materials – a work in progress. Upon completion, the finished space is as close to a 'bespoke' design as can be made: the project is personal, and intimately reflects the occupier's requirements.

This project was situated in the primarily residential Turtle Bay area, in upper Manhattan. The area had first been developed in the late nineteenth century, then, through progressive legislation in the early twentieth century, had remained a small, private residential enclave, attracting film stars, artists and writers.

This context was an important factor in the design of the rooftop insertion. Rudolph conceived the building as though it were a framing device for the spectacular views looking westwards across the city or east towards the river. The 6-metre (20-foot) width of the existing building, reinforced by walls on the north and south sides, defined the width of the enclosure, but not the height. Therefore through careful, and sometimes difficult, negotiation of the planning laws and structural surveys, the four-storey extrusion grew up into the Manhattan sky.

Organization

Rudolph was a committed Modernist. At a time when many of his contemporaries were interested in Postmodernism, Rudolph persisted with explorations in configuring abstract space whilst experimenting with industrial processes and materials. The penthouse was a testament to the production of free, open, Modernist interior space. It was formed from a series of steel frames that were clamped on to the rooftop and which allowed a free plan to be organized within their boundaries. The north and south flank walls of the building had to be rebuilt in order to accept the new structural load of the steel frame. The top part of the west end of the façade was demolished and the new building was cantilevered out towards the city to a length of almost 6 metres (20 feet) from the building. A cantilever on the east side was smaller. The frame was engineered to support multiple terraces, mezzanines and levels within which the functions of the house could take place. In all, 17 differing levels were present within the building, all of which were compacted into four main floors.

The west end of the apartment contained the guest bedrooms and their bathrooms and private terraces. The opposite east end contained the library, kitchen, dining room and master bedroom. This 'split' was joined by circulation that included stairs and a transparent bridge. Amongst this seemingly straightforward organization Rudolph created endless vistas, views, level changes and openings between floors. These facilitated views between rooms and the spaces within the interior.

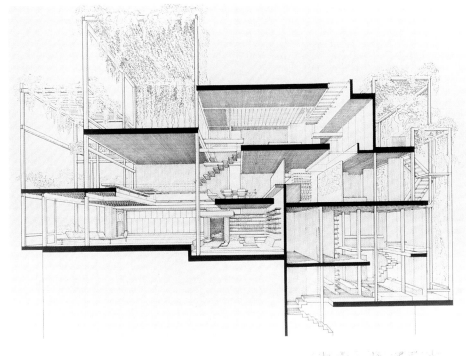

Left The 17 different levels of the interior are expressed in this section through the apartment looking south.

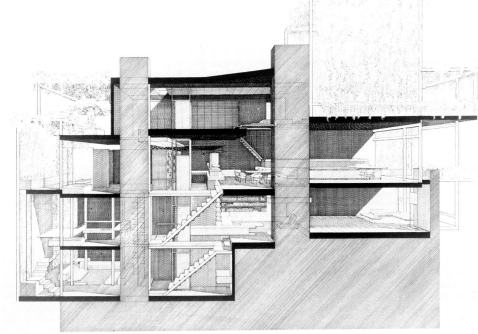

Left Section looking north. The garden terraces to the right frame the view to the East River.

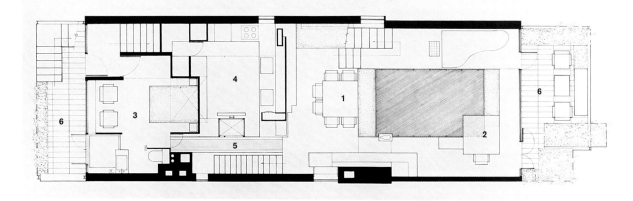

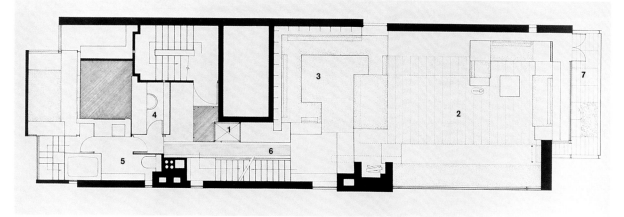

The penthouse was entered at the western end on the sixth floor, via its own private lift. At this point a two-storey guest bedroom was contained within the lower level of the western cantilever. A set of stairs led up into the library, which was lined on three sides by books. The fourth side of this open room consisted of a framed view east across the river. Moving towards the view, a two-step level change towards the terrace led into the double-height living room. The upper level consisted of a mezzanine office. The sleeping quarters of the upper level west-end guest room were accessed across the bridge. The next level contained the kitchen, dining room and another guest room in the front, or west-end, cantilever. The kitchen occupied the centre of the floor whilst the dining table was positioned at the edge of the void, looking down on to the lower-level living space. The balustrade at this edge formed a bench of seating for the table. A stair that was placed against the north wall accessed the master bedroom above. Its placement away from the main stair denoted its invitation-only status.

Whilst high above the ground, the apartment had a unique relationship with landscape. Each level was connected to the exterior by a terrace. There were five distinct outdoor spaces on four staggered levels. The largest terrace faced east and was connected to the master bedroom.

Above Lower-level plan.
1 Lift
2 Living room
3 Library
4 Study
5 Bathroom
6 Bridge
7 Terrace

Middle Main-floor plan.
1 Dining room
2 Drawing table
3 Guest room
4 Kitchen
5 Bridge
6 Terrace

Top Upper-level plan.
1 Master bedroom
2 Bathroom
3 Terraces

Detail

In the Rudolph apartment entire rooms are hidden within the structure whilst others are boldly exposed. The richly reflective and transparent surfaces of the interior aided the architect's vision, making him master of all he surveyed while deliberately half-concealing other sections of the house from the visitor.[1]

The main materials used in the construction of the exterior of the apartment were concrete, glass and steel. The interior was different. Here, Rudolph developed a complex spatial language by combining shiny and transparent materials such as stainless steel, formica and chrome with white marble, opaque and transparent plastics, and pale leather upholstery. The result was a sharp and geometric interior. The shiny and reflective surfaces also promulgated the endless flowing views through the space and through the interior to the terraces – an attribute that was emphasized by the positioning of strategically placed mirrors and the lack of any doors in the apartment, which reinforced the intimate nature of the relationships between Rudolph and his guests.

1 Tim Rohan, 'Public and Private Spectacles', *Casabella*, vol. 673/4, 1999/2000, p.138

Top left The main living space overlooking the East River. The drawing table in Rudolph's study projects into the void on the right-hand side of the upper mezzanine.

Above left The shiny and reflective surfaces used in the guest room at the lower entry level.

Top right Bridges link the east and west sides of the apartment, demarcating the public and private elements of the house.

Above right The master bathroom arranged around the sunken bath.

Above The sunken courtyard to the rear of the house.

Left The exterior of the four-storey nineteenth-century building after it was repaired and restored.

PROJECT	**Pawson Family House**
DESIGNERS	John and Catherine Pawson
LOCATION	London, UK
DATE	1996–9

Context

The original mid-nineteenth-century building, in London's Notting Hill, was a modest, end-of-terrace house constructed over three floors with a basement. It had originally been intended for as many as eight people, plus a number of servants, but was redesigned internally to provide a family home for two adults and two children.

Concept

'Minimum is maximum in drag', writes Rem Koolhaas: a consciously inflammatory comment, but all too true, I think, where simplicity is crudely translated into a decorative effect. Drag implies spectacle. There is of course a place for theatre, but for architecture of this type, theatre is not the principle on which everything is hung.[1]

The notion of a work of art, such as a painting, a piece of music or a sculpture, that transmits an underlying set of values, or fundamental principles, by reducing its palette of elements, is often referred to as Minimalist. Minimalism in interior design is often regarded as an ideal of simplicity based on the qualities of space, proportion, light and materials; in other words, a reduction of a space to its fundamental qualities. The work of John Pawson is often described as 'Minimalist' but it is a label that overlooks the depth of ideas and the level of thought that goes into the work – a level of understanding space and the rituals of its occupancy that makes each project unique and bespoke.

Pawson cites influences such as the Yorkshire countryside and the power of the nearby Cistercian monastery ruins at Fountains Abbey, near to where he grew up. Just as important were his formative years working in Japan with Shiro Kuramata (see page 106). In all of the projects Pawson and his office undertakes, whether a monastery or a piece of furniture, values such as the careful measure of proportion, the sensual properties of materials and the rituals of the occupants are of paramount importance.

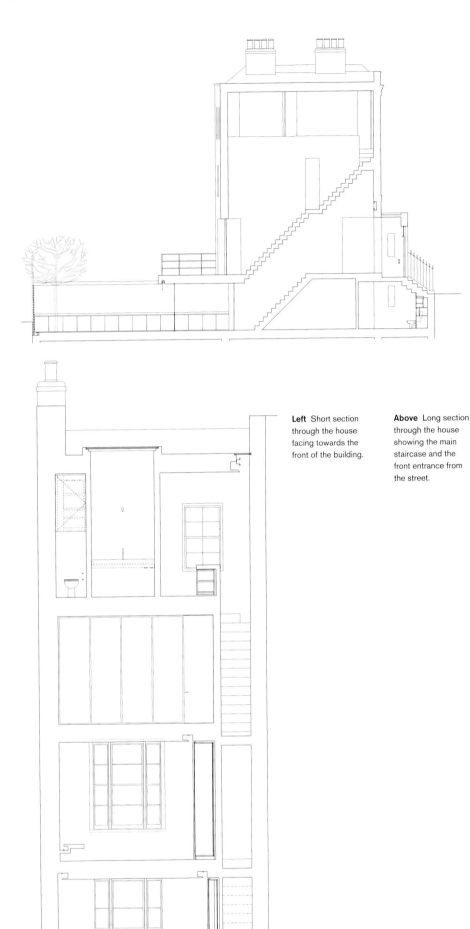

Left Short section through the house facing towards the front of the building.

Above Long section through the house showing the main staircase and the front entrance from the street.

Organization

The Pawson family house involved the extensive reworking of a typical mid-nineteenth-century four-storey end of terrace. The project was surprisingly compact at just over 150 square metres (1,615 square feet). The house formed part of a rectangle of buildings that enclosed a private communal garden. The original building, like many London terraces of the time, had two rooms per floor, linked by a winding staircase that was attached to the party wall of the next terrace. A slate-clad pitched roof completed the building. It had been unoccupied for many years and had suffered terrible subsidence, compromising the structural walls and cracking many of the lintels above the windows.

The original small rooms of the house, its prescriptive circulation and the structural issues of the building enforced a robust remodelling strategy. Pawson stripped out the interior and reconfigured the house in a radical way. A period of living in the house before its remodelling allowed the Pawsons to appreciate that the aspects from the house were significant. Framed views out towards the trees and landscape at the front and the communal garden to the rear ensured that the house felt like a free-standing building and not a terrace. This influenced the final arrangement of the interior.

Both back and front listed façades were retained, whilst the interior of the building was hollowed out and replaced with a new concrete frame. This was inserted into the building in order to underpin and take the loading of the new floors. This allowed the basement to be excavated to create a sunken garden to the rear of the house. The circulation through the house was rearranged as a long, solid stair, starting from the rear of the house and linking all three floors. The first floor is accessed via a landing at the halfway stage of the stair and contains the master bedroom and en-suite bathroom. The stair continues to the top-floor children's rooms and rooftop bathroom, with its glass roof that can be opened to the sky. The living room is on the ground floor, while the kitchen and dining room are located in the basement, accessed by a stair from the front-door entrance.

Below The long, linear kitchen in the basement is organized along the side wall of the house and has a worktop that flows out into the courtyard garden.

Right Plans, from top to bottom: second floor, containing children's rooms and bathroom; first floor, containing master bedroom and bathroom; ground floor, containing entrance hall and lounge; basement, containing kitchen and dining room.

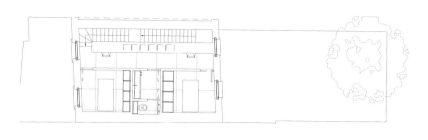

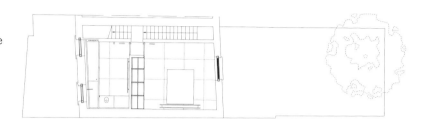

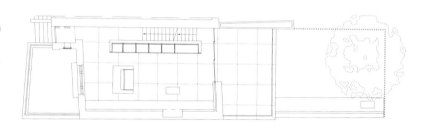

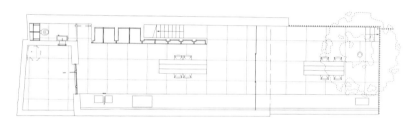

Detail

The details and materials of the house reflect a desire to create simple spaces to accommodate the routines of everyday life. Pawson used a limited palette of materials in order to complement the straightforward layout of the house. All floors were clad in pale, honey-coloured Italian limestone. The new structural frame of the building was required to accommodate this heavy loading, which was the equivalent of the existing house. This stone was also used for the stairs, benches, baths and basins. Walls were rendered to meet the floors with sharply detailed shadow gaps and no skirting boards. Elegant oak chairs and tables were designed for each room. The everyday clutter of the house is secreted in floor-to-ceiling cupboards in each room. In the basement the kitchen was lined up against the wall. Its worktop slides effortlessly into the garden through the frameless glass floor-to-ceiling doors. Everywhere in the house the materials radiate a cool and calculated atmosphere, exuding a sense of calm and serenity that returns the scale and proportions of the house back to what they once were.

1 John Pawson, 'The Simple Expression of Complex Thought', *John Pawson 1995–2005*, El Croquis, 2005, p.7

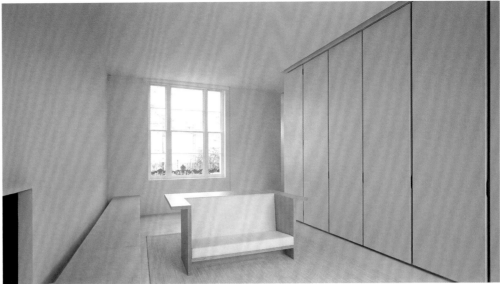

Left The ground-floor lounge. Clutter is hidden away in floor-to-ceiling cupboards.

Below left The living space leads to a small terrace overlooking the basement garden.

Left A continuous stair, running through the house, links the upper-level bedrooms and bathrooms to the ground-floor lounge. The stair to the basement begins at the front door.

PROJECT	**Bunny Lane House**
DESIGNERS	Adam Kalkin and Albert Hadley (interior design)
LOCATION	New Jersey, USA
DATE	2001

Above The existing house has been completely enclosed by the prefabricated shed.

Left The industrial building looks incongruous in the verdant New Jersey landscape. The garden terrace contains the 'hearth' chimney, now used for barbecues.

Context

This project involved the retention of a two-storey clapboard cottage that was already on site. This was subsequently enclosed within a large prefabricated metal shed to create a family house in 1.2 hectares (3 acres) of New Jersey landscape.

Concept

A point which I want very much to establish is that the choice of these 'readymades' was never dictated by aesthetic delectation. This choice was based on a reaction of visual indifference with at the same time a total absence of good or bad taste … in fact a complete anesthesia.[1]

Marcel Duchamp proposed the idea of the 'readymade', the notion of utilizing off-the-peg objects with which to make statements about the production and consumption of art. Objects such as a urinal, a bottle rack, a shovel and a bicycle wheel were reconfigured to provoke reflections on the making and understanding of art and the contexts in which it was placed. 'Readymade' is a term that applies to the reuse of an existing object that is reconfigured to be read in a different manner from that intended.

Adam Kalkin's work often involves the appropriation of standard industrial forms, such as shipping containers, scaffolding and electricity pylons, which he then manipulates to create new housing. The choice and processing of these materials provokes reflection upon the usual themes of domesticity – in particular, the notion of the home as a place of stability, comfort and security. This is particularly relevant to the Bunny Lane House, where a two-storey clapboard house, in many ways the idealized image of domesticity, was enclosed within a portal-frame prefabricated industrial shed.

Above The usual thresholds between inside and out have been rendered ambiguous by the strategy of enclosing the house within the new industrial shed.

Top The glazed sides and end of the shed frame the view of the internalized house.

Organization

The enclosure of the existing undistinguished house inside the new shed provoked a series of surprising relationships between the old and the new building. What was previously exterior became interior, and what was once inside become even further internalized as the house was covered by the prefabricated hut.

The interior was organized into three parts. The existing house was enclosed at one end of the shed. At the opposite end a new three-storey block was built, consisting of a grid of nine 3 x 3 metre (10 x 10 foot) rooms to house bedrooms, studies and offices. These two main elements of housing were then separated by a full-height, open informal lounge 'courtyard', decorated with carefully placed furniture and a large rug.

The existing house contained the normal rooms of a house – kitchen, bedrooms, bathrooms and study. The doors and windows were retained, even though they no longer needed to keep out the wind and rain. The residual spaces around the sides of the house, between the old and the new, became on one side an enclosed studio space and, on the other, a doorway leading to the garden.

In a final twist on the relationship between the interior and the exterior Kalkin created a garden terrace, edged by a large masonry chimney. The traditional hearth of the family home now resides outside in the garden and is used for barbecues.

Above Between the old and new houses a 'courtyard' lounge is arranged around a large rug with a set of furniture formally laid out in the space.

Top At the opposite end of the shed to the house, a new three-storey construction accommodates extra bedrooms, studies and offices.

Left The rooms of the existing house are intensified by their internalization in a shed, a feature that has been embellished even further by their colourful and surreal decoration.

Detail

The spatial ambiguity of the house, with its variety of enclosures, intensifies the elements of a normal family home. Within this context the traditional furnishings and features look surreal and out of place. The porch, once an outside space, is now a raised level with a roof. The view from the balcony of the house once took in the surrounding fields; it now overlooks the studio and the skin of the shed.

The language of industrial buildings is maintained with large roller doors. Openings in the shed correspond with some of the openings in the old house, retaining landscape views, and large windows and doors in the shed can be pulled back to frame the existing building and open up the interior, reinforcing the link to the gardens. The startling contrast between the industrial prefabricated shed and

traditional clapboard home shows an extraordinary approach to the readymade object that transforms and augments a conventional structure in a striking manner.

---

1 Marcel Duchamp, 'Apropos of Readymades', lecture at MOMA, 1961. Reprinted in David Evans, *Appropriation*, MIT Press, 2009, p.40

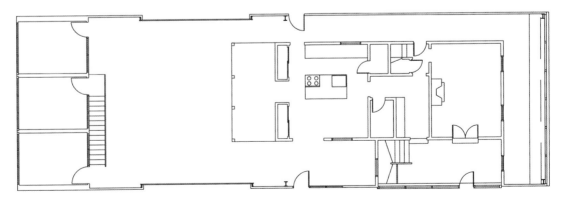

Above The section through the house accentuates the suprising relationship between the shed and the house.

Above right The ground-floor plan of the house. The 'old' home is on the right.

Glenlyon Church

PROJECT **Glenlyon Church**

DESIGNERS Multiplicity: Tim O'Sullivan (architect) and Sioux Clark (interior designer); Mel Ogden (landscape designer); Allom Lovell & Associates (conservation architects)

LOCATION Victoria, Australia

DATE 2004

Top The inserted free-standing double-height boxes dominate the interior of the church building.

Above The new asymmetric glass-and-steel front door, set into the existing arched doorway, provides a night-time beacon of warming light on the approach to the house.

Context

The Glenlyon church was a small former Catholic church in rural Victoria. Unused since 1980, it was derelict until the clients, a professional couple with young children, acquired the property, intending to convert the building into a small weekend retreat.

The church had been designed in 1860 by the English architect Charles Hansom and was built on a small hill surrounded by a wood of existing cedar trees. The church measured 200 square metres (2,150 square feet), and had been constructed from bluestone, a local rock. The interior consisted of a main double-height single room with a single-storey entrance annexe on the west side of the hall. It was punctuated by a series of exposed timber trusses and featured a number of tall, elegant stained-glass windows.

Concept

It's a form of madness. But our practice spends a great deal of time just measuring and getting a sense of the space.[1]

The design of the new interior was based upon an intimate examination of the original building and the requirements of the family for their new living space. The designers' detailed

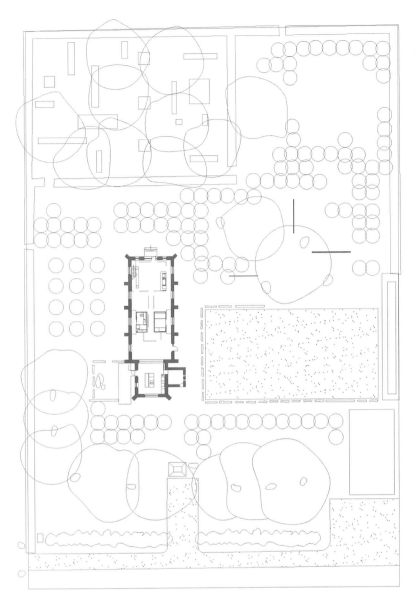

Left The site plan shows the house in the surrounding landscape.

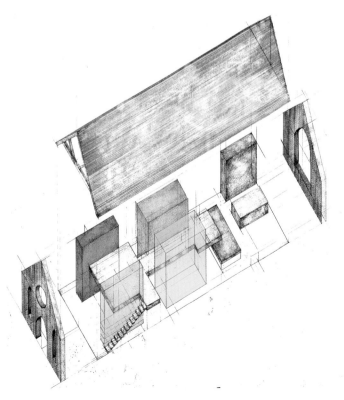

Right This concept sketch shows how the new inserted elements occupy the main hall of the church building.

study of the building initially involved measuring and surveying the host, even drawing each individual stone in the building's envelope. This close reading of the characteristics of the host building acted as the generator for a carefully crafted insertion that was built to correspond with the internal dimensions of the church. The insertion consisted of two large boxes that stand free of the existing building. The use of this type of design strategy creates an unusual mixture of clearly defined enclosures set against freer, less prescribed space.

Organization

The two new double-height boxes contain the children's bedrooms, a two-storey stacked bathroom that services upstairs and down, and on the ground floor, storage and services such as laundry and a kitchen pantry. The first-floor mezzanine level houses the master bedroom, which hangs above the ground-floor lounge, creating a canopy and helping to enclose and make this relaxing area more intimate.

This is supported on one side by a third element, a free-standing concrete and black steel fireplace block. This delineates the edge of the lounge area and rises to become storage for the master bedroom.

The study was placed at the opposite end of the bedroom and, like a modern pulpit, hangs over the dining and kitchen area. The kitchen and dining table occupy the south-end altar space of the church, the formal entrance of the original building. The lounge occupies the north end under the rose window and is defined by its loose arrangement of furniture and the stairs to the upper level.

Detail

The predominantly masonry and timber existing building acts as a simple backdrop to the new elements, while the flat surfaces of the rendered walls, the dark exposed timber roof and the reclaimed Tasmanian oak floor provide a neutral scene to contain them. The bold new cubes are of a

steel frame construction and are clad, one in clear green-tinted Perspex and the other in a ceramic tile, creating a stark, modern counterpoint to the host space. The bridge and mezzanine floors, hung between the cubes, are a steel and timber construction with glazed balustrades. The new elements are designed to act as an allegorical reworking of the proportions and textures of the host building.

The new elements do not touch the old building yet they derive their form from its scale and proportions. Specified pieces of furniture sit alongside new custom-designed pieces. The kitchen is where the old altar was and is organized around a large concrete, steel and timber free-standing bench. New 4-metre (13-foot)-high oak cupboards mirror the ceiling's scissor trusses. The dining table was made from steel, green Perspex and timber, utilizing the palette of materials used throughout the house. The stair balustrade to the upper level consists of a bookshelf made from steel, timber

and Perspex. A new steel and glass asymmetric front door replaces the old solid timber one and allows views into the interior from the landscape.

The original character of the church was retained and allowed to infuse the charm of the new living space. The building retains some of its pious qualities whilst the new remodelling breathes life back into the old place.

1 Tim O'Sullivan of Multiplicity, quoted in Stephen Crafti, 'Sanctity of Place', *Indesign*, vol. 20, February 2005, p.141

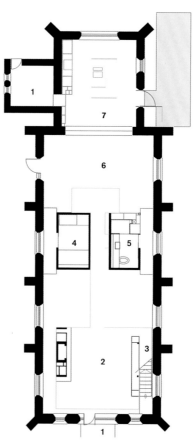

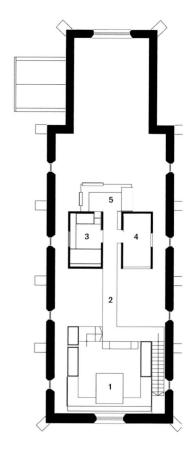

Above and top Long sections through the interior of the house.

Right Ground-floor plan.
1 Entrance
2 Lounge
3 Stair to upper level
4 Bedroom
5 Bathroom
6 Dining room
7 Kitchen

Far right Upper-level plan.
1 Master bedroom
2 Bridge
3 Bedroom
4 Bathroom
5 Study

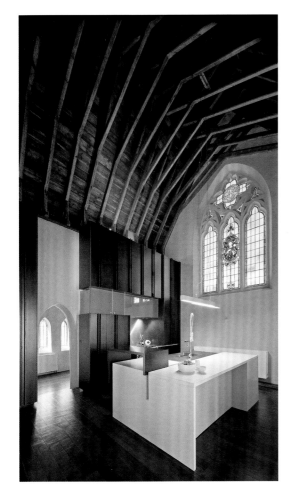

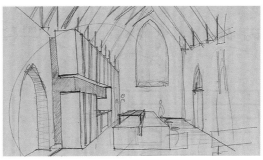

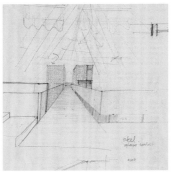

Top Early sketch of the kitchen.

Left Sketch of the upper-level walkway and the towers.

Right An elevation of the ceramic-clad tower.

Left The stark white concrete-and-timber bench of the kitchen and the tall oak cupboards contrast with the dark timber of the church ceiling.

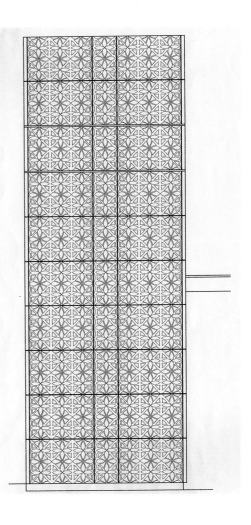

Above The lounge beneath the master bedroom mezzanine, which is partially supported by the concrete and steel fireplace on the right of the image.

CHAPTER 2

Work

For nearly 100 years, from around 1890 until 1990, the office was an archetype of modernism, a place of rational production and administration, its design almost entirely determined by considerations of management efficiency and its importance to contemporary culture marginalized by a fixation with mechanistic process.[1]

In this chapter the generic term 'work' is used to describe occupations of space that include a multiplicity of forms of production and manufacture – buildings may be adapted to facilitate work that is knowledge-based (e.g., educational and cultural), or they may house office-based production, administration, headquarters and community spaces. The case studies in this chapter reflect the history of reusing buildings in order to provide workspace, while in this introduction, the office is used as the spatial exemplar for exploring patterns of change in the colonization of existing buildings.

In the late nineteenth and early twentieth centuries the contemporary office environment underwent a radical change. It became a place of rational and efficient administration and production. Rapid increases in trade and concomitant increases in the numbers of workers with which to process this work meant that office sizes grew. These were all changes that accelerated hierarchical pay structures and the division of labour, which was required to achieve the new volume of work: structures that were already prevalent in factory production lines. This was manifested in rationalized and efficient structures of clerks, workers and managers, divided into departments and responsible for one section of work before it was passed to the next. In short, the early twentieth-century office resembled the production line of a factory in its organization and structure.

The spatial implications of this arrangement were clear. At the turn of the century, offices for large companies such as insurance firms, mail-order businesses and government

administrations occupied large and open spaces with rows of clerks at their desks, usually closely supervised by managers in strict work-flow systems. These interiors were often arranged along the principles of scientific management systems, principles that were mostly popularized by Frederick Winslow Taylor, who had studied factory line production and, in particular, Henry Ford's principles of car manufacturing. He then applied these ideas to the processes of the office workplace. In these systems the efficiency of the workers was carefully gauged, then often maximized by the

reduction of their work to the simplest of repetitive tasks.

The model office

Frank Lloyd Wright designed the Larkin Administration Building in 1904 in Buffalo, upstate New York, for a mail-order soap company of 1,800 workers. It was considered the first purpose-designed environment for a large organization. The Larkin family commissioned Wright to create an environment for the workforce that was progressive and would accept yet challenge the dominant Taylorist principles. The interior of the building

Opposite The central light-filled atrium of the Larkin Building, designed in 1904 by Frank Lloyd Wright.

Left The striking rooftop extension to a solicitor's office by Coop Himmelb(l)au, Vienna, 1989.

Above left Changing old churches into work and community spaces is a viable alternative to demolition. St Paul's, Bow, London, by Matthew Lloyd.

Above Office for Jack Lang by Andrée Putman, Paris, 1984.

was dominated by a tall, top-lit central atrium that ran the full height of the building. The interior was organized in a manner that challenged the hierarchical spatial orthodoxies of the day. Company officers occupied the ground floor at the bottom of the light court, with the workers arranged above them, in tiers, effectively reversing prevalent hierarchical structures and allowing them to observe the managers below.

The highest point of the building contained the employee restaurant, which could seat up to 600 workers and was connected to a roof terrace so

that workers could take some fresh air. The restaurant furniture consisted of specially designed eight-person tables that emphasized the democratic nature of the office by having raised posts at the narrow ends, ensuring that nobody sat at the head of the table.

Wright took great care over the design of the interior and the furniture of the office. The large amounts of natural light and the development of an innovative air-conditioning system embodied the client's and Wright's intentions to create a progressive building that had a healthy, and thus

principled, attitude to its workforce. The Larkin building was a manifestation of the identity and ideals of its owners, and a building in which the interior and the building envelope were conceived together in complete harmony.

The contemporary workspace

Far more money is now being spent on the relatively short-life interiors of offices. It is in these interiors that restlessness is easily accommodated. Conversely the shell and the exterior of the office building are dwindling in both architectural and economic

significance. Architecture, in this financial sense at least, is rapidly becoming a branch of interior design – the neutral shell within which the real dramas are played out.[2]

In stark contrast to the Larkin building, the latter part of the twentieth and the early twenty-first century can be characterized by the desire for workspaces that are flexible, adaptable and responsive. The contemporary office is distinguished by its ability to change much more quickly – as fast as market forces, workers and their requirements, technological

developments and their impact on space enforce them. Interior spaces are, by their very nature, flexible entities. As described by Duffy above, they can respond quickly and be adapted far more readily than the building envelope in which they are located.

The 'office landscape' strategy (Bürolandschaft) was an attempt to move away from a fixed, rigid organization, towards an interior that represented flows of people and information. The Bürolandschaft office was designed to incorporate a new model of space that responded to diversity and complex human relations, rather than the rigid Taylorist model of a production-line work-flow. The importance of the design and arrangement of office furniture within the Bürolandschaft strategy – for example, flexible partitions, plants and break-out areas, such as coffee bars – allowed offices not only to be more egalitarian but also easily reordered when needed. This flexibility was hindered by fixed entities such as power and light sources but it

nonetheless heralded a new form of democratic spatial representation in the workplace. The need to create more flexible, responsive and fluid environments in which to work reduced the importance of the building envelope and placed a new emphasis on layout and furniture, and the technological and environmental impact on the workspace and workforce.

Workspace furniture

Throughout the early twentieth century, the emphasis on increasing efficiencies in the workplace meant that furniture was designed to increase effectiveness and raise production; the evolution and development of office furniture is a constant theme of the attempt to create expedient environments in which to work. The industrial designer Raymond Loewy designed the 'Model Office and Studio for an Industrial Designer' for the Metropolitan Museum's exhibition 'Contemporary American Industrial Art' in New York in 1934. The streamlined plastic laminate and gun-metal fittings incorporated technologies that were prevalent in the

design of modern appliances such as fridges, aerodynamic cars and steam trains – objects that Loewy was familiar with designing.

Office furniture design and construction continued to evolve through the century. Studies on hand–eye coordination, desk sizes and the further fragmentation of work processes were all undertaken in order to increase efficiencies. Changes included the replacement of roll-top desks with flat surfaces, to eradicate lost papers or files, and the removal of pigeonholes, which were found to hinder filing (itself now a separate process in the office). Pedestal bases on chairs and tables were replaced with legs so that cleaning was made easier, reducing germs and possible sickness in the office. Even silence became a requirement in the office, as it encouraged concentration and the flow of work.[3]

The fluid workspace

In the twenty-first century, a space in which to perform work will often take

the form of an office environment of some kind, but it might also include a variety of other environments. The influences of information technology – the widespread use of the internet, laptops and mobile phones – has had by far the greatest effect on recent developments in workspace requirements and has created a much more fluid and limitless work environment. The erosion of such boundaries, along with the development of various wireless technologies, now means that work has become much more mobile and can take place away from the office – in your home, in a café or even in a car.

The beginning of the fluid workspace was evident in the 'casual' office environments pioneered by software firms in Silicon Valley, in the United States, in the early 1980s. Workers were encouraged to occupy non-personalized workspaces and operate fluidly via 'hot-desking' and 'desk surfing'; activities that suited flexible shifts and long hours spent programming. The dress code in these offices also became much more relaxed, as the boundaries between home and work became much more fluid. This approach became widespread, especially in creative industries and the 24-hour office – a flexibility that enabled working patterns to change, redefining rigid orthodoxies of work times and space.

The adaptable workspace

Architectural design in the context of existing buildings extends the use of buildings over multiple phases of use, and in the process, carries over the existing qualities of the building into the future.[4]

As Breitling and Cramer state, building retention ensures the continuity of a city's urban fabric. As the importance of the building envelope dwindles, the reuse of existing spaces becomes more of a question of how to create a suitable interior landscape in which workers can be productive and also happy. This has led to more innovative forms of interior space, as well as the reuse of existing buildings that were previously disregarded or seen as unfit for any purpose. Rather than demolish redundant spaces, they can be reworked and reused. Churches can become community spaces whilst retaining their religious requirements; nineteenth-century buildings can be reused to house new teaching spaces for a university, and so on.

Adapting existing buildings also places an emphasis on developing new ways of understanding the complex interactions of the workplace. In *The New Office* by Francis Duffy, new strategies of interior workspace inhabitations are defined by the analysis of patterns of working and the requirements of new occupation. He suggests that there are four types of office – hives, cells, dens and clubs:

'Hive' because such offices can be compared to beehives, occupied by busy worker bees; 'cell' because these recall the monks' cloister ... 'den' because these are busy interactive places where it's easy to work in teams; 'club' because one of the nearest models to the new transactional office ... is the old-fashioned gentlemen's club.[5]

Reconfiguring buildings to house workspaces may use furniture-scaled schemes, such as the office for the French Minister of Culture Jack Lang: an elegant 'club' tastefully considered and installed in a period room.

Other office environments fuse the envelope with the interior to create dramatic statements for the company that it houses. A 'den'-like solicitors' office in Vienna, created by Coop Himmelb(l)au, is located in the attic of a polite eighteenth-century building. A central glass and steel sculptural conference room dominates the 400 square metres (4,300 square feet) of office. The adaptation of unusual existing spaces and buildings provides an occupant with the potential for new and innovative spatial configurations with which to communicate their company's identity.

These strategies have led to the development of entirely new interior terrains with a mixed landscape of spaces, enclosures, pods and rooms in which work can take place. In a project by Fashion Architecture Taste (FAT), a disused church in Amsterdam has become a space for the Dutch advertising agency KesselsKramer. The interior contains a number of elements that form a landscape in which to work, relax and present agency work – a fort, a shed, a lifeguard's watchtower and fragments of a football pitch, picnic tables, hedges and fences. Several ornaments, objects and pieces of furniture were also bought by the client from flea markets. Behnisch Architects 'Haus im Haus' project constituted a reworking of Hamburg's neoclassical chamber of commerce to contain a new business start-up centre and consultation, exhibition, club and meeting room facilities for members, guests and visitors. Both of these projects are considered as independent elements within the envelope of the buildings that contain them.

In the modern workspace environment the changing relationship between the building envelope and its interior is mirrored by developments in technology and sustainability. Computers, digital filing systems, wireless, home working and cloud technologies have virtually negated the need for any enclosure at all. Sustainable and healthy work environments have become important considerations in order to reduce the impact on the planet's resources and ensure that a space is not detrimental to the health of workers. Sustainable office design is partly about using materials (such as timber from sustainable forests, or recycled plastics) and also about exploiting natural daylight and air, using energy-efficient technologies.

The conversion of a 1930s former laboratory building for Greenpeace by Feilden Clegg Bradley Studios was an environmental and ecological remodelling, incorporating a variety of low-energy design features and materials. Materials were carefully selected to minimize their impact on the environment in manufacture, in use and ultimately, when the office was remodelled, disposal. The project makes maximum use of the substantial window areas in the existing building to provide controlled and natural lighting and ventilation, and uses a combined heat and power plant to provide both heat and electricity. A new internal stair was inserted through the centre of the building to provide closer connection between the different parts of the organization on the four floors as well as enhancing the movement of air through the interior via 'stack effect' ventilation.

Whether sustainable, technologically advanced, a den, club, hive or cell, this chapter presents buildings that have been adapted to create a whole diversity of workspaces.

1 Jeremy Myerson, 'After Modernism: The Contemporary Office Environment', in Susie McKellar and Penny Sparke (editors), *Interior Design and Identity*, Manchester University Press, 2004, p.191

2 Francis Duffy, *The Responsive Office: People and Change*, Steelcase Strafor/Polymath Publishing, 1990, p.8

3 Adrian Forty, *Objects of Desire: Design and Society Since 1750*, Thames and Hudson, 1986, p.126

4 Stefan Breitling and Johannes Cramer, *Architecture in Existing Fabric*, Birkhäuser, 2007, p.199

5 Francis Duffy, *The New Office*, Conran Octopus, 1997, p.61

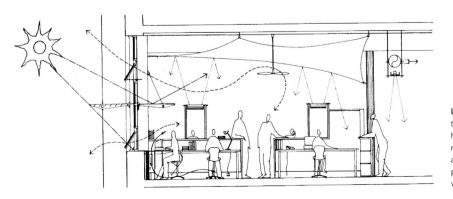

Left Section through the new Greenpeace headquarters shows the movement of light and air through the office, promoting a healthy working environment.

Bürolandschaft

PROJECT **Bürolandschaft**

DESIGNERS Eberhard and Wolfgang Schnelle/ Quickborner Team

LOCATION Germany and elsewhere

DATE 1959–

Above and left The large deep-plan of the Osram building in Munich, designed in 1965 by Walter Henn, contained a Bürolandschaft interior office space.

Context

Since the late nineteenth century the design of the workplace has seen radical experimentation and innovative strategies with which to plan, manage and accommodate its occupants. One such strategy is 'Bürolandschaft', or 'office landscaping', a strategy devised in 1959 by the brothers Eberhard and Wolfgang Schnelle, whose organization later became known as the Quickborner Team.

Bürolandschaft was utilized in a number of office environments, particularly for many large corporations needing to radically rethink their working environment and processes. German companies such as Osram, Krupp, Boehringer, Ninoflex and Mercedes were early adopters of this interior planning strategy, which then also became very popular in Europe and the USA from the late 1950s through to the early 1980s.

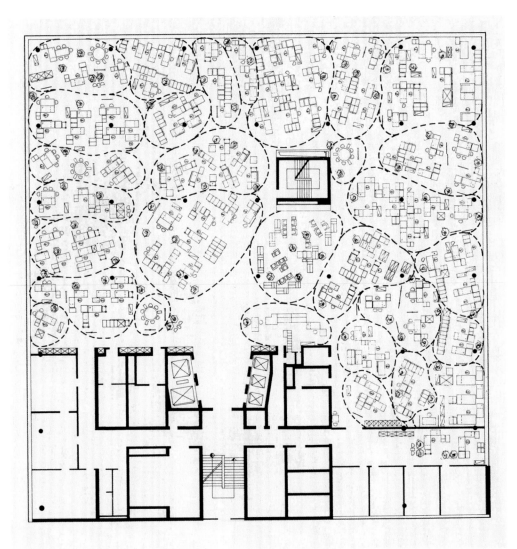

Left The plan of the Osram office with clusters of furniture organized to promote the free flow of both people and information.

Below Organization of the informal and seemingly random interior of the Osram office was based on a deep analysis and understanding of the interaction between people and information throughout the firm.

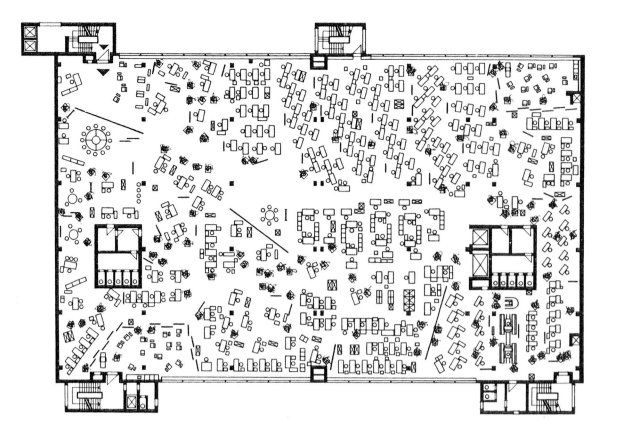

Left The strategy was utilized in many office spaces with similar effects. The Bertelsmann office, Gütersloh, 1961.

Left The interior of the Bertelsmann office. Routes through the space are formed by the placement of furniture and plants.

Concept

Bürolandschaft … reflects the realization that office work is essentially a ritual in which people do things together, involving a continuous flow of work from one group of tables to the next.[1]

Until the mid-1950s, the design of office space was generally organized along Taylorist principles. This involved the application of scientific management values to the organization of the workplace in order to increase efficiencies in movement and flows of information amongst workers. The idea was named after Frederick Winslow Taylor, an American engineer who, like his contemporary Henry Ford, devised systemized patterns of production.

In the late 1950s Eberhard and Wolfgang Schnelle developed a set of principles based upon more egalitarian and humanely structured beliefs. Bürolandschaft was a rational, systemic theory that structured companies in a spatially freer environment – one that was based upon non-hierarchical office floor-plan arrangements. Values such as appearance, status, recognition and tradition were considered to be of minor importance.

This type of interior organization allowed buildings to be serviced and mechanically controlled throughout, which led to a complete rethink of the ways that large businesses could be organized and accommodated within large, deep-plan interior spaces – a typology that was rapidly becoming the norm for large-scale office design.

The first aim of the strategy was to establish the existing circle of communications within the company. It would then analyse the 'commerce' between each different department and any others over a period of time, establishing the frequency and importance of connections. Numerous diagrams of the network of people and departments would be produced with furniture and technological requirements slowly added. Even phone calls and coffee breaks were added into the equation. This information was then used to develop a series of plans for the office that would eventually become its new layout.

Organization

The typical plan of a Bürolandschaft office involved free and open planned space with furniture arranged in large, seemingly unstructured, arrangements. The planning could be moulded into a variety of forms but essentially these arrangements were intended to propagate the free flow of people and hence information. This strategy had a number of benefits. It negated the necessity for clearly separated circulation routes as the planning of the floor combined both movement and workspace. This was a highly efficient way of planning and it also eased social interaction as people passed by each other's desks more regularly. Another innovative idea was the *Pausenraum* (break room), a conveniently located space where anything from coffee to a full canteen service was provided. Dispensing food and drink at all hours enabled workers to break when they wanted to rather than waiting for the 'official' regulated break, a Taylorist norm.

Bürolandschaft evolved from work–study research and the development of office furniture. It was designed to permit easy change and to facilitate the addition and subtraction of groups of people in the workspace. The flexibility of this strategy, as well as the breaking down of barriers between managers and workers, was key. The idea that all ranks of the company staff could sit and chat together and also break from their work whenever they wanted to was revolutionary and was in sharp contrast to Taylorist principles, which insisted on highly regimented workplaces.

Detail

Prior to developing the Bürolandschaft, the Schnelle brothers had been furniture designers and had also run a company specializing in paper, furniture and office equipment, including filing systems. It was the very lack of harmony between these products and systems that inspired them to investigate the workspace as a whole. Bürolandschaft was a strategy that was very much based at the furniture scale of design, and the key issues to be dealt with were privacy and noise.

Bürolandschaft was one of the first strategies to attempt to domesticate the workplace. It did this by arranging furniture in groups that replicated domestic settings and using the trappings of the home, such as thick carpets, plants and low screens with which to divide large, open-plan areas. This allowed a certain level of privacy without cutting workers off from each other. The acoustic properties of these surfaces and materials were also very important and helped to deaden the noise of the interior. Ceilings were also generally kept low (2.7 metres/9 feet) to help counter noise.

By eliminating partitions Quickborner got rid of the enclosed office and the geometric grid. This overturned the traditional hierarchies of an established workspace and thus provided an egalitarian office planning system that was to remain very popular for another two decades.

---

1 Francis Duffy, 'Skill: Bürolandschaft', *Architectural Review*, February 1964, p.148

PROJECT	**La Llauna School**
DESIGNERS	Enric Miralles and Carme Pinós
LOCATION	Badalona, Catalonia, Spain
DATE	1984–6 and 1993–4

Above The ground-floor playground of the school is accessed from the upper floors via the scissor stairs and ramps.

Left The southwest masonry wall of the factory was removed to accommodate the insertion of a new steel and glass entrance with a large curved sliding door.

Context

This project involved the transformation of an old printing factory in the city of Badalona (part of the metropolitan area of Barcelona) into a boys-only primary school. Phase one of the project, carried out between 1984 and 1986, was to redesign the entrance and foyer. Unexpectedly, the project grew owing to a change in the budget, and this resulted in the commission in 1993 to redesign the whole school.

The three-storey steel-framed host building was locked into its site by surrounding buildings. The unrelenting structure of the building and the basic budget meant that the designers needed to come up with an inventive solution to accommodate the requirements of the programme.

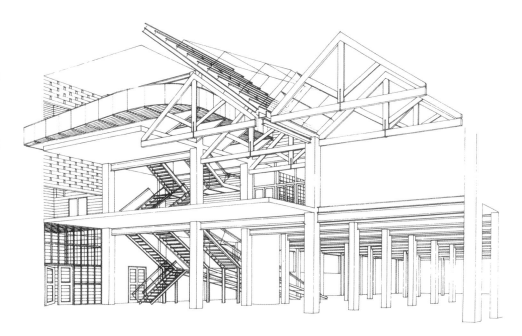

Left The perspective of the interior shows the ground-floor playground and the new stair inserted into the existing structure of the building. The removal of the top-floor roof trusses facilitated a new upper-level landing.

Left New lights, concrete and glass-block walls and a polished concrete floor complement the lattice-beam structure and jack-arched industrial quality of the interior of the building.

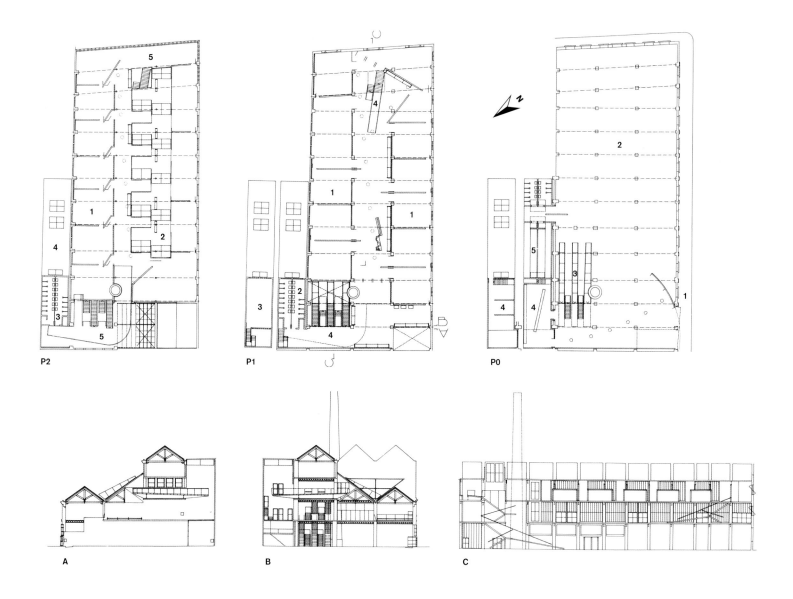

P2

P1

P0

A

B

C

Concept

Existing architecture acting as impetus to the architect's imagination: a host of new ideas, the pleasure of designing and building, materials treated in a straightforward, direct manner – these are all factors which, taking as a starting point the existing factory, have contributed to the design of this project.[1]

The existing factory building provided a space that was imbued with a robust industrial quality. It fitted the requirements of the brief for providing an environment that was tough enough to contain large numbers of energetic small children. When Miralles and Pinós remodelled the building they responded to the tight budget and restricted timescale for the build by focusing on three strategic interventions: a new service block, a new entrance and the reworking of the circulation throughout the building. They formulated this pragmatic arrangement by extracting the maximum theatricality from the lively and animated occupants, arranging the various interior spaces of the school around a large indoor playground. This would allow the schoolchildren to expend their energies in the safety of the building, and prepare them for the quiet focus of the classrooms and workshops, where they were expected to concentrate on their studies.

Above left Both short sections show how the new second floor could be accommodated via the roof-truss change.

Above The long section shows how the structure of the building influenced the layout of the rooms in the interior.

P2
1 Classrooms
2 Staff rooms
3 Toilets
4 Roof
5 Circulation

P1
1 Classrooms
2 Toilets
3 Offices
4 Circulation

P0
1 Entrance
2 Playground
3 Circulation
4 Offices
5 Toilets

Above The top landing of the stairs.

Above The new upper-level balcony with the now virtually redundant roof truss.

Organization

The building was organized in a simple yet effective manner. The ground floor was left empty to provide the indoor playground. Here the kids could run amok amongst the columns of the building whilst protected from the weather. Above the ground-floor level are two floors of classrooms and staff rooms. The regimented structure of the building informed the layout of the interior on all floors; the structural proportions allowed classrooms, workshops and offices to be organized within the grid of the columns.

Slight modification of the structure took place on the second floor, where a few roof trusses were removed in order to allow the headroom for a set of new stairs that were inserted to connect all of the floors. The new vertical circulation consisted of a series of playful scissor-ramps and stairs that were slotted into a void cut between the bays of columns.

The new dramatic entrance to the school required the removal of two bays of the exterior south-west masonry wall, leaving only the supporting column intact. A large glass and steel wall was inserted into the space and contained an automated curved steel-mesh gate that, when opened, swung into the playground. A new addition on the north-east side of the building filled a small, thin plot of land available to the school with a three-storey service block of administration offices and toilets.

Detail

The industrial qualities of the existing building meant that the designers could utilize its hard and tough surfaces in order to develop a robust environment suitable for kids. Where possible, the structure of the building was exposed, revealing iron columns and a lattice-beam structure that supported small masonry jack arches, common in factory buildings that were required to take heavy floor loadings.

The designers complemented these raw surfaces with exposed blockwork screens and glass-block walls for the classrooms, offices and workshop enclosures. They used polished concrete for the floors, and servicing elements, such as radiators, lighting and air-conditioning ducts were left exposed and treated as sculptural objects in the space, adding to the industrial atmosphere of the environment. Furniture such as benches and classroom seating was over-scaled and robustly detailed in order to be hard-wearing and able to take a battering from the children. The stairs were constructed from steel sections with mesh balustrades and thick timber treads. As they descend from the upper floors they turn into three elongated ramps, projecting into the playground and allowing the kids to reach maximum speed as they run into their play area.

1 Philippe Robert, *Adaptations: New Uses for Old Buildings*, Princeton Architectural Press, 1989, p.70

PROJECT **Metropolis Recording Studios**

DESIGNERS Powell-Tuck, Connor & Orefelt

LOCATION London, UK

DATE 1990

Above The café level of the recording studio.

Left The Edwardian brick and Portland stone exterior of the power station.

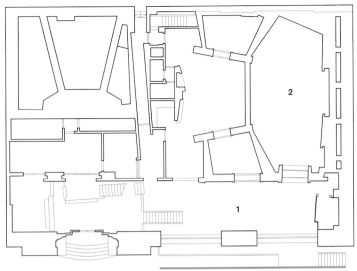

Ground

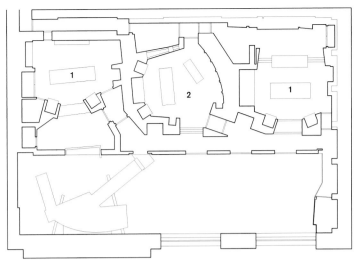

Second Floor

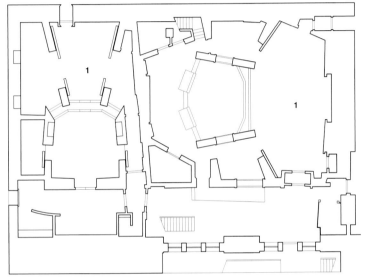

Basement

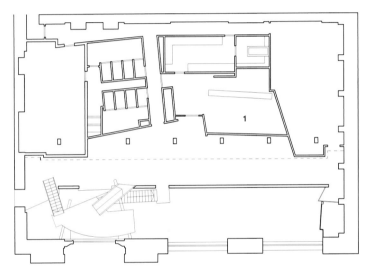

First Floor

Context

The substantial Edwardian brick and Portland stone Chiswick power station was designed by William Curtis Green at the end of the nineteenth century. It went into operation in 1901, providing electricity for the new West London tram service, but was rendered obsolete by 1911, after just ten years in service. The turbines were removed from the listed building and it remained empty until 1985, when permission was granted to fill the site with apartments and offices.

In 1986 the still-empty power station was taken over by Metropolis, and Powell-Tuck, Connor & Orefelt were selected from a four-practice competition shortlist to design a new recording studio.

Top left The ground floor containing one studio (2) and where the internal 'street' (1) is accessed via the front door and the reception.

Top right The top floor with 2 studio spaces (1) linked by a central control room (2)

Above left The basement studios (1).

Above right First-floor plan with café. (1)

Right The cinematic quality of the interior circulation is exaggerated by the under-stair lighting..

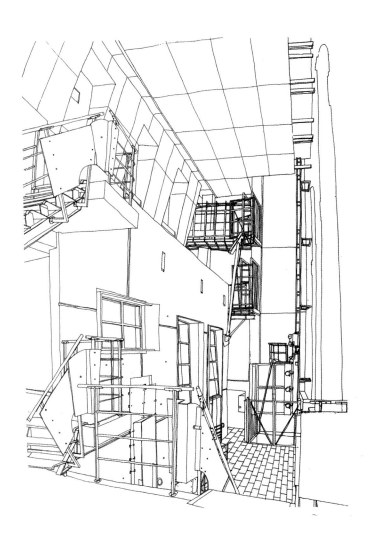

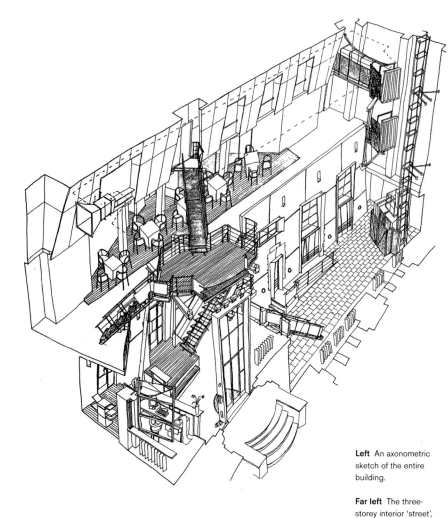

Left An axonometric sketch of the entire building.

Far left The three-storey interior 'street', viewed from the reception.

Concept

What we're after is evoking the spirit, without picking up turbine details or bits of old equipment, which would become pastiche. It's an interior with the ghost of what went before. [It is] an expression of movement between a timeless shell and something passing through it. Our imagery reflects things passing through things and time.[1]

Much like the imagery of the film from which the studio derived its name, the interior of the power station, once the scene of a dynamic and noisy intensity, formed the concept for the new studios. Ironically, recording studios are usually based in rooms where sound can be contained and recorded with the utmost precision, free from distracting noise and compromising external clatter. They are often found in tucked-away spaces, such as basements or environments that are heavily insulated from external commotion. This means that studios are often without daylight, fresh air and a view to the outside world.

The designers' impulse was to change the insularity of the recording process without compromising the quality of space and equipment required for a high-specification studio. This manifested itself in a dynamic 'split' in the building, one part semi-public and one private. The new studio was part of the city whilst at the same time accommodating the secluded and insulated space that was required to make and record music in a specialized environment.

Organization

The organization of the interior was based around the physical separation of the private, insular recording studio spaces from a series of open 'break-out' spaces. This was manifested in the form of a new three-storey wall inside the building that stretched from the basement to the second floor. The wall allowed the designers to create a huge vertical 'street' that not only facilitated all of the circulation but also allowed light, air and the view to pour in through the building's original tall, arched windows.

The brief requested five recording studios/mixing rooms, recreation and leisure spaces, a bar/restaurant and offices for the management of the studio. Three recording studios, complete with control rooms, booths, machine and amp rooms, were located in the basement and on the ground floor of the interior. The other two were placed on the top floor of the construction. The material division of the secluded and the open is counterpointed by visual connections through the wall. These take the form of a series of openings, allowing the seclusion of the inner workings of the building to be alleviated by light, view and, when needed, fresh air. The restaurant and bar sit atop the block of lower studios and spill out on to the deck. This affords views back into the street. Vertical circulation takes place at both ends of the street in the form of a highly engineered steel and timber staircase, with landing, bridge and ramp at the reception end and a deconstructed exposed service lift at the other.

Detail

The condition of the fabric of the existing building inspired an equally robust and tough detail strategy for the new interior. The combinations of masonry, glazed engineering brick, faience tile, steel and heavy machinery inspired the raw design language of bush-hammered concrete, exposed painted blockwork, bare and painted steel sections, thick timber floors and unpainted plaster walls.

The 'street' is a space of 'live' sound lined with echoic materials, filled with the chatter of people moving through the space or enjoying a drink at the bar. The acoustic properties of the studios required a different but also very particular set of surface conditions. The rooms – irregularly shaped in order to avoid awkward echoes – were finished with different materials. One was finished with linen in order to 'deaden' sound; another was finished with panels of maple-veneered timber sheets, giving a warm sound; yet another was finished with raw plaster to give a 'live' sound, and so on. The surface conditions of each space were carefully calibrated in order to give a range of sonic properties.

With 19 apartments on the site, and the five studios capable of producing huge amounts of noise, the isolation and confinement of the interior had to be carefully considered. Concrete floors were floated upon rubber pads and thick walls were braced with rubber, separating the studio partitions from the building structure, a possible source of noise transference. Ceilings were suspended upon rubber mounts and walls were insulated. The overall effect was the juxtaposition of the isolation and serenity of the studio space against the vitality of the city and the interior street.

1 Julian Powell-Tuck, quoted in *Designers Journal*, November/December 1990, p.6

Top left The highly engineered steel-and-timber staircase links all floors of the studio.

Top right Opposite the staircase is a former service lift, now deconstructed in order to expose its mechanics.

Above The café.

Right Sheets of maple-veneered timber line the studio and eradicate corners in the room in order to deaden any reflective qualities in the sound.

Above left The ethereal
atmospheric double-height
39th-floor reception area.

Above The main boardroom with
its stunning views towards the
skyscrapers across the city.

PROJECT   **DE Shaw Offices**

DESIGNERS   Steven Holl Architects

LOCATION   New York, NY, USA

DATE   1991–2

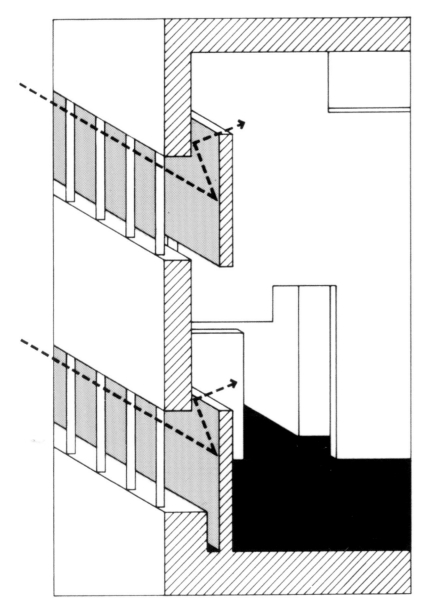

Context

The host building for this project is a nondescript ziggurat-shaped skyscraper, satisfying strict Manhattan zoning and light regulations by stepping back as it rises to its full 40-storey height. The DE Shaw offices occupied the top two floors of the office block. The project had a budget of $700,000 and the office space available for remodelling was 1,115 square metres (12,000 square feet).

Left The light was carefully controlled and manipulated by painting the back of the screen lining the interior with luminous billboard paint.

Below An axonometric sketch of the project showing how the notched-wall strategy connects all areas of the office.

Concept

I would say that I am very interested in the philosophical nature of ideas as an origin, but I couldn't just stop there. My struggle is to try to find the phenomenal potential of the idea.[1]

DE Shaw is a financial trading firm, founded in 1988 by David Shaw, a doctor of computer science. It is an unusual company, conducting hundreds of daily trades by analysing stocks and shares data on the world markets using an elite group of mathematicians.

Because of the need to respond to the various opening and closing times of stock markets around the world, the office remains open 24 hours a day, seven days a week. Staff work both day and night shifts throughout the week, resting in the few hours between the closing of the Tokyo stock exchange and the opening of the London exchange.

The intangible quality of the business, the working hours of its employees and the unusual location of the project inspired Holl to create an interior based on the manipulation of space utilizing natural and artificial light. The end result was an ethereal, atmospheric interior space in the sky.

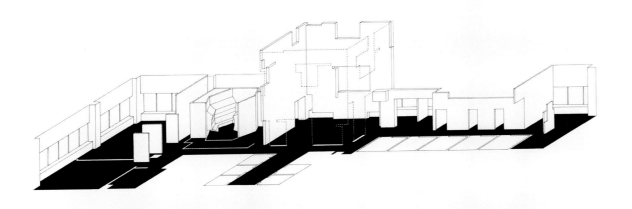

Organization

Stepping out of the lift on the 39th floor, the interior begins with a double-height reception. In an allusion to the flow of invisible data through this office space, the 10-metre (30-foot) cube reception is treated as a huge microchip with framed indentations, carved apertures and recessed notches. The double-height space was lined with a screen of white-painted plasterboard, chosen to mediate light into the space, creating an ethereal glow during both the day and at night. The new lining acts as a filter that screens the light and also frames the view to the city; the notches condense the view towards neighbouring skyscraper façades, rendering them as abstract computer motherboards.

The secretive and focused nature of this business meant that the main office had to be organized as a series of cellular spaces in which the mathematicians could reside undisturbed. These were placed on both levels of the office space at the end of the building and are accessed from the reception. Natural light is utilized, although it is also carefully controlled in order to alleviate glare on the computer screens. West of the reception is a hexagonal trading centre and two executive offices. The stunning views across Manhattan are exploited in both of these spaces.

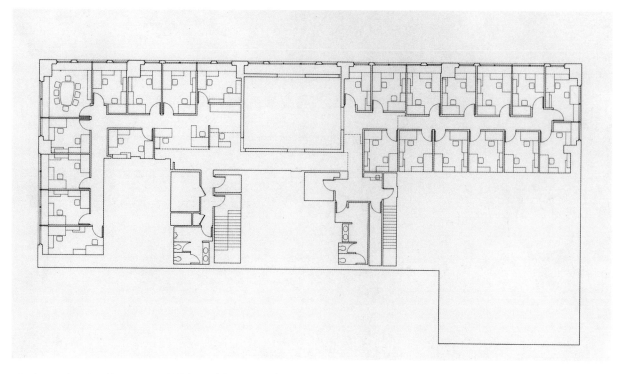

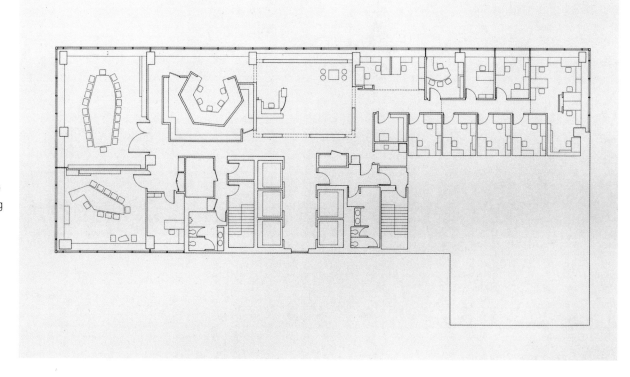

Top The cellular offices of the traders dominate the upper-level plan.

Above The ground-floor plan. The reception is at the centre of the space adjacent to the lifts and stair core. Meeting rooms and boardrooms are to the left, with offices to the right.

Detail

The unique location for the project afforded the designer a number of site-specific advantages. However, it also came with particular site-specific difficulties, which, along with a limited budget, regulated the choice of materials.

Holl chose panels of 'sheet rock' or plasterboard formed in a stud wall construction for the reception area wall. These panels were light enough to be carried up in the lift but when assembled and rendered took on the appearance of a solid masonry wall. The abundant natural light was a given and was supplemented by artificial light. Rather than use any filters or colours, the notched reception screen was painted with luminous billboard paint that acted as a reflector, throwing soothing coloured light back into the interior and giving the space an iridescent glow. The effect of this is a

calming, restful space, no matter what time of day workers begin their shifts.

In the executive office and meeting room the designer carried on the language of the geometric reception by introducing its proportions into the design of custom furniture and lighting. In the main boardroom a large brushed-steel meeting tabletop, inset with panels of sandblasted glass, shares the same golden-section proportions as the reception wall. Cupboards that house presentation equipment were also constructed using notched cut-outs and irregularly shaped doors. The pendant lighting above the table was specially designed due to the lack of suitable existing models; these consist of sandblasted Pyrex cylinders suspended from slender black electrical wires.

The unusual location of the existing space, the limited budget and the

unusual qualities of the programme ensured that Holl created an atmospheric office space for the workers to utilize at any time of the day.

---

1 Steven Holl, *Steven Holl 1986–1996*, El Croquis, p.17

Below and below left
The iridescent glow of the notched wall of the reception changes throughout the day and is reflected by the the black-gloss resin floor.

PROJECT	**Reactor Studios**
DESIGNERS	Brooks + Scarpa (formerly Pugh + Scarpa)
LOCATION	Santa Monica, CA, USA
DATE	1998

Above The company's meeting room has been housed in a deconstructed shipping container placed in the window of the existing building.

Left The tall, single-storey open space of the Art Deco garage building with its large windows facing onto the boulevard.

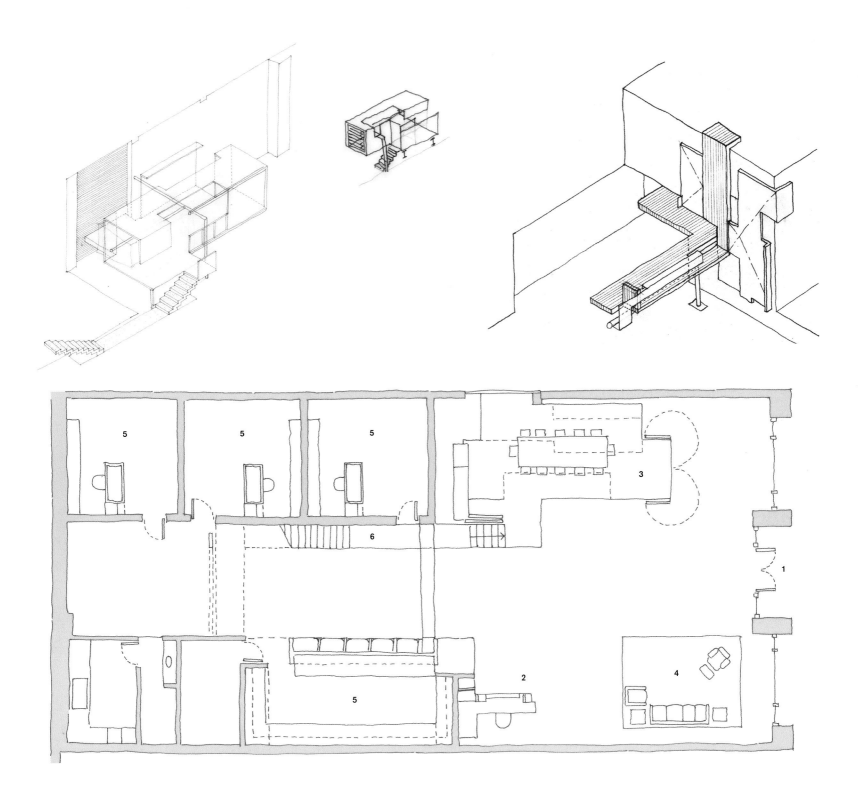

Context

Pugh + Scarpa were commissioned to adapt an existing Art Deco garage in a prominent Santa Monica street to house Reactor Films, a production studio for television commercials and music videos.

The 1930s garage, with its generous double-height ceilings, had previously been used as an art gallery and photographic studio. An unusual by-law, applying to the bayside pedestrian district of downtown Santa Monica, stated that a zone at the front of the building, 15 metres (50 feet) deep and running parallel to 4th Street, was required to continue the public boulevard. This rule meant that a startling addition to the streetscape had to be conjured up by ensuring that the first part of the interior of the building engaged with its immediate context.

Top left Exploratory sketches detailing the deconstruction of the shipping container in order to make the meeting room.

Top right An axonometric sketch of the reception desk.

Above Ground-floor plan.
1 Entrance
2 Reception
3 Meeting room
4 Waiting area
5 Offices and production spaces
6 Stairs up to mezzanine

Above The open-plan space is easy to comprehend upon entering the former garage.

Above right A folded steel table and elegant designer chairs are placed on the rug in the reception space.

Right The timber surface of the top-lit reception desk is folded up in order to announce its location in the room.

Far right The meeting room is raised off the floor on concrete plinths and is accessed via a set of concrete steps.

Concept

A familiar thing seen in an unfamiliar context can become perceptually new as well as old.[1]

A 14-week schedule from preliminary design to move-in, combined with a limited budget, meant that the designers were obliged to avoid large amounts of time-consuming and expensive new-build. They concluded

that the ideal solution would be something prefabricated and adaptable.

As mentioned earlier in this book, 'readymade' was a term first invented to describe aspects of the work of Marcel Duchamp. His most famous readymade was *Fountain*, a porcelain urinal placed on its side and signed 'R. Mutt'. Its appearance at an exhibition of the

Society of Independent Artists in 1917 provoked a storm of protest and it was hidden from view at the opening of the show. 'Readymade' is a term that is now used to describe an off-the-peg object, a familiar thing that can be placed in an unfamiliar context. In this short, fast and cheap project the designers selected a corrugated steel readymade shipping container with which to satisfy the constraints of the job and the zoning laws attached to the building. The dimensions of the container allowed 16 people to be seated around a table. Its simple, prefabricated, inexpensive construction offered an eye-catching solution to the dynamic installation needed to create a suitable space for the company.

Organization

The studio includes offices, conference rooms, film production spaces, an archive in the form of a video vault, and staff facilities such as a kitchen and rest room. The façade was characterized by large floor-to-ceiling windows, elements that, when removed, facilitated the installation of the shipping-container conference room. The space was organized around an open entrance lobby with two aisles of cellular office space set deeper into the plan. A concrete and steel stair positioned to the side of the room and

against the wall of director's offices connected the upper and lower floors. The simple organization of the room and the large open-front lobby of the office allow visitors to enter the space and quickly become familiar with where they are. This is accentuated by a reception desk positioned deep into the lobby.

Detail

As well as the budget and timing considerations it was important that the adaptation of the 650-square-metre (7,000-square-foot) space created the right image for the company. In an industry that is image driven, the comfort and identity of the interior needed to match its artistic and technical capabilities.

The shipping-container conference room was just one part of the unique identity that was created for the company by the designers.

The recycled container was deconstructed by cutting open the panels of corrugated steel. Sheets of glass, timber and Corten steel were then attached to it to create a three-dimensional puzzle of voids and surfaces. The container can be unpacked and unfolded or closed up and shut down as needed. It was installed early one Sunday morning and fork-lifted on to its precast in-situ concrete plinths through the large front windows.

Overall, the interior was conceived as a fluid surface, connecting up all of the office spaces and enhancing the daring elegance of the conference room. A neutral palette of rendered white walls and a polished concrete floor created the interior's main backdrop, making the conference room even more prominent. The reception desk was fashioned from a series of folded timber planes that form a desk and also flip up to form

a thin, vertical screen, announcing its existence to any unwary visitors as they come through the front door. A large rug was placed on the floor in order to delineate the waiting area in front of the reception. An elegant folded mild-steel table was placed on the rug and was bordered by a series of designer chairs, thus creating a comfortable setting to offset the harsher surfaces of the surrounding environment.

---

1 Robert Venturi, *Complexity and Contradiction in Architecture*, Butterworth Architecture, 1977, p.41

Below and below left
The container can be reconfigured in a variety of ways depending on what levels of privacy the meeting-room occupants require.

PROJECT **Utrecht Town Hall**

DESIGNERS Enric Miralles and Benedetta Tagliabue (EMBT)

LOCATION Utrecht, The Netherlands

DATE 2000

Top The wedding room of the town hall. The informal quality of the room is exemplified by the placement of the redundant fireplace and the collection of odd chairs, reminiscent of a time when guests brought their own furniture to a marriage celebration.

Above The new entrance to the hall has been created by turning the building 180 degrees, a move that reorientates it towards a new public square.

Context

With surgical precision EMBT carefully reworked a number of extant buildings in order to create the new Utrecht town hall. The designers were amongst 31 invited competition entrants and, from a shortlist of two, they won first place with a series of sketch proposals detailing their strategy for creating the new building. The site to be remodelled contained a number of buildings that dated back to the thirteenth century. They ranged in age from medieval housing to sixteenth-century guild- and cloth halls, through to a nineteenth-century neoclassical conversion. EMBT proposed that this complex site be carefully analysed and then 'filtered' in order to decide what to retain and what to demolish. The resultant new building would be a combination of both new and old.

Concept

If collage is described as the placement of a fragment next to a similar fragment and then the two are spliced together in such a way that the net result is greater than the sum of its parts, one might wonder how this differs from any other artistic activity.[1]

A collage strategy can be an effective way of renewing disparate fragments. The complexity of this project was added to by the 700 years of extant building stock on the site. The original town hall, facing the Oudegracht, the main canal in Utrecht, was located in a series of townhouses. The houses contained the council rooms, the cloth hall, guildhall and exchange. Houses added to the site in the sixteenth century contained the city archives, orphanage, post office, fire station and even a prison. In the nineteenth century a neoclassical conversion took place that was incorporated into the site to cater for municipal receptions and marriages. Various earlier plans, formulated to wipe the slate clean and start again, had not been carried through, leaving an incoherent combination of spaces and buildings.

Above left The new square on the north side of the building (right) relieves the congestion on the Oudegracht-facing elevation (left) and links the building back to the city.

Above right The newly built staff canteen located in the northwest wing of the building culminates in a glass box that pops out of an old doorway.

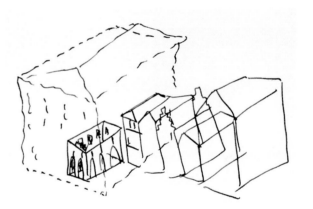

Top The incorporation of the existing houses on the site is demonstrated in this early concept sketch.

Above Finding a way to reintegrate the neoclassical extension into the rest of the project was an important element of the design strategy.

From their analysis the designers formulated a strategy that was based on three major decisions. The first was to accept the series of extant buildings that made up the site, celebrating the idea of the town hall as a gathering of different houses with their different scales and rooms. The second decision was the retention of the monumental canal-side face of the building and its public side on Stadhuisbrug (town hall bridge). This led to the creation of a new entrance on the other side of the building and a new square. The third decision was to accept the recent insensitive neoclassical addition but to develop and better integrate it into the whole composition. Together these three ideas would rejuvenate the site.

Organization

The change in orientation of the building resulted in a significant modification of the whole site. The new main entrance connected to a newly created public square on the opposite elevation to the congested Stadhuisbrug side of the building. This square provided a new focus for the building, facing the cathedral, and created a place that was to be inhabited with cafés and bars.

Offices for the civil servants were placed in a long extension on the north-west side of the building facing the Ganzenmarkt. The offices were located in the front of a series of existing buildings which had their backs removed and replaced with a set of new constructions. The square-facing façades – using a collage of recycled fragments of existing buildings – created the new offices. Windows were constructed from lintels and beams found on the site held together with new concrete infill panels and reused bricks. The wing culminated in a new staff canteen with the best seats in a glass box poking out into the street through an old doorway.

The designers connected up a new zone of interior circulation through a sequence of spaces that stretched between all of the existing buildings. The existing entrance on the new square was not big enough to

Right The site plan demonstrates how the building was to be reworked to reintegrate it into the city.

TOWN HALL
STADHUS UTRECHT

Left Second-floor plan.
1 Offices

Below left First-floor plan.
1 Circulation
2 Balcony
3 Council chamber
4 Central circulation corridor

Below right Ground-floor plan.
1 Entrance
2 Neoclassical hall
3 Wedding rooms
4 West wing

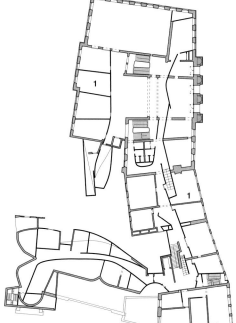

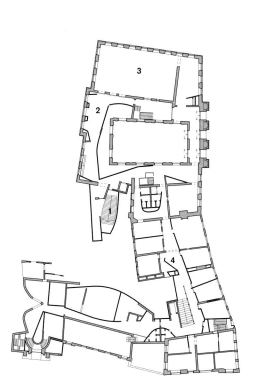

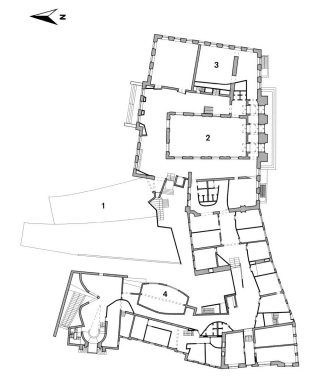

accommodate a new internal stair, so EMBT created a bold new entrance, which connected up the circulation in a much better fashion.

Detail

The interior of the new town hall has the same collage-like characteristics as the exterior. The collection of assorted buildings provided an interior landscape that comprised a number of unique rooms, of different sizes, shapes and outlooks. Rather than ameliorate this condition EMBT decided to embellish the disparity of rooms and create an interior that was much like the city of spaces in which they were housed.

There are now two wedding rooms, one formal with a coffered ceiling and prim furnishings, and another arranged around a surreal fireplace and an unusual assortment of chairs (recalling a time when guests brought their own chairs to a wedding). The main hall was retained and conserved in all of its neoclassical glory. The double-height entrance around the central hall forms an exhibition space full of paintings and photographs of the city's history. The council chamber ceiling was removed to let light in and improve the acoustics, but the timber structure of the roof was left in place to remind occupants of the room's history.

The whole interior abounds with playful details, and the selection of furniture, lighting and surfaces exemplifies the simple, unified strategy of a collage approach to the building.

1 Ben Nicholson, *Appliance House*, MIT Press, 1990, p.18

Top The council chamber has exposed ceiling beams and specially designed furniture.

Above left New circulation connects the buildings via stairs and corridors.

Above Both levels of the exterior wall of the central hall are animated with paintings and photographs of people and events from the history of the city.

PROJECT	**TBWA\HAKUHODO**
DESIGNERS	Klein Dytham Architecture
LOCATION	Tokyo, Japan
DATE	2007

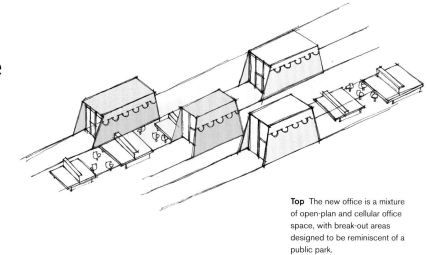

Top The new office is a mixture of open-plan and cellular office space, with break-out areas designed to be reminiscent of a public park.

Above The informal relationship between the desks and the enclosed meeting rooms is counterpointed by the formality of the bowling lanes within which they are arranged.

Context

A new collaboration between two established advertising agencies – one American and one Japanese – led to both companies seeking a location that would not only accommodate the new, larger workforce but would also show their clients that they were a company that stood out from their competitors. The chosen location was a large, anonymous eight-storey building in Tamachi, downtown Tokyo, that housed an amusement arcade. The fifth and sixth floors contained a disused ten-pin bowling alley that became the new office space.

Concept

The design of the new office for the two advertising agencies was a deliberate attempt to communicate the ambition and philosophy of the new collaboration. The location had to be a place that would dispel any preconceived notions of what an ad agency should be like. This resulted in the designers being employed not only to design the office but also to find the new premises. This led them to the choice of an unusual location – a selection that subsequently influenced the concept and organization of the interior.

Klein Dytham persuaded the clients that the bowling alley could be their new home. The new offices would still share a lobby with their immediate neighbours: another bowling alley on the floors above them and a golf driving range below. Clients would have to fight their way through gaudy neon signs and the carnival lights of the 'Tokyo Port Bowl' entrance lobby until they reached the reception. The concept for the interior was derived directly from the qualities of the host building, with the bowling alley providing a conveniently column-free space. The designers decided to treat the hall as an interior landscape or park, with desks and offices, meeting spaces, cafés and vegetation arranged neatly in rows like a playing field in a busy city.

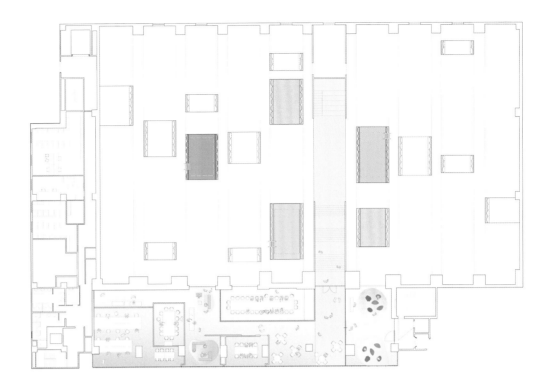

Above Lower-floor plan. The linear qualities of the previous function of the building have directly influenced the organization of the new advertising agency. The office is arranged in rows, following the pattern of the lanes in the bowling alley.

Top Upper-floor plan. The entrance to the office is from the communal stairwell of the building. Workers and guests then descend to the lower-floor workspaces.

Organization

The lower level 3,300-square-metre (35,500-square-foot) space was organized utilizing the existing grain of the linear 30-lane bowling alley. Offices and workspaces were lined up following the outlines of the old lanes. The column-free interior had been achieved by using a number of 2-metre (6-foot)-deep beams that spanned the entire hall. These deep beams reinforced the direction of the alleys and thus suggested the arrangement of the workspaces. In order to aid the mechanical servicing of the deep-plan office the beams were exposed and reworked in order to accommodate lighting and ventilation. In the aisles the open-plan office was occasionally interrupted by a series of folded planes that grew up from the floor, folded over the alleyway and enclosed a series of trapezium-shaped rooms. The sides of these 'huts' were transparent, allowing light in yet increasing the level of privacy needed for such a big open-plan office. The 16 huts were fashioned from larch and lime-wood veneered timber and glass and enclosed meetings rooms, offices and the library. The tops of the huts were covered in artificial grass in the form of a shaggy green carpet and were designed as accessible break-out spaces for people to climb up on and work with their laptops, thus adding to the overall park-like atmosphere.

The main reception is on the sixth floor. This level contains administration, a gallery of current works and meeting spaces for clients and external visitors. It affords the visitor a view across the park before they descend into the main studio. An over-scaled stair connects both levels of the office. This wide corridor-like passage incorporates a row of stepped seating and can be quickly transformed into a presentation or party space.

Detail

The biggest challenge was to create an outdoor atmosphere indoors.[1]

The former life of the building is easy to discern and the designers have playfully reiterated the linear characteristics of the host building in their arrangement of the new interior. Playful and witty details also complement the clarity of the space's layout. Lauan veneered timber strips were used for the new wooden floors to recreate the sprung smoothness of the lanes of the alley whilst at the same time suggesting the decking found in an ordinary back garden. Panels of roughly hewn Douglas fir were used to create low walls separating office departments. White plastic garden furniture was placed in the public break-out spaces, making meetings look like gatherings around a barbecue. The balustrade of the main stair was formed from playful steel loops and the treads were edged with white rubber nosings. The steel loops also form the edges of the tops of the huts on the main office floors. The roofs of the huts consists of a drape that, whether timber, artificial grass or white vinyl, adorns the lid and wraps down the sides of the element, finishing with a cut edge reminiscent of a circus-tent fringe.

The novel details and cut of the material of the space lend a playful air that is conducive to a fun, spirited, unorthodox environment – a space that encourages thinking in an innovative and unconventional manner.

1 Astrid Klein, quoted in *Frame*, September/ October 2007, p.124

Top White plastic furniture and interior landscaping is redolent of the language of the suburban back garden.

Above Some of the break-out spaces on the rooftops of the 'huts' are covered in artificial grass and encourage people to climb aboard and work whilst looking over the office.

Below Short section. The mezzanine-level reception and meeting rooms (left) offer an overview of the large open-plan office. Note the large beam spanning the two-storey work space.

Top Conventional open-plan office space is organized in between the huts.

Above The edging of the tops of the huts has been cut in a playful manner, reminiscent of circus-tent fringes.

Below Long section. The rows of offices, meeting rooms and the library follow the rigorous orthodoxy of the existing building's structure.

Top The huts fold up from the floor and enclose private spaces that are quieter than the open-plan office.

Above The atmosphere of the office can be dramatically changed by adjusting the lighting in the interior space.

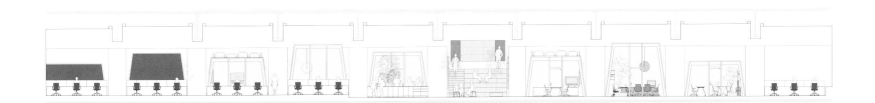

PROJECT **Birkbeck Centre for Film and Visual Media Research**

DESIGNERS Surface Architects

LOCATION London, UK

DATE 2007

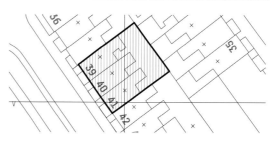

Above The dynamic flow of the interior is counterpointed by the deep-red break-out space of the auditorium foyer.

Left The centre occupies three Grade II listed terrace houses facing Gordon Square in Bloomsbury, central London. The windowless extension is at the back.

Below The location of the three terraced houses facing the park in Gordon Square.

Far left The stripped-out back extension prior to the commencement of remodelling.

Left The sharp, angular, dynamic colours of the interior reinforce the flows of circulation through the space.

Below An axonometric line drawing reveals the three-dimensional qualities of the forms and colours employed in the extension.

Context

The site for this project consisted of three joined-together Grade II listed Georgian terraced houses on Gordon Square in central London's Bloomsbury area, near Euston Station. The building was once home to Virginia Woolf and the Bloomsbury Group. A two-storey windowless brick box extension was added to the rear of all three buildings in the 1970s.

The Centre for Film and Visual Media Research is part of Birkbeck, a school of the University of London.

Concept

A lot of film and narrative thinking deals with the idea of a journey. In a sense this is a journey too. You're in another world, but you're constantly connected to things that are in the real world as well.[1]

The processes of designing three-dimensional space and making film share many similar preoccupations. They both explore a formal language with regards to matters such as structure, sequence and framing. Both processes create distinct environments in which the narratives of their occupants are played out. This is done by making distinct atmospheres using objects and surfaces, light and shadow. Both processes create rich and complex narrative and spatial journeys through a series of particular environments. Film and the process of editing also allow completely different moments in time and space to be pushed next to one another in the form of montage. This creates sequences that might be joined as narrative but that do not necessarily share the same space or moment in time.

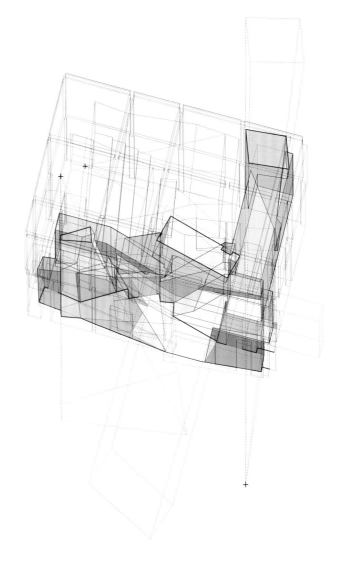

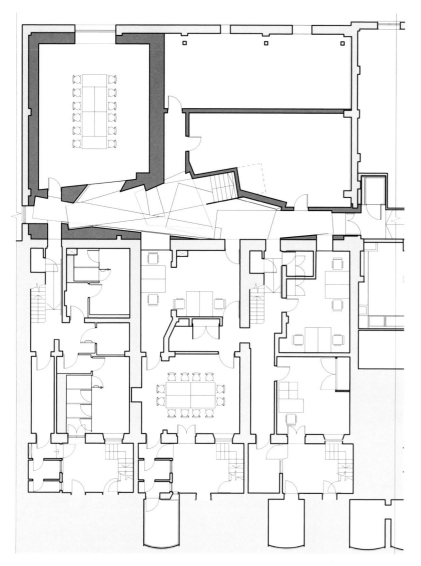

Above The basement plan shows the contrast between the organization of the rooms in the terrace and the sculptural qualities of the extension on the back of the building.

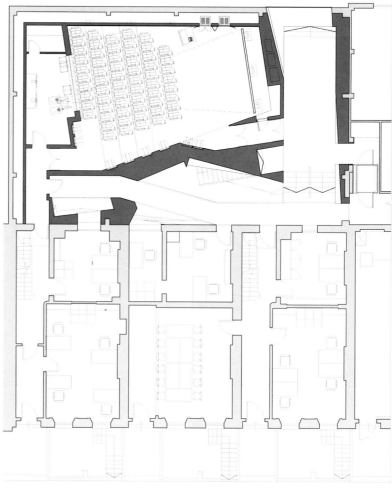

Above Ground-floor plan. The offices and tutorial spaces are positioned in the formal rooms of the terraces. The auditorium is located in the back extension.

In this project Surface Architects leant heavily on the language and formal requirements of the screen – and in particular the idea of montage – to create a unique space in which students can study film and cinema.

The designers treated the existing listed terrace and the 1970s extension as a 'montage': they were stitched together yet each offers a very different spatial experience. The terraced houses were left relatively untouched and reused to accommodate the more mundane requirements of the brief. The extension was treated as series of 'stop-frame' instants that were carved from the solid entity of the form of the extant building.

Organization

The designers were required to remodel the basement and ground floors of the terrace and extension in order to house an 80-seat state-of-the-art cinema/auditorium, seminar rooms, offices for staff and a library/archive with previewing facilities for the centre's collection of DVDs and videos. The existing building suggested a two-part strategy for the new reorganization of the interior.

The offices, one seminar room and the DVD library were all placed in the rooms of the terraces facing the street. The two-storey blank-walled extension on the back of the building offered scope for a more radical remodelling. It was here that the designers dramatically altered the building by stripping it back to its shell and then inserting the new auditorium and seminar space in the shape of a folded, carved room. The threshold between the terrace and the extension was a break-out space or foyer where students can sit, chat and catch up before entering the black-box auditorium. This space consisted of a double-height void through which a stair and a cranked steel bridge form the circulation. An over-scaled window offers one of the rare glimpses to the outside world. The view from the extension frames the brick walls of the Bloomsbury neighbours, and an upholstered ledge allows students to sit and think, away from the insular focus of the auditorium interior.

Detail

The disjunction between the terrace and the extension was heightened by the use of panels of dynamic, highly coloured surfaces. These panels were applied to a series of laser-cut sheets that were craned into the space and then connected to the new steel framework of the building. The steel and glass bridge and stairs braced the whole structure. Both are bathed in natural light pouring through a new rooftop skylight.

The explosive colouring of the interior has its basis in the choice of surfaces and the logic of movement through the space. Shiny and hard surfaces and colours are used to reflect natural light and movement, whilst tactile surfaces are used to exemplify stasis and signify places of repose. Grey and yellow poured resin was used to create the shiny and reflective basement floor. Walls were painted in fuchsia pink and orange, marked out in sharp, triangulated shapes. The underside of the bridge was finished with shiny stainless steel panels. Away from the movement spaces the corridor leading to the window seat was painted in a soothing crimson and the seat upholstered in a dark velour. The inside of the auditorium was finished in black upholstery, creating a distinct and moody environment in which students can relax and enjoy the film.

1 Sam McElhinney (Surface Architects), quoted in *Frame*, September/October 2007, p.102

Above left The underside of the bridge is clad in reflective steel panels with lighting sunk into its underside.

Above Lurid colours have been chosen to dramatically enhance the interior's angularity.

Left Sketch models of the development process reinforce the sculptural and folded qualities of the space.

The history of modern consumer culture is therefore in essence also a history of the continuous evolution and the ever increasing sophistication of commercial display and presentation methods. From the Bon Marché in 1850s Paris to Rem Koolhaas's recently opened Prada store in New York, retail has always been an extravagant spectacle … what counts is the successful attraction of attention and awakening of unknown desires.[1]

The inherent nature of an interior space that is designed to display goods is one of constant change. Shop interiors are responsive, adaptable environments that can be altered quickly and readily – much more so than the architectural enclosure in which they are often contained. This is particularly acute in the design of fashion showrooms, where the environments that contain and display goods such as clothing and shoes are designed to reflect an innate sense of transformation, replicating the constant need to be fashionable. Shops are reflections of many desires, not least the wish to consume, but they also express the need to communicate identity whilst conferring status on both the product and the consumer. The many different ways in which shops incorporate social and cultural rituals offer compelling lessons for designers who want to make spaces that are sharply defined communicative environments. Shop interiors pinpoint an exact emphatic visual language in order to entice a customer. In these instances the spatial environment can be viewed as an event that is an extension of the visual identity of the chosen item or product. This includes the paper in which the goods are wrapped and the bag into which they are placed.

The reuse of existing buildings to create spaces for the display and consumption of products often results, therefore, in short-lived and extravagant temporal micro-environments. These are spaces that stylize cultural, economic and social phenomena. They are transitory spaces designed to invite attention and stimulate desire. This introduction examines the history of the display of goods, in order to contextualize the spectacular transformative qualities of the adaptations of spaces that have contained them.

The arcades and department stores

The arcades are a centre of commerce in luxury items. In fitting them out, art enters the service of the merchant.[2]

Late nineteenth- and early twentieth-century retail spaces revolved predominantly around arcades and large-scale department stores. Whilst traditional forms of commerce such as stalls in markets and commercial streets still existed, covered streets such as the Galleria Vittorio Emanuele II in Milan and the Burlington Arcade in London, along with large department stores such as Le Bon Marché and

CHAPTER 3 **Shop**

Printemps in Paris and the Wertheim department store in Berlin, evolved in response to the needs of the emerging bourgeoisie. They were constructed in order to allow shoppers to browse amongst masses of goods, free from the vicissitudes of the street and protected from inclement weather.

These spaces and their goods evolved in response to the late nineteenth- and early twentieth-century development of the distribution and consumption of goods. This was a rapidly developing network of technological advances that included expanding mass transport systems, new methods of communication and increases in disposable income and leisure time, much of which had developed during the Industrial Revolution, which began in the eighteenth century. These factors were recognized as conditions that were central to an evolving consumerist economy, and ultimately resulted in an accelerated expansion of the retail sector.

Arcades and department stores would service the needs of the well-off, who would spend their leisure time browsing amongst the goods on sale. The interior environment would unify the surroundings in which the goods would be displayed, yet the variety and quality of products would emphasize the distinctions between them.

The increasing significance of shopping as a leisure activity was encouraged by the provision of extra spaces such as restaurants, reading rooms and gardens. These were designed to alleviate the relentless flow of consumption and entice customers into lengthier excursions, ironically leading to more time being spent in the stores and ultimately lengthier bouts of consumption.

Other significant spatial developments included the adaptation of arcades and stores to house temporary events and themes. Extravagant spectacles such as London's Great Exhibition in 1851 and the World Exposition in Paris in 1900 influenced these excessive occasions, where the 'event' interiors

of stores were staged theatrical entities that would keep customers coming back for more.

Arcades and department stores were amongst many emerging forms of entertainment in the early part of the twentieth century that transformed the form and appearance of the city and its streets. Fairs, expositions, music halls, theatres, arcades, cinemas, bars and restaurants all vied for the attention of the new leisure classes. The spectacle of the street, with its variety of goods and sellers, shops, stalls and booths had been to some extent interiorized and sanitized by the arcades and department stores, so the external representation of the interior of the arcade and store to the street thus became an important element with which to attract attention and direct custom. Shop windows therefore became important devices, showcasing the interior of a building to the street, competing with the other forms of urban entertainment. Within the new streetscape of artifice and spectacle the fantastic arrangements of ever-changing goods in brightly lit windows became an art form in itself. Austrian-American designer Frederick Kiesler arranged the windows for Saks, on Fifth Avenue in New York. He described it as a process that was designed to:

Simulate desire. That is why shop windows, institutional propaganda, and advertising were created.[3]

The shopping centre and the high street

In the middle of the twentieth century, post-war governments, industry and businesses encouraged consumerism with cheap loans, credit and cash. High street stores and shopping centres transformed both the main streets and suburbs of major cities across the world. Whilst still prevalent on the high street, the arcade and the department store model evolved into the shopping centre or mall: a covered space with a generic collection of products and retail environments, refreshment areas and entertainment centres. The shopping centre was a department store with its own internal street. It could often be

Left The atrium of the Wertheim department store on Leipziger Platz in central Berlin, built in 1896.

Below left Displays of goods such as clothing and furniture in the Wertheim store were designed to seduce customers into spending their money as well as their leisure time in the store.

Bottom The enigmatic and dynamic Saks shop window on 5th Avenue, New York, designed by Frederick Kiesler.

Opposite The Burlington Arcade, London, designed in 1819 by Samuel Ware.

Right The simplicity of the interior and the well-chosen yet affordable products on sale made Habitat an instant high-street success.

Far right The Joseph store by Eva Jiricna in London was dominated by a centrally placed, highly engineered sculptural steel-and-glass staircase that linked all three floors of the space.

found out of the town that it imitated and was usually designed to be accessed primarily by car. Technological developments such as air-conditioning, artificial lighting and escalators were used to create controlled spaces within which the movement and flow of goods and people could be carefully choreographed.

In London in the late 1950s and early 1960s the boutique – originally a concession or stand-alone space in a department store – appeard as an independent shop on the high street. Alongside the boutiques, retailer Terence Conran started Habitat, a shop offering utilitarian goods in a simple, whitewashed, quarry-tiled space.

The emergence of the boutique as a 'one-off' established a pattern of growth on the high street, a model that is still prevalent today. This is alongside its antithesis, the chain store, a series of shops selling the same goods in various cities, often on a global scale, often with the same spatial identity. Ironically, many of today's chain stores started as one-off boutiques themselves.

The language and appearance of retail spaces changed significantly in the 1980s when marketing and advertising strategies seized on the socio-cultural and technological changes taking place across the world. One manifestation of these changes was that the designers of retail spaces began to appropriate the visual language and display strategies of white-cube art galleries and museums. Interior spaces became cool and crisp and acted as scenography for the display of objects, usually clothes, that were artfully placed within minimalist environments of glass, timber, concrete and steel. Events or signature details became elements that signified the identity of the products on display.

Japanese fashion designers such as Issey Miyake and Rei Kawakubo (of Comme des Garçons) commissioned stores across the world that were extreme versions of their minimalist and highly detailed clothing. The Comme des Garçons shop in the Axis building in Tokyo was so extreme that none of the clothes were on display – garments were only brought out of glass-panelled drawers by staff upon request. Other shop interiors, such as the Joseph stores in London designed by Eva Jiricna, were highly engineered environments, characterized by signature steel staircases, formed from steel and glass suspended by tension wires. The reuse of existing buildings to create shop interiors had reached a point where clothing, identity and the spatial environment were intrinsically linked, with each part reinforcing the other, regardless of the architectural envelope in which they were located.

The destination store

Shopping is doubtless the last form of public activity.[4]

After the discreet environments of minimalist interiors drifted out of fashion, the use of existing buildings for retail spaces became enthralled by the notion of the 'event', a retail experience that made the store into a 'destination'. The Prada Epicenter shop in New York, by Rem Koolhaas/OMA is not just a shop but also incorporates a stage for performances, catwalks, a moveable display system that allows the shop to be completely reconfigured, and a whole range of technical devices such as stock-check screens and changing-room doors whose opacity can be adjusted at the flick of a switch. Koolhaas and OMA even completed their own guide to shopping during the time that they were designing the shop.

Koolhaas developed the shop along the lines of other public spaces, such as the museum, the shopping centre and the airport (in fact the New York Prada shop was located in the former downtown Guggenheim gallery). He utilized their design language and conflated these public spaces to make one public interior event environment. The oki-ni shop in London by 6a architects was designed on a fraction of the budget of the Prada shop but also utilized an existing building. It was located on Savile Row, the heart of tailoring in London, and was designed as a small shop where the space became a stage-set 'experience' for the customer and the display of the clothing. The 'event' dimension of the store was that the garments on display were only for trying on. If bought, a pair of jeans or shirt would be immediately shipped to your door via a warehouse.

The most recent development in the design of retail spaces is in essence a distillation of many of the aspects of shop interior design. The transience and temporal aspects of retail design, along with the desire to capture a fleeting moment or 'zeitgeist', is represented by the development of the pop-up or guerrilla shop model. In many retail interiors the host space is designed in order to narrate the brand identity. This distillation of a visual language is often constructed from particular materials, colours and spatial devices.

The development of the pop-up shop is regarded as an antidote to the saturated and potentially jaded palette

of the high street landscape. The consumer is challenged to find the space; it is often in an unusual location in an unorthodox district of the city, and often only open for a short period of time. The guerrilla or pop-up shop can act as a 'refresher' of a brand as well as a bold signifier of the ambition of the company, and of course as a radical promotional tool.

Comme des Garçons opened the first guerrilla shop in Berlin in 2004. Along with social media and word of mouth, the attention that the space received ensured large amounts of publicity. The pop-up shop is a form of occupation of an existing building. It does not involve an expensive redesign, but simply utilizes what fixtures, fittings and furniture are left behind. It often revels in the theatrical element of the tension between the previous and the new use. After the Berlin shop, Comme des Garçons went on to open other guerrilla shops across the world, and the strategy itself has since been co-opted by many other brands attempting to alter and refresh their identities.

This chapter explores several case studies that demonstrate ways of reusing existing buildings to create spaces for the display of goods. All of the studies communicate the essential elements of shop-space design – the

particular spatial identities with which to attract and define custom, and to stimulate desire.

1 Christoph Grunenberg, *Wonderland: Spectacles of Display from the Bon Marché to Prada*, cited in *Shopping: A Century of Art and Consumer Culture* (exhibition catalogue), Tate Publishing, 2002, p.20

2 Walter Benjamin, *The Arcades Project*, translated by Howard Eiland and Kevin McLaughlin, Harvard University Press, 2002, p.220

3 Frederick Kiesler, *Contemporary Art Applied to the Store and its Display*, Bretano, 1930, p.79, cited in Christoph Grunenberg, *op cit.*, p.27

4 Judy Chang Chuihua, Jeffrey Inaba, Rem Koolhaas and Sze Tsung Leong, *Harvard Design School Guide to Shopping*, Taschen, 2001, inside cover

Top The Prada Epicenter store in New York, designed by Rem Koolhaas/OMA, with its stage open, ready to facilitate a performance.

Above oki-ni by 6a in London allowed customers to try on clothing and shoes, but then had their purchases shipped to their homes via a remote warehouse.

Left A disused warehouse in Berlin was the first guerrilla store for Comme des Garçons in 2004.

PROJECT	**Knize Tailors**
DESIGNER	Adolf Loos
LOCATION	Vienna, Austria
DATE	1910–13

Above The upper salon of the store, designed to resemble a gentlemen's club or library. The mezzanine contained the workshop and staff spaces.

Left The enigmatic Swedish black granite of the abstract three-part portico façade.

Context

Knize tailors was the first of many shops Loos designed. It was completed for Gisela Wolff. The premises was located in a prominent building on one of the main shopping streets in central Vienna. The two-storey space consisted of a narrow ground floor with a helical staircase that led to the upper-level tailor's salon, spread across three neighbouring spaces. The existing building was a solid masonry construction with timber-beamed ceilings – a typical nineteenth-century Viennese construction.

Concept

Well dressed: who doesn't want to be? Our century has done away with sumptuary laws, including those including dress, and everyone has the right to dress like a king … Somewhere an American philosopher says, 'A young man can count himself rich if he has a brain in his head and a decent suit in his wardrobe' – that is a philosopher who knows the world. What use is a brain if one doesn't have the clothes to set it off.[1]

With the Knize shop, the enigmatic Viennese designer Adolf Loos created an interior that matched the style of his writing: concise, well formed and utterly inscrutable. In a series of essays published in *Das Andere* ('The Other'), Loos explored topics as diverse as plumbing, short hair, gentlemen's hats and underwear. His most famous essay, 'Ornament and Crime', published in 1908, expressed his distaste for superfluous ornament in design, architecture and clothing; he associated ornamentation with a degenerative impulse, appropriate only for savages. The Knize shop allowed Loos to invent an elegant, functional space that dignified the customer, whether they bought a shirt or were fitted with a bespoke suit. The design of the shop combined many of Loos's interests whilst simultaneously expressing many of the ambiguities that were apparent in his thoughts and writing.

Organization

The shop was located on the Graben ('ditch'), a long, wide central street in Vienna, lined with luxury shops and banks. The façade of the new shop was conceived as a powerful statement within the context of the street and the city. It was constructed by using black Swedish granite formed into an abstract three-part portico consisting of plinth, columns and frieze. The columns housed two inset glass display cases. These curved inwards towards the door, yet the plinth upon which they sat did not. This meant that the visitor had a clear view of the goods, but to get a closer view had to move around the knee-high plinth and towards the central opening of the shop. This simple device propelled potential customers towards the narrow front door and, from there, into the shop itself.

The interior of the shop was designed to be modern, although it expressed many traditional elements in both its materiality and organization. The ground floor occupied a thin, narrow space that sold shirts and accessories. These were displayed in floor-to-ceiling oak cabinets, with some in drawers and others in glass vitrines. The space was completed with a waist-high island glass display cabinet in the centre. Set into the far wall of the room was the cash desk. The accessibility of both the products and the space meant that the ground floor was popular and open to all. The upper floor was a different matter. This housed the men's tailoring salon with a sewing area, drapery, fitting rooms, tailoring spaces and a cashier. A private mezzanine level held the workshop, staff room and accounts offices.

Loos conceived the upper level of the shop as a private club, and the enfilade, or suite, of rooms was designed as an exclusive space where customers could spend time and potentially part with their money.

Above The protruding knee-high plinth of the base of the shopfront was designed to draw customers around the display case and in through the front door.

Detail

Knize catered for men only, so Loos designed the space with its masculine clientele in mind. He used oak panelling and cherry for the cabinetry and walls, whilst Persian rugs and leather armchairs recreated the atmosphere of a gentlemen's salon or library. The two levels differed in both their role and their materiality. The lower level, designed to attract customers with cheaper off-the-peg goods, employed materials such as cherry, plaster and green linoleum on the floor to reflect its accessibility. In order to alleviate the restrictions of the ground floor Loos set mirrors into the wall at a high level, suggesting infinite space within the small interior. Glass and timber was highly polished, reflecting the intimacy and scale of this small room. Cherry panelling with inset mirrors lined the helical staircase, framed next to the cash desk, making the small space appear bigger and also allowing surveillance, as visitors could be seen ascending the stair. The mirrors also denoted the subtle shift from public to more private space. A large mirror placed on the wall of the stairwell suggested a 'second' façade of the shop, one that contradicted the solidity of the exterior granite façade. Instead of conveying solidity, the mirror projected unpredictability, demonstrated by the transitory reflection of the customer as they tentatively ascended the stair to the tailoring salon.

On the upper floor, amongst the displays of goods, Loos arranged free-standing furniture, as though imitating small domestic scenes. Luxurious leather chairs, sofas, coffee tables and rugs all suggested a more relaxed atmosphere and a place where plenty of time could be taken for selecting and fitting clothing. Loos reinforced these small stage sets with intricately carved oak ceilings that contained light sources.

The Knize shop still exists today – intact and almost identical to the day it first opened.

---

1 Adolf Loos, 'Men's Fashion' (1898), in *Ornament and Crime: Selected Essays*, Ariadne Press, 1998, p.39

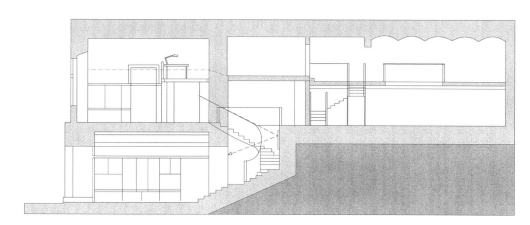

Left The section shows the central stair that articulates the threshold between the public space of the ground floor and the more exclusive upper-floor 'club' environment.

Below left The ground floor occupies one 'bay' of the host building. It is organized by a central display case and is lined by cabinets displaying shirts and accessories.

Below The upper floor is organized across three bays of the host building with each room containing a 'stage set' arrangement of tables and chairs.

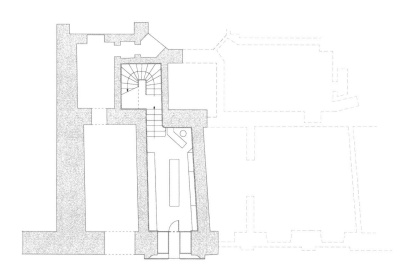

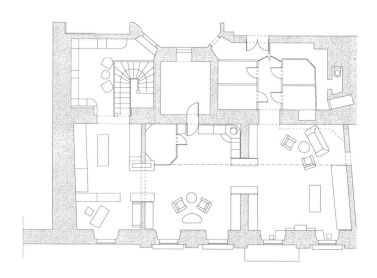

Far left The ground floor contained off-the-peg items such as shirts and accessories. The space was dominated by a central display case. The cashier was located at the far end of the room to the right of the stair.

Left To encourage customers to spend time in the space, the interior was arranged to resemble a series of domestic scenes, with carpets, comfortable chairs and coffee tables strewn with magazines.

Far left A mirror set into the stair between the upper and lower level of the shop made it possible to watch customers as they ascended to the salon.

Left The upper level of the shop occupied three buildings and was arranged as an enfilade of rooms through which customers could walk and browse at leisure.

Olivetti Showroom

PROJECT	**Olivetti Showroom**
DESIGNER	Carlo Scarpa
LOCATION	Venice, Italy
DATE	1957–8

Above The Olivetti showroom viewed through the front display window facing Piazza San Marco.

Left The shop occupied the lower floors of the Procuratie Vecchie and was recessed into the colonnade, sheltering it from the main square.

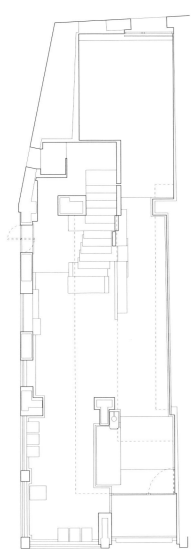

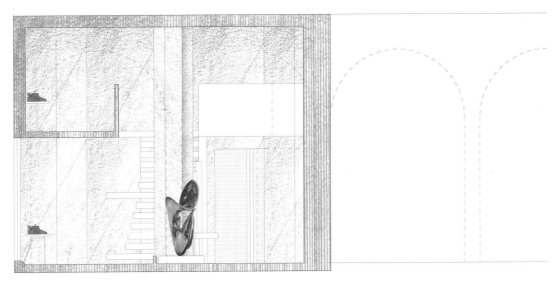

Left The logic of the interior was derived from the immovable columns of the existing building. The relationship of the space to the piazza was articulated by the deep entrance threshold. The stair dominated the composition.

Above The view through the space from the entrance was articulated by a series of elements such as the sculpture by Alberto Viani, the cascade of stone that formed the central stair and the latticed screen at the back of the showroom.

Below The typewriters are displayed on cantilevered trays in the window facing Sottoportico del Cavaletto. The sculpture by Alberto Viani is in the background to the right of the immovable column that Scarpa had to work around.

Context

In the late fifties, Adriano Olivetti, president of the Italian office equipment firm, commissioned Scarpa to remodel a small showroom in the centre of Venice. The showroom was located on the ground floor of the Procuratie Vecchie, at the intersection of Sottoportico del Cavalletto and Piazza San Marco. It was recessed into the colonnade and shielded away from the bustle of the main piazza. The difficult site was 21 metres (69 feet) long, 5 metres (16 feet) wide and only 4 metres (13 feet) high. Nevertheless, it had an interesting corner location and significant front and rear vistas, which Scarpa used to dramatic affect.

Concept

There were spaces you couldn't change, a central pillar, two windows – where should the stairs go? I decided to put them wherever I could gain elbowroom … by putting them at the most difficult point I could throw something out – and I was interested in getting rid of things. In this way I could make better use of the length.[1]

Organization

As with many of Scarpa's projects, the qualities of the site, its location and the possibilities of the new function afforded him a series of reflections on the possibilities for the new interior. Once the existing interior was stripped out, he introduced a series of interventions that accepted the vagaries of the host building. He set about manipulating the long, thin room into a clearly ordered, sequential space that opened up to the light and a view of the piazza at the front of the building, and which carefully filtered the reflections from the canal at the back of the showroom. Light and views were key to the new space. Scarpa believed that the gradual modulation of light – from the display windows in the arcade, to the latticed screen at the back – allowed the visitor to see the whole space as a reflection and abstraction of Venetian light.

The front façade of the showroom consisted of a large glass display window that could be viewed through the colonnade from the piazza. The side façade was formed from two large glass windows, situated towards the square. Away from the piazza the façade was clad extensively in large panels of concrete. These culminated in a side door for staff, demarcated by a panel of Istrian stone, carved with the trademark Olivetti name. The glazed front door of the space faced the piazza and was set deep into the masonry arch of the building. An elaborately woven steel gate, which folded back eloquently when the showroom was open, protected it.

The occupation of the double bay of the inner colonnade of the Procuratie meant that Scarpa had to organize the interior around immoveable constraints such as a central column, positioned at the front of the space. He adopted an asymmetrical organization that, to the right of the column, opened the interior to the piazza and afforded the visitor a straight view through the interior. The back wall was clad with a delicate lattice screen that offered selective views of the canal. The column also created a deep threshold, one that drew the visitor into the room. This open entrance 'hall' was dominated by an abstract sculpture by Alberto Viani, reflected in a shallow basin of water that was slightly raised from the floor. Once inside the hall and past the column the visitor was free to follow a direct route through the space or drift into the other side of the room.

Scarpa also inserted a mezzanine into the interior that created a narrow, galleried upper level, accessed by a sculptural marble staircase. This staircase, with its expressive cascading 'tumble' of large slabs of Aurisina marble, formed the dominant feature of the space and disrupted the formality of the interior, enticing visitors into the heart of the room. The huge, irregular slabs of stone invited the visitor up the stair, yet they appeared to rest on nothing but a thin brass rod placed through the riser-less treads. After promenading through the space and up the stairs to the mezzanine the visitor was offered a view back to the piazza through two almond-shaped 'eyes'.

Above The low teak soffit compresses the space under the mezzanine, an effect only relieved by the view from the interior back out onto Piazza San Marco.

Right The glass-inlaid mosaic-tiled cement floor undulates through the space, directing the eye towards the lattice screen at the back, which filters light from the adjacent canal.

Detail

The progression of movement through Scarpa's interior was elaborated by the deployment of a variety of exquisite materials and surfaces. The ground-floor walls on the entrance side were lined with an ordered sequence of polished plaster panels, bordered with wooden frames. The mezzanine balustrades were also rendered in pale plaster, whilst the soffit and the interior of the gallery walkways were lined with a veneer of dark African teak. The floor of the showroom was elevated 310 millimetres (12 inches) above that of the piazza and was made from cement with a glass mosaic inlay. The coloured tiles were laid in four distinct colours and patterned in order to simulate water, one of Scarpa's constant preoccupations and symbolic of the city of Venice. This created what appeared to be a gently ebbing floor, just like a sheet of water.

As for the products themselves, typewriters were displayed on small wooden trays in the showroom's large windows. These were cantilevered from the base of the windows and then hung from a steel rod connected to the ceiling. Lighting was recessed into the walls and covered by vertical strips of satin glass.

1 Carlo Scarpa, interviewed by Martin Dominguez in May 1978, in Francesco Dal Co and Giuseppe Mazzariol (editors), *Carlo Scarpa: The Complete Works*, Rizzoli, 1985, p.297

Left The tumbling slabs of stone unfold from the upper level and appear to float down to the floor, inviting the visitor up to the mezzanine.

Above Two almond-shaped apertures frame the view back towards the piazza.

PROJECT	**Retti Candle Shop**
DESIGNER	Hans Hollein
LOCATION	Vienna, Austria
DATE	1965

Above The axial view through the interior was carefully articulated in order to express the contrast between the first and second rooms of the shop.

Left The brushed-aluminium façade of the space was inserted into the lower floor of the Baroque Viennese building in an incongruous and collage-like fashion for maximum contrast between the old and the new.

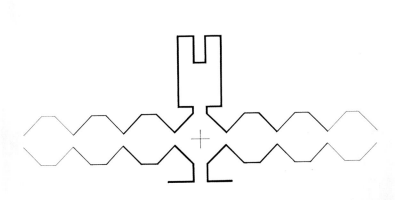

Context

This retail space was designed for the candlemaker Marius Retti. The shop was inserted into a richly detailed Baroque building on the Kohlmarkt, a main shopping street in central Vienna. A small 14.8-square-metre (160-square-foot) footprint was arranged into two rooms in the one-storey ground-floor space of the existing building.

Concept

To do justice to Hollein, one cannot ignore the Viennese reality …Vienna possessed a tradition of aesthetic heightening of reality, a long praxis of artificial remoteness. The techniques of montage, collage, alienation, striking allusions and disarming quotation are not cultivated in language alone.[1]

In 1965 Hollein wrote 'Zukunft der Architektur' ('Future of Architecture') in which he examined the role of history, technology, modernity and ideology. He published a series of collages entitled 'Transformations' (1963–ß8), which placed objects such as aircraft carriers, railway carriages and spark plugs into images of cities and landscapes in a strikingly incongruous manner. This combination of urbanism, technology and montage is a strategy that was realized in the Retti shop.

The compact aluminium façade stood out and announced its presence amongst the other shops in the busy street. The shop appeared to have been 'plugged in' to the host building. Various meanings and symbols have been attached to the form and appearance of this façade: some have likened the doorway to a candle or an abstracted impression of a column, a response to the Baroque detailing of the existing building. Others have described the façade as the combination of two Rs

Top left The playful advertising hoardings of the shop announcing its opening and the designer as the building work was undertaken.

Above left The basic geometrical concept of the plan of the shop is shown in this sketch by the designer.

Above The importance of the axial view into the shop through the abstracted column of the doorway and the acute angle of the window displays is shown in an early drawing of the façade.

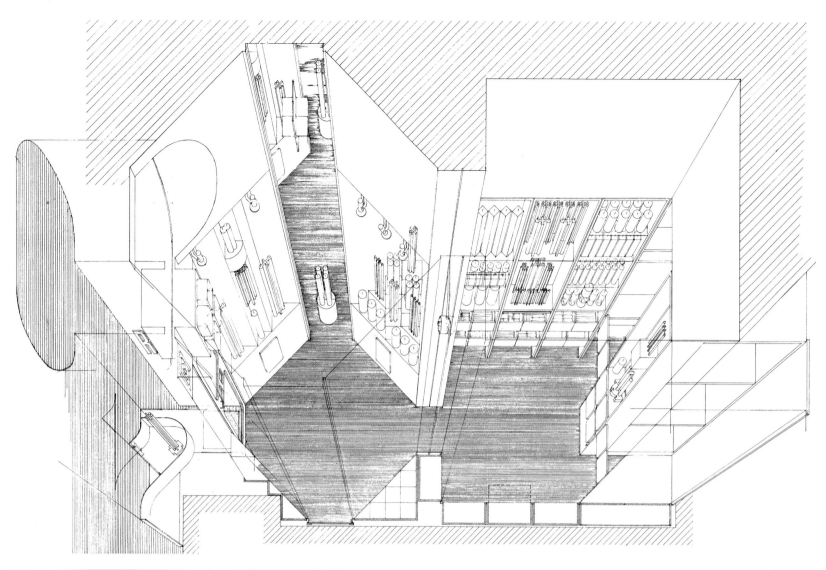

placed back to back, announcing the surname and owner of the shop to the street. Sketches of the façade by Hollein show how he accepted the formal arrangement and decoration of the existing building and allowed it to influence the new arrangement. The new entrance was a subtracted version of the central column of the upper level, recessed into the flat metal façade.

Organization

The lack of external advertising heightened the quality and value of the shop and its products by making them appear exclusive. Hollein conceded to one form of external display by placing two small shop windows in the façade. These were set at angles to the street, making them difficult to see straight on, suggesting that this was not the place for casual browsing or impulse buying. Placed at the centre of the façade was a glass door, which allowed axial views directly into the shop.

The interior was organized into two rooms that corresponded to this direct central axis. The first room was octagonal and exhibited candles on polished aluminium cubes. The cubes

were set within a series of niches that were created by the newly formed angular walls. The slightly larger second room conformed to the rectangular shape of the existing building. It displayed candles in a less reverential manner, utilizing regular shelving units that lined the walls. The second room also contained the cash desk, wrapping area and storage.

Detail

The narrowness and diminutive size of the shop meant that Hollein had to consider carefully every small detail and choice of material. Brushed aluminium was used predominantly on the façade and into the interior, expressing a continuity between inside and out. It was also used to line the ceiling and cover the lower and upper levels of the walls. In the first room display area, a series of silk-lined niches were coloured a vivid orange. This created a dramatic backdrop against which the colourful candles could be positioned. The floor of the shop was finished with a vibrant orange vinyl, contrasting with the clinical appearance of the brushed steel skin. In the second room, formica panels were used to line the shelves and clad the

storage units, creating a subtle contrast between the front and back of the space. The front door manifested an important deep threshold between inside and out and framed the view through the interior to the back wall display. The threshold between the first and second room, in turn, was expressed as an open slot, framing the view towards the backlit display of candles. At the sides of the first room, at the junction between the existing building walls and the angle of the new niched planes, Hollein applied two floor-to-ceiling mirrors. These gave the effect of endless space within the narrow shop.

Lighting and ventilation was integrated into the space. The metal skin of the façade and interior housed the ducts and channels of the air movement systems. Hollein exposed the grilles of the system above the front door and below the candle displays, giving the impression of a technologically advanced machine, one that contained and carefully looked after the soft, waxy candles. The view through the front door was punctuated by a set of lights and a backlit wall of candles at the far end of the space. The niches were lit by spotlights hung from the

soffit of each recess. Each junction and view was thus articulated carefully and coherently throughout this small but incredibly efficient interior space.

1 Friedrich Achleitner, 'Viennese Positions', *Lotus* 29, 1981.

Opposite, above The axonometric view of the shop demonstrates the 'two-room' concept of the interior.

Opposite, below left Endless reflections are created by corner mirrors in the initial octagonal room.

Opposite, below right The well-controlled lighting in the tiny shop space illuminates the silk-lined niches, making the colourful candles stand out.

Below left The soft, malleable candles and the silk-lined niches contrast with the cold brushed-aluminium panels and the technological aesthetic of the grilles of the air-circulation system.

Below The lights are endlessly reflected through space.

Issey Miyake Store

PROJECT	**Issey Miyake Store**
DESIGNER	Shiro Kuramata, Kuramata Design Studio
LOCATION	Shibuya, Tokyo, Japan
DATE	1987

Above The free-standing metal-mesh cage was intended to communicate a sharp and well-defined image of the identity of the designer and the clothing, in order to stand out from the other fashion outlets in the department store.

Left The cage's double-layered skin was meant almost to disappear within the harshly lit interior of the store.

Context

The fashion brand Issey Miyake was established in 1970 and named after its creator. Miyake and the designer Shiro Kuramata collaborated on many designs, ranging from shop interiors to furniture – both found common ground in the transient nature of fashion, a respect for the properties of particular materials and an understanding of how the past informs the future. From the 1960s onwards, Kuramata designed over 300 boutiques and restaurants, yet because of the fast-changing pace of fashion and the transient nature of Tokyo's infrastructure, hardly any remain today.

The men's boutique Kuramata designed for Miyake was located in the Seibu department store in the Shibuya-ku district of Tokyo.

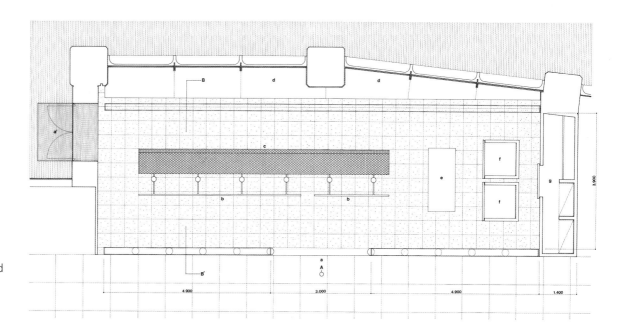

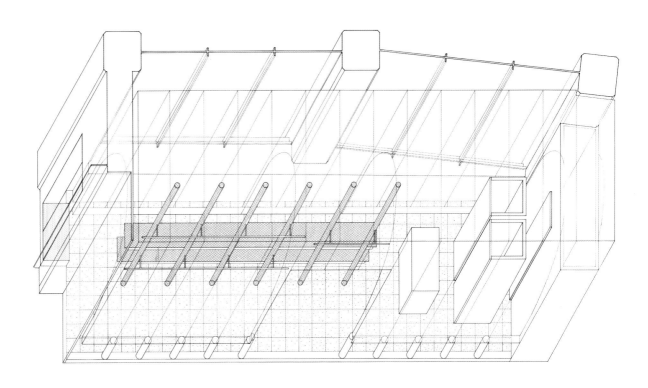

Top The plan of the store with the outer wall at the top. The cash desk and changing rooms are square and heavy and are deliberately articulated in order to counterpoint the light and airy mesh covering.

Above The axonometric of the store shows the fundamental components of the scheme: the central shelves, supported by the columns and the cash desk and changing rooms.

Concept

Designing is an act of transience. In this sense design is very similar to Tokyo. There are no concrete or eternal things here.[1]

Retail spaces designed to reflect fashion are generally essays in transience: they are spaces that are intended to mirror the shifting patterns of seasonal fashion and style. The Seibu department stores are the oldest and most established in Japan. The individual showrooms within this type of interior are quite different in nature to ordinary high street boutiques; they are an exaggerated type of shop that seeks to imprint a defined image of its contents upon the customer. Each shop must do this whilst jostling alongside other retail spaces, all seeking to deliver an impressive identity and entice customers into their space. In this context, novelty can become the norm, but other methods of communication are possible. Kuramata decided that in order to stand out he would adopt the strategy of invisibility. Thus, he created a light, floating, immaterial structure with which to showcase Miyake's sharply defined garments.

Organization

The long and narrow installation covered just 80 square metres (860 square feet) of display space. It was contained within two bays of the large floor of the department store building. It was enclosed by glazing on one side and by the entrance to the shop floor on the other. The simple layout of the project belied the visual complexity of the interior.

Kuramata lined the space with a free-standing expanded metal mesh box. Within this cage he placed a steel-mesh 'vault'. Six steel-mesh columns were positioned in the centre of the space, from which a rail and two long shelves were hung in the form of a cantilever. Clothing was displayed in two ways: it was either hung from the steel rail or carefully folded and laid upon the shelves. A solid granite cash desk and two changing rooms were placed at the end of the room and were positioned to deliberately counterpoint the weightlessness of the shimmery, floating interior space.

Detail

The choice of mesh with which to articulate the interior created a space that resonated with light and shadow and one that appeared to disappear before the customer's eyes. Kuramata used baked black metal mesh for the skin of the space, such as the walls and the vault. The shelving was constructed using chrome-plated metal mesh. The result was that, as the customer passed around the shop floor and through the installation, the two layers of mesh appeared to shimmer. The shiny inner layer would sparkle through the veiled black envelope of the showroom. The counter and changing room were constructed from hard, solid blocks of stone. This was to provide a sharp contrast to the ephemeral quality of the enclosure in which they were contained.

The floor was covered by a coarse-ground emery tile. These small flecks of ground glass granules created a surface that was rough and abrasive underfoot, but sparkled under the lighting of the showroom, offering an intriguing contrast of grit and glitter within the small space. The existing integrated ceiling lighting system of the showroom gave a general wash of light to the shop. This bland light was counteracted by a series of downlighters set between the mesh cage and vault. These illuminated the garments with pinpoint accuracy and added to the sensation of shadowy emptiness that invigorated this corner of the bright and brash department store.

---

1 Shiro Kuramata, quoted in *Domus*, April 2003, p.110

Right The shelves are cantilevered from the columns. Garments are either neatly folded and laid on the shelf or hung on hangers suspended from the columns.

Left The simple layout of the store belies the visual complexity of the interior.

Below left The shimmering mesh is designed to attract the attention of the passing customer in the store.

PROJECT	**Mandarina Duck**
DESIGNERS	Renny Ramakers and Gijs Bakker (Droog); NL Architects
LOCATION	Paris, France
DATE	2000

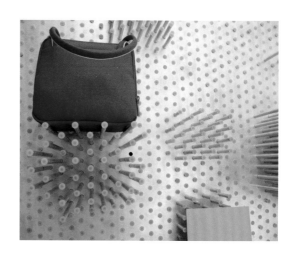

Above The upper-floor curtain room encloses a display of bags on a free-standing unit and is wrapped by screens of hanging steel balls.

Left The shop-window view of the pinwheel-bag wall.

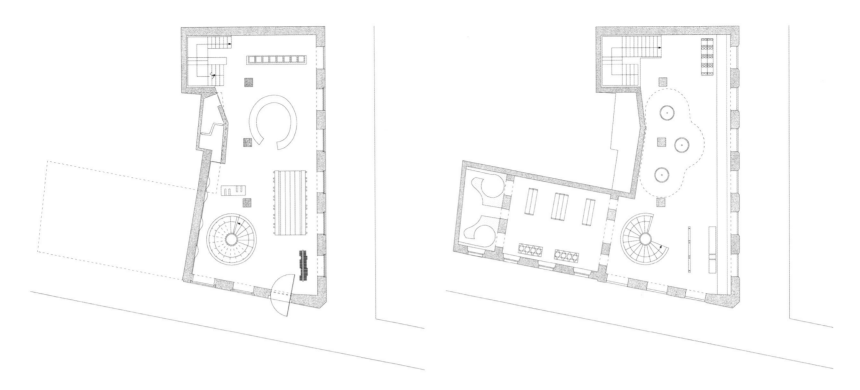

Context

Mandarina Duck is an Italian fashion label, formed in 1977 and specializing in luggage. The mandarin duck is a colourful bird, known for flying long distances non-stop, and it provided the perfect emblem for the company and its sophisticated, jet-set clientele. The host building for their flagship store was a nondescript nineteenth-century building on the fashionable Rue St-Honoré.

Concept

I think the whole policy of corporate brand image is slightly outdated. There is now so much competition that shopping has to be entertainment. You need to do more than sell your products, or perhaps in order to sell your products, you need to give people an experience. Stamping out the same shop in every city is not necessarily the most effective way to do this.[1]

Above Lit by curved low-energy bulbs, the cash desk is situated on the ground floor at the back of the shop.

Top left Ground-floor plan. The building is sited on the corner of the street. Its interior is organized around a series of elements, each with their own specific character.

Top right First-floor plan. The shop's upper level also occupies the first floor of the adjacent building, and is also arranged as if it were an interior landscape of unique objects.

Droog ('Dry' or 'Sober') is the name of a loosely bound collective of designers formed in 1993 by Renny Ramakers and Gijs Bakker. Sensing a shift in ideas and, in particular, the preponderance of recycling existing objects, Droog was formed to showcase things and their designers. Both Ramaker and Bakker work as art directors and commissioners of new work that they then distribute under the Droog umbrella.

Mandarina Duck commissioned Droog initially to work on a bag, then a shop window. The success of these collaborations then led to a commission to work on a new shop in Paris. The shop was part of a strategic reorganization of the company's outlets around the world, a strategy manifested as three different types of shop. 'Embassies' were to be flagship stores, autonomous units in both style and character. 'Consulates' were medium-sized outlets and 'corners' were shops in department stores or within larger boutiques. Droog were asked to design the Parisian 'Embassy', a prominent shop approximately 300 square metres (3,230 square feet) in size. Ramakers and Bakker saw the interior project as an opportunity to 'curate' a series of objects placed within the interior in order to animate the display of products. The concept was, therefore, a furniture-based strategy: treating the interior as a 'landscape' of interior elements through which the visitor browses.

Organization

The shop was situated on the corner of Rue St-Honoré and the Rue d'Alger. It occupied the ground and first floor of the existing building. The ground-level front and side of the shop consisted of large display windows. The upper floor extended across the ground floor of a neighbouring shop. Apart from a series of columns to the rear and side of the space the interior was unfettered by any internal structure.

The interior of the shop was organized as a series of elements that were called 'cocoons'. These allowed the space to be understood as a series of distinct display environments – the customer moved between each of them in a random sequence, experiencing the products in a different setting each time. Circulation between the ground and first floors was at the front of the shop and took the form of a highly engineered steel spiral stair, revolving up, like an over-scaled corkscrew drilling through the space.

Detail

The general surfaces of the store were relatively neutral, with white walls and a tastefully pale poured resin floor. The idea was that this tasteful backdrop would accentuate the eccentricity of the new furniture. Bags are displayed on an oversized 'pinwall' of aluminium pipes placed at the entrance of the shop. When pushed into its spiny surface from the shop side a positive outline of the bag is revealed on the reverse side of the wall in the shop window. The revolving spiral stair, painted white, yellow and green, was designed to catch the visitor's eye and lead them to the upper level. A tunnel, displaying bags in a backlit channel of stacked plastic pallets, entices visitors deeper into the shop. The choice to use pallets for this was a meditation on the transient nature of travel – relating to the lifestyles of the customers who were buying the luggage. An incubator, complete with fixed rubber gloves, displays small, precious items that are usually not to be touched. A large steel 'doughnut' hides a display rack of clothes within its shiny steel shell. Its outward appearance suggests exclusivity, yet the inside of the object is packed with clothes and bags.

The witty display games are carried on upstairs with a curtain wall made from metal rods for changing behind, vacuum-formed display walls with clothes sandwiched in between them and a 'curtain room' that consists of a series of hanging steel-beaded screens. The whole of the experience is like passing through a landscape of furniture, with each area offering a different way of viewing and interacting with the objects on sale.

1 Simon Foxton (Creative Consultant, Mandarina Duck), quoted in Paul Hunwick, 'An Open and Shut Case', *Blueprint*, December 2000, p.51

Left The large and playful pinwheel bag wall as seen from the shop interior.

Top left The 'incubator', where precious objects are housed that can only be touched with rubber gloves. The spiral stair is in front.

Above left The shiny steel 'doughnut' is used for discreet displays of bags and clothing.

Top right The colourful lime-green spiral stair is designed to stand out and attract visitors to the upper level.

Above right A tall wall of swaying steel rods screens the changing room and customers from the public space.

PROJECT	**Alexander McQueen**
DESIGNER	William Russell
LOCATION	New York, NY, USA
DATE	2002

Above Clothes are displayed in what appears to be a carved and glacial environment where floors become walls, walls become ceilings, and so on.

Left A small canopy over the front door announces the entrance of the shop in the gritty environment of New York's meat-packing district.

Context

The innovative fashion designer Alexander McQueen commissioned designer William Russell of Pentagram to design his new flagship store on West 14th Street in New York. This subsequently became the blueprint for his London and Milan shops.

The shop occupied the ground floor of a four-storey warehouse in the Meatpacking District of lower west-side Manhattan. This area was historically the location of the city's abattoirs and warehouses, and by the 1980s it was run-down and notorious for prostitution and drug dealing. Its gentrification, in the late 1990s, started with artists and designers, followed by designer boutiques and hotels. Today it is considered one of New York's most fashionable neighbourhoods, with only a handful of slaughterhouses and packing plants left.

Concept

In contrast to established traditional upmarket New York shopping streets such as Madison Avenue, the choice of this gritty downtown district for the new flagship store was a deliberate attempt to reinforce the identity of McQueen as an 'edgy' designer. McQueen and fellow British fashion designer Stella McCartney established the first high-end fashion shops in the district. Now many other fashion designers, along with restaurants, hotels, nightclubs and even an Apple shop, have ameliorated what was once a challenging location.

McQueen was famous for his exquisite tailoring – the result of his formal training at the traditional Savile Row tailors Anderson & Sheppard and Gieves & Hawkes, both masters in the technical construction of clothing. Russell's design was required to reflect McQueen's fashion and also capture some of the essence of his renowned

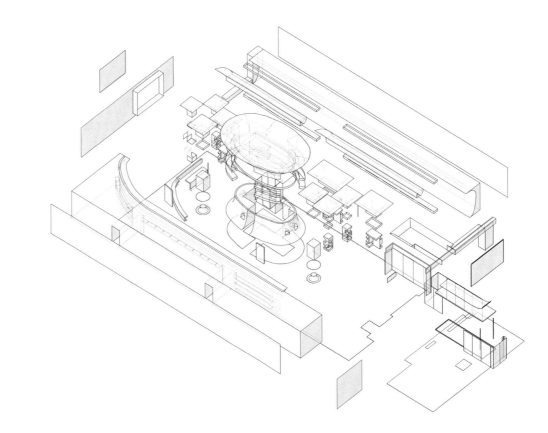

Top The axonometric sketch of the space shows how the interior is organized around the central hub – the 'mother ship' containing changing rooms and displays of couture.

Above Strategically placed mirrors endlessly reflect the shiny surfaces of the interior.

Organization

shows. These were often incredibly extravagent, lavish productions staged in unusual places, such as municipal swimming pools and historical palaces. Russell conceived the interior as an elegantly constructed piece of scenography that incorporated a journey from the gritty environment of the Meatpacking District into a glacial sculptural interior.

A small canopy over the front door of the shop discreetly announces the 335-square-metre (3,600-square-foot) space to the street. One large window display, with a panel of floor-to-ceiling advertising, indicates the entrance. The existing building was hidden, its structure covered by the new interior, and the internal columns within the shop were clad and then incorporated into the new display systems. A deep entrance threshold accentuated by a recessed front door disconnects the

visitor from the context as they enter, and allows them to adjust to the stark white interior.

The interior was imagined as a dynamic centrifuge of space. Curved walls, floors that slope up to become walls, which in turn curve into ceilings and hanging displays, have created a restless space that propels both the eye and the customer perpetually forwards. The interior was organized around a central 'hub' that the designer referred to as

'the mother ship'. This hub contains three changing rooms and a series of cut-glass boxes where couture items are displayed. The changing rooms were clad in walnut, a luxurious and detailed timber surface that offers a relief to the relentlessly white interior. The reception area was recessed into the thick lining of the wall at the back of the space. The cash desk was formed to appear as though part of the sculpture as it rose seamlessly from the shiny Terrazzo floor.

Above The shop is inserted into the lower floor of a nondescript warehouse building. It draws no influence from the surrounding architecture.

Right Each short section through the space reveals the continuous surfaces of the floor/wall and the ceiling/wall.

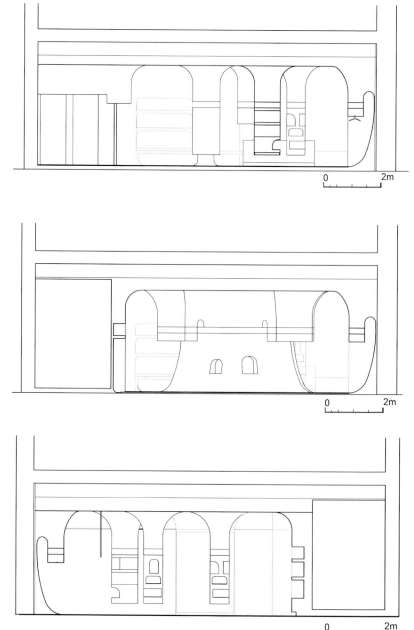

Detail

The space was conceived as if carved or hollowed out of a solid block rather than constructed piece by piece. Therefore, conceptually there are only two surfaces – the ceiling/wall and the Terrazzo carpet. The walls curve seamlessly into the ceiling, which in turn arcs down to form the floating display cabinets as if they are all from the same homogenous block.[1]

The language of the interior hints at the eclectic and theatrical influences that McQueen included in his work. The shop is a tightly tailored construct that fits the identity of the McQueen brand and creates a stage set that displays each object in a very deliberate manner. The walls are lined with curved screens that morph from the floor towards the ceiling and are recessed with niches in which to display clothes, shoes and bags. The ceiling is vaulted and forms a series of hanging display units, some recessed, some mirrored. The impression is one of a space that is carved from a solid block or which has been excavated from the ground. The white plaster and pearlescent Terrazzo flooring were sculpted and smoothed to form a continuous lining that conflates ceiling, wall and floor into a glaciated landscape.

This language of vaults, niches, carved recesses and arched alcoves used to display the elegant clothes evokes religious environments, where precious reliquaries are set into the walls. All lighting is recessed too and takes the form of thin glowing strips of etched glass, thus adding to the glaciated qualities of the interior.

1 William Russell, *Frame*, Shonquis Moreno article, *Frame* 31, March/April 2003, p.86

Top Like precious reliquaries, shoes and bags are set into niches that are recessed into the walls of the hanging display units.

Above The interior is reminiscent of a glacial landscape, an impression heightened by the sparkle from the recessed lighting reflected in the Terrazzo flooring.

Top The cash desk is recessed into the sinuous curved walls that line the interior of the shop.

Above Dresses and clothing are enigmatically lit and hung within the organic curves of the space.

PROJECT

Santa Caterina Market

DESIGNERS

Enric Miralles and
Benedetta Tagliabue
(EMBT)

LOCATION Barcelona, Spain

DATE 1997–2004

Above The undulating vaults of
the market's new roof.

Left The roof is supported by
twisting tubular steel columns as
it folds and surges over the top
of the existing walls of the old
marketplace.

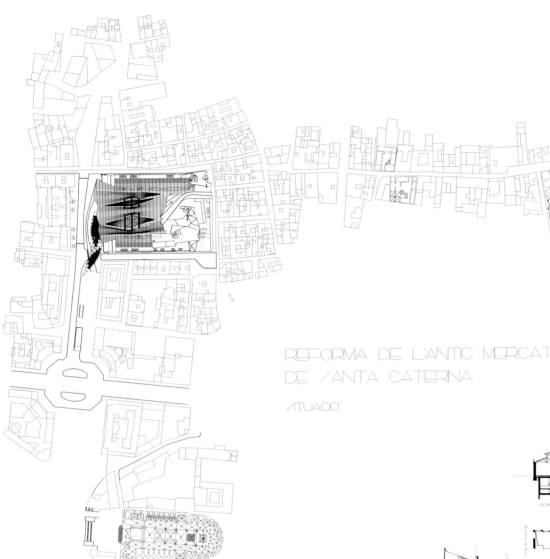

REFORMA DE L'ANTIC MERCAT
DE SANTA CATERNA

SITUACIÓ

Left The new market is just north of the cathedral and it occupies an important location in the Gothic quarter of Barcelona.

Below The orthogonal rectangular plan of the building is reinforced by the organization of restaurants and bars on the south and north-west corners of the market. This is offset by the fluid and dynamic layout of the market stalls. The housing blocks sit at the southern corner of the building.

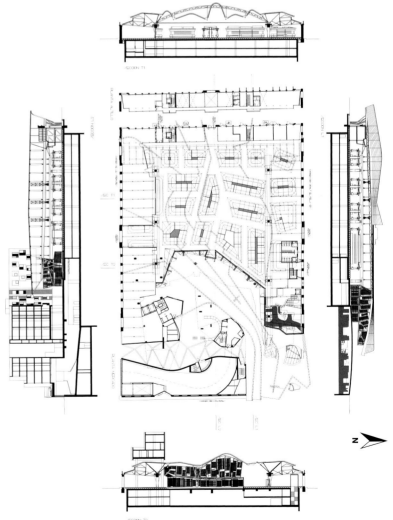

Context

Located in the Gothic quarter of Barcelona, this covered market is one of the city's oldest, dating back to 1848. The nineteenth-century market building had been constructed on top of the remains of the medieval Dominican convent of Santa Caterina, which burned down in 1835.

In the early 1990s a campaign to save the market from demolition was backed by the designers themselves, who lived close by. In 1997 they won the competition to redesign the building. The project suffered many delays, including the uncovering of the ruins of a Roman necropolis beneath the building, and the untimely death of Enric Miralles during its design.

Concept

Supporting demolition as the only way to 'solve' things is another mistake. On the contrary. The key is using and using again. It is like thinking, and rethinking things. Architecture is just a way of thinking about reality. Therefore new buildings cover existing ones. They mix up; they blend in order to make the best qualities of that place appear. So it is logical to use terms like conglomeration, hybrid, etc. Terms that go beyond the black and white dichotomy.[1]

In the Catalan language *plaça* (*plaza* in Spanish) means 'place', an abbreviated form of 'marketplace'. Santa Caterina marketplace was considered to be a key element of a new masterplan for the city's Gothic quarter. Rather than facilitate large-scale clearance and demolition, a strategy used with limited success in the Raval (a nearby quarter of Barcelona), EMBT developed a plan that understood the historic city and attempted to weave its components back together. At the centre of this plan was the market.

The site was a palimpsest: a series of compressed layers of ruined buildings, denoting centuries of occupation and built on top of each other. The designers were aware of these layers. It prompted the notion that the site was a set of narratives – the superimposition of a new layer would connect the building to its place and allow a new story to be formulated from the mix of old and new elements. Based on this reading of the site the designers retained three sides of the market and a series of trusses were used to support the existing roof. These were then incorporated into the new building, acting as a reminder of the old place.

Organization

Parking and the servicing of the market take place underground in an excavated basement. On the south-west corner of the market two towers were built containing 59 units of housing for displaced elderly residents. The south-east fourth façade of the original market was cut back and a new plaza configured around the dissolved edge of the building, reinforcing the public dimension of the building and connecting it intrinsically to the city. The 'fifth' façade is the magnificent roof that loops and folds over the market and covers the 60 vendors' stalls below.

Large, deep trusses, some new and some existing, facilitate wide spans of open interior space with supporting columns to the sides of the building. This allowed the market interior to be organized as a free plan, flowing through the space, underneath the undulating vaults of the roof. Market stalls were arranged in an array of prismatic shapes that formed aisles and internal streets throughout the space. Bars and restaurants form a

solid edge of occupation on the most public south and north-west façades of the building. The existing walls of the market contained many arched openings that were already accessible to the surrounding streets. Granite pavers, matching those laid in the surrounding streets, were used in order to ensure continuity between the city and the interior.

Detail

The exterior of the roof was clad in 325,000 vibrantly coloured ceramic tiles, arranged to form pixellated abstract images of the fruit and vegetables being sold below. The whole roof was completed using hexagonal and flat tiles. Broken tiles were mixed in with these – a 'Gaudí-esque' method of tiling called *trencadís*, one that is closely connected to Catalan history. The 5,500-square-metre (59,200-square-foot) roof underwent several computer simulations in order to overcome the difficulty of assembling the tiles into a satisfactory covering. The soffit of the roof was clad in cedar ruptured in two

places to form clerestories, allowing natural light to pour into the large hall. The new south-west façade was clad in an array of seemingly erratic slatted timber cladding that resembled a mass of deconstructed loading palettes. Tree-like structural columns twist and turn as they rise from solid concrete plinths to support the new tubular steel roof trusses.

This colourful, vibrant building provides a suitable backdrop for the gaudy, graphic, fluorescent-lit landscape of vendors' stalls and traders' booths, with their overflowing displays of meat, fish, fruit and vegetables.

---

1 Benedetta Tagliabue, quoted in *Architecture & Urbanism*, May 2005, p.90

Right One of the many entrances into the market interior through existing openings in the old market façades.

Far right The gaudy colours of the market-stall advertising and food contrast with the rib-like vaults of the timber-and-steel soffit of the roof.

Above left The eroded south-east end of the market is enclosed by a series of timber panels that resemble deconstructed loading palettes.

Above A new square is formed round the bottom of the sheltered housing block.

Left The multi-coloured pixellated patterns of the abstracted images of fruit and vegetables dominate the tiled roof and the views from the surrounding apartments.

PROJECT	**Dover Street Market**
DESIGNER	Rei Kawakubo
LOCATION	London, UK
DATE	2004

Above The interior is reminiscent of a market, incorporating a variety of design elements.

Left At night the informality of the interior is emphasized by its contrast with the ordered structure of the building's windows and doorways.

Context

Dover Street Market is a reworking of the idea of a department store by the Japanese fashion designer Rei Kawakubo. Kawakubo established her own fashion company Comme des Garçons in Tokyo in 1973, opening her first fashion boutique in 1975. The host building for this project was a nineteenth-century block on a side street in London's West End – a stone's throw from upmarket shopping areas such as the Burlington Arcade and New and Old Bond Streets.

Concept

I want to create a kind of market where various creators from various fields gather together and encounter each other in an ongoing atmosphere of beautiful chaos: the mixing up and coming together of different kindred souls who all share a strong personal vision.[1]

In early 2004, Rei Kawakubo and Comme des Garçons pioneered the 'guerrilla shop'. These temporary flagships were designed to last precisely one year and often 'popped up' in run-down spaces in unfashionable parts of large cities. Carrying on the idea of unusual, idiosyncratic fashion retailing, Kawakubo opened Dover Street Market in 2004 in a disused office building on the edge of the more established shopping centre of London's West End. Taking inspiration from the hustle and bustle of marketplaces, and in particular the recently closed Kensington Market, Kawakubo broke with the traditional established retail and marketing concepts of 'corners' and 'brand', and instead allowed the building to be adapted and changed as the host designers saw fit.

Above right Different designers stamp their individual identity on the space through constructing their own micro-environments in the market.

Right The product displays are sometimes arranged as if they were stage props. In this case, a large mirror and furniture placed on its side are used to narrate the story of the clothing and the shoes.

Dover Street Market originally started as 12 designers displaying goods alongside various Comme des Garçons ranges. This has now evolved to contain a multitude of both well-known and fledgling designers under the umbrella of Dover Street and Kawakubo. The designs of Kawakubo's shops have always reflected her radicalism in fashion, often dispensing with what is expected in construction, form and choice of materials. Her first American outlet in New York, designed with Takao Kawasaki in 1983, had no merchandise in the window and hardly anything in the shop. This radical gesture shocked Americans and only the intrepid would venture through the doors – effectively a process of self-selection as to who might wear the clothes. Since its conception, the idea of the guerrilla, or pop-up, shop is now part of the official language of mainstream retailing.

Organization and detail

The market is located in a Georgian-fronted office block on Dover Street. It was arranged over six floors, occupying 1,000 square meters (10, 760 square feet) of space. The understated shopfront on the ground floor contrasts with the elegantly designed showroom windows around the corner in Bond Street, with the only concession to any signage being a hastily arranged title on the glass windows.

The building was left in its original 'found' condition, with bare brick walls and concrete floors. Even a standard office-style suspended tiled ceiling was left intact in various parts of the space. The atmosphere is of dereliction and a semi-stripped-out interior space. In amongst this rough and ready chaos, designers impose their showroom spaces by utilizing bric-a-brac, found objects, bits of materials and furniture that they have found or have asked friends to create for them. The effect is unsettling as each space and floor level houses completely different ideas, creating a sense of dislocation throughout the interior. This achieves the desired effect of a bristling, bustling marketplace – the antithesis of the sleek, over-produced, fashion-branded showroom.

Top and middle Found display elements such as trolleys and former museum display cases are salvaged and incorporated into the retail spaces.

Left Occasionally a designer will contrast the worn-out aesthetic with an element that is deliberately new and cleanly defined.

The market is constantly changing. It shuts twice a year for three days in order to change the interior and create new scenography, so a visit at one time of the year will be different to another visit at a later point. Like the seasonal changes in fashion, the market is also redressed twice a season. During one visit, a hastily cobbled-together shed, made from scraps of wood and corrugated steel, housed the cash desk on the ground floor. On an upper floor a chandelier hung from the suspended ceiling. Scaffold pipes, MDF boxes and ex-museum exhibit cases displayed clothes, shoes, jewellery and furniture. Random pieces of furniture – some contemporary, some vintage – were placed around the building.

Whilst other fashion stores such as Prada and Gucci open increasingly expensive monuments to their brands, Comme des Garçons is opening guerrilla shops around the world, each with its own inimitable atmosphere and quality.

1 Rei Kawakubo, Dover Street Market website

Right and above right
Vintage furniture is reworked and placed alongside timber-yard offcuts in order to construct display elements in the space.

PROJECT
Selexyz Dominicanen Bookshop

DESIGNERS
Merkx+Girod: Evelyne Merkx (interior architect) and Patrice Girod (architect)

LOCATION
Maastricht, The Netherlands

DATE
2007

Above The dramatic black steel bookcase is inserted into the main hall of the church interior.

Left A new entrance to the church is constructed from Corten steel and contrasts dramatically with the exterior of the old building.

Context

The Selexyz bookshop is located in a deconsecrated Dominican church in Maastricht. The church was built in the thirteenth century and was an important friary in the town until the Dominicans were driven out by Napoleon in 1794. The deconsecrated building had then lain dormant for many years, being used as a city archive, a florist, even a bike pound, until being purchased by the Dutch bookseller BGN in 2005.

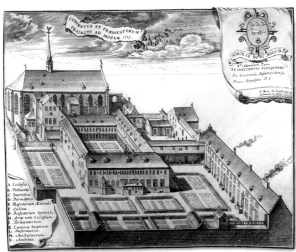

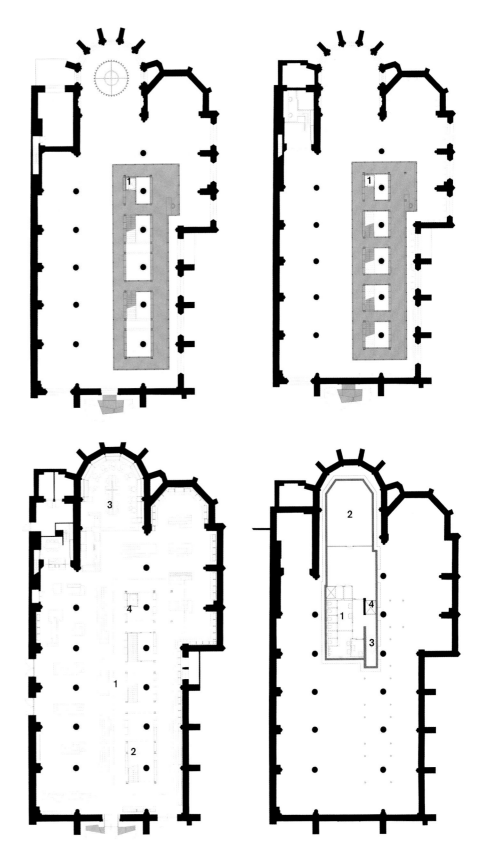

Above left In previous incarnations, the church was used as a bicycle pound and even as a flower shop.

Left The church when it was part of the Friary of Maastricht.

Top left Plan of second mezzanine.
1 Lift

Above left Ground-floor plan.
1 Main hall
2 Bookcase
3 Café
4 Lift

Top Plan of first mezzanine.
1 Lift

Above Basement plan.
1 Toilets
2 Storage
3 Stairs
4 Lift

Concept

The retention of the character and qualities of the elegant Gothic interior of the church was of paramount importance, yet the commercial imperative of the project required a floor space of over 1,200 square metres (12,900 square feet); twice the surface space available in the church. A strategy was needed that would satisfy the client's requirements whilst respecting the integrity of the interior.

Merkx+Girod decided to utilize the height of the church and suggested that a large-scale inserted 'bookcase' structure would both create the necessary amount of selling space, and retain the host building's scale, detail and atmosphere. The client's reservations about customers utilizing upper floors were assuaged by the notion of the bookcase as a platform, affording fantastic views across the church. These elevated views conclude at the top with the striking 1619 ceiling paintings by Jan Vessens, depicting biblical images of saints and sinners. A 'stack' concept was completed by the

installation of a lift that connected the newly excavated basement storage area to all levels of the bookcase, allowing heavy stock to be moved conveniently between the different floors of the shop.

Organization

The reuse of the church as a bookshop allowed the designers to create a space that resonated with many layers of meaning. The rich, semi-ruinous fabric of the existing building made an unusual

backdrop for the books and for the café. Any new intervention into the building needed to be comparable to the colossal scale of the great church hall.

The multi-level black steel walk-in bookcase, situated orthogonally in the main hall of the church, was constructed to equal the mass of the building whilst being demonstrably of a different material quality. The journey up through the 'case' allows visitors to move up through the stack – a sequence of

compression and expansion – before exiting into the open space of the main hall. The bookcase is a monumental gesture that matches the grand scale of the church and adds to its dimensions. Although huge, the case appears light, its steel-frame construction and black perforated-steel cladding sitting lightly against the sandstone mass of the church interior.

Counterpointing the elevated bookcase, yet in keeping with the orthogonal plan

Below Part of the basement of the church was excavated to facilitate installation of services and a new lift for the bookcase stack.

Below right The bookcase is framed by the colossal structure of the Gothic church.

Right A short section through the church and the bookcase shows the proposed lighting scheme.

Far right The top of the bookcase houses concealed lighting that illuminates the vaulted painted ceiling.

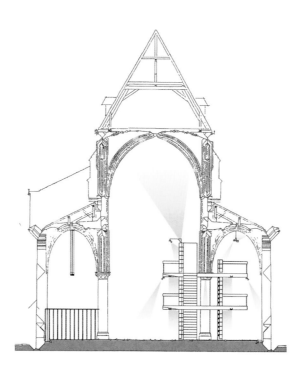

of the interior, a series of low-level display plinths were positioned between the exposed columns of the nave. These terminate in a wall-mounted bookcase set below the side windows of the nave and into the flanking walls of the church. The café was installed in the apse of the church. At its centre there is a large crucifix-shaped table, reminding the user of the building's previous function.

Detail

I have more respect for good interior architecture than I do for good architecture. An interior architecture needs to have both an understanding of architecture and an eye for specific subtleties. Refinement, care, detail – three core values.[1]

A small and carefully chosen palette of materials was utilized in the realization of the new interior. Black steel was selected for the structure of the bookcase because it contrasted with the heavy sandstone of the church. Perforated black steel was used for the balustrades of the bookcase to maximize the view up to the upper levels of the stack. The horizontal display plinths, placed on the ground floor of the interior, were formed from a modular system that is constructed from simple industrial-standard fibreboard and employed in all Selexyz bookshops across the Netherlands,

although it was configured in a different way here. The new entrance to the church was constructed from Corten steel and was designed as a sculptural box that contrasted dramatically with the building's exterior. The lighting of the interior was also carefully considered. It was concealed within the steel bookcase construction to ensure that all levels of the display space are adequately lit. The structure also conceals ambient lighting systems that illuminate the church interior and, most dramatically, the painted ceiling.

The dramatic location of this bookshop demanded an equally spectacular approach from the designers. The huge bookcase was accommodated within the interior of the church, without dominating it, but equally, without being overshadowed by the sheer scale of the existing building. The scheme revels in the character of the existing building, and the insertion of this massive, dramatic unit, accentuating the qualities of both old and new.

---

1 Patrice Girod, quoted in Birgitte van Mechelen, *Merkx+Girod*, Birkhäuser, 2003, p.4

Left The new café is placed in the apse and is organized around a large, symbolically shaped table.

Below Each bay of the nave contains a bookcase recessed into the wall and set below the side windows. Low-level modular plinths complete the book-display strategy.

Below left The upper levels of the bookcase interact with the arches of the church interior and give the visitor framed views through the space.

Display is an innate part of human behaviour, constantly practised in our daily lives.[1]

The projects in this chapter concentrate on the design of spaces that are adapted for 'display' – to host collections of objects arranged in the form of an exhibition. Exhibition design is a creative form of expression that can include artistic practices such as performance and installation art. It can also consist of more commercial endeavours such as trade fairs, brand experiences and world expositions. Events that involve the display of objects can be the size of a city, as is usual at world expositions, or at the scale of a small and intimate room. The exhibition or display may be permanent or temporary. Whatever the size and timescale might be, however, the fundamental concern in the practice of the display of objects is two-fold: the communication of the narrative of the collection, and their relationship to the environment in which they are displayed.

Reusing an existing building to display an exhibition usually manifests itself in one of two ways – the reuse of the space as a passive container, or the adaptation of the building to form a narrative instrument. Both strategies will articulate the dialogue of the collection of objects through the presentation, arrangement and sequence of object and space. The passive container will not take a prominent role in this exchange; the narrative instrument approach will often accentuate and take an active part in it.

Neutral or 'passive' containers are often used as display spaces because they do not overpower a collection. They might also be chosen if they offer the right-sized environment, are in the right location or perhaps offer climatically controlled spaces in which the objects can be displayed with maximum efficiency and free from any interference from the immediate environment. These types of spaces might be described as housing 'non-site-specific' exhibitions. These

may take place in formal or informal galleries, warehouses, factories or anywhere that a collection of objects can be displayed. This will often be for a short space of time, before the objects are removed and the space is returned to its original condition. Some existing buildings are deliberately chosen to emphasize the communication of the narrative of a particular collection. These types of spaces and their resultant exhibitions could be described as 'site specific'; the collections are displayed in particular types of galleries and museums so that object and environment are closely connected.

Whichever method of display is utilized, the objects and elements of a collection, along with the building that houses them, form the language of display, where the relationship between object and environment is of paramount importance.

CHAPTER 4

Display

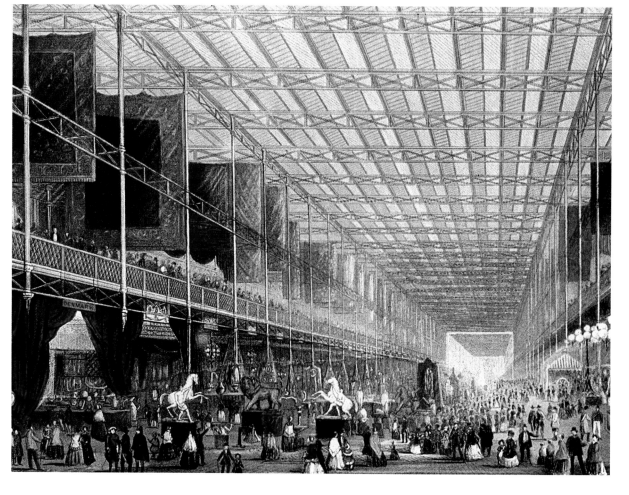

The origins of display

Once the exclusive province of the rich, the powerful and the elitely educated, both access to and participation in the development of exhibitions has gradually come to include people at all levels of society.[2]

The practice of display, and in particular the exhibiting of collections of objects in museums, has its roots in the Renaissance. Wealthy and powerful families patronized artists and collected art in order to show them to other prosperous families, often to demonstrate their affluence and authority. The rapid expansion of bespoke new museums and galleries in the industrialized eighteenth and nineteenth centuries was in order to provide a home for existing old collections. Private collections that were either acquired or bequeathed were housed in grand buildings that were designed to both reflect the status of their owners and educate the general public. Early museums such as the Louvre or the British Museum were akin to warehouses, crammed with paintings, often arranged on the walls in such a way as to cover the entire space.

As well as the development of the public museum, 'expositions' or great event exhibitions were an early catalyst in the development of municipal museums and galleries. They were an important development in the idea of democratizing the display of collections for the consumption of the general public. These colossal events were usually housed in specially designed buildings. They would often revolve around the demonstration of a particular country's power and technological ability, all wrapped up in an unforgettable large-scale spectacle.

The Great Exhibition of the Works of Industry of All Nations took place in 1851 and was housed in an enormous glass and cast-iron building in London's Hyde Park. Designed by Joseph Paxton and engineered by Charles Fox, the Crystal Palace, as it became known, was 560 metres (1,848 feet) long and 125 metres (408 feet) wide and displayed a diverse collection of objects, ranging from precious stones and textiles to appliances and machinery imported from around the world. The exhibition was so successful that the entrance fees of its six million

visitors not only repaid the costs of the building and the exhibition, but also raised enough money for a legacy of three buildings to be built to the south of the park; the Victoria and Albert, the Science and the Natural History Museums. The exhibition set the trend for the world fairs and expositions that followed, where great expanses of land in various cities throughout the world would feature themed pavilions, usually sponsored by countries or industry. Still prevalent today, world fairs were precursors to themed entertainment parks, themselves examples of the often ostentatious display of leisure.

Opposite The main hall of the Great Exhibition in Hyde Park, London, designed by Joseph Paxton in 1851.

Above left The Machine Art exhibition designed by Alfred H. Barr in 1934 at the Museum of Modern Art, New York.

Above The 'City in Space' by Frederick Kiesler.

The new museum

If a new museum building can eclipse the objects it is intended to display – a betrayal of its purpose, it might be argued – old buildings can equally become exhibits in their own right.[3]

The informative and communicative dimension of exhibits, the method of their display and the environment in which they are contained characterize display and exhibitions in the twentieth and twenty-first centuries. In particular, the defining strategy of the last 50 years has been the shift from a didactic relationship to one that is interactive. The role of the building in this relationship is of paramount importance. The engendering of a new aesthetic in the twentieth-century museum and gallery gave rise to new forms of display, ones that developed a requirement to move away from the eighteenth- and nineteenth-century desire to catalogue and taxonomize a collection. Instead the contemporary gallery or museum became a space in which the aesthetic judgement of experts, such as curators and designers, was incorporated to ensure that the display communicated the message of the work. Early display design work by the art historian and first director of the Museum of Modern Art in New York, Alfred H. Barr, encapsulated the notion of museum displays arranged to communicate the ideas of a collection so that it resonated with visitors.

Throughout the last century, the desire of the designer and curator to engage the viewer with the objects of the contemporary display space has taken the form of a number of interesting methods. In 1924 Frederick Kiesler pioneered a free-standing, transportable display framework for the 'International Exhibition of New Theatre Techniques' in Vienna, which he called the L&T (Leger und Trager; 'lying' and 'supporting') system. The system was installed in the space and could display hundreds of objects such as paintings, models and costumes within its frame. Kiesler adapted and developed the system in the design of the Austrian section at the International Exposition of Modern Industrial and Decorative Arts in Paris in 1925. He created a monumental structure that inhabited the pavilion interior called the 'City in Space'. The exhibition incorporated models of buildings, paintings, set design, plans for theatres, drafts for scenes and costumes by Austrian architects and artists. The system was adaptable and allowed visitors to adjust the display of the objects so that they could read and interact with them in a much easier way. The exhibition was described thus:

Left The Gare d'Orsay in Paris, a former train station, after remodelling in 1986 by Gae Aulenti to become the Musée d'Orsay.

Below left The Museo del Tesoro di San Lorenzo in Genoa by Franco Albini. Statues and relics were housed in three circular rooms.

Below The *Merzbau* by Kurt Schwitters, the solidification of detritus into a spatial construction.

Variability, combinability and movement are the design components that manifest Kiesler's conception of an architecture of 'continuous tensionism' in the object.[4]

In the early 1920s the German painter and Dadaist Kurt Schwitters created abstract collages from collected everyday detritus such as bus tickets, old letters and tin lids. He would nail them together and add colour. He termed these assemblages *Merz* pictures and would attempt to make sense of current events by using these found elements. He went on to build a series of *Merzbaus*, the first of which was in his hometown of Hanover. It was:

A huge architectural-sculptural column that eventually pierced the ceiling of its original room and climbed to the next storey.[5]

The *Merzbau* was a conglomeration of collages, paintings and detritus all incorporated into an undulating sculptural growth that inhabited the rooms of Schwitter's own house. The columns of the sculpture would grow from the basement to the attic and fill the rooms and interior spaces of the house. Friends would bring objects and Schwitters would add them to the *Merzbau* along with other found detritus and objects. The fluid condition between the sculpture and its contents – its propensity to be adapted to house new finds – was symbolic of the interaction between visitor and exhibit. Both the 'City in Space' display system and the *Merzbau* were early prototypes of an interactive relationship between the object and viewer.

Narrative environments

Each time a memory is triggered, it is renewed and revised by the new experience, and our sensitivity to buildings becomes an amalgam of recall and reinterpretation.[6]

In the last 60 years or so the reuse of existing buildings has become an increasingly viable solution for housing contemporary cultural spaces such as galleries, museums and theatres. It is a strategy that promotes continuity and resonance in the urban fabric of a city.

In the adaptation of buildings for new uses, such as display and exhibition, the designer or curator creates a composite of old and new meanings, through the arrangement of a collection, amongst the extant rooms and spaces of the building. This becomes particularly marked when working with a building in order to use it as a device in the narrative of the collection. The story of the building and the objects can be reinforced, or edited out, by the designer. This intertwining of environment and object can be integral to the new interior space. Carlo Scarpa was the master of this approach. In the restoration and remodelling of the

Castelvecchio Museum in Verona, he uncovered the various historic strata of the building through the use of creative and selective demolition. The castle was a complicated confusion of many eras of construction and Scarpa strove to explore and isolate the various phases of building to reveal the complex and rich poetry of the place.

Scarpa achieved three things with his adaptive reuse project. First, he accepted and presented parts of the building complex as historically pre-existing, therefore maintaining their original integrity. Second, he laid bare through conceptual surgery all the genuine survivals of the Castelvecchio. Finally, he added new parts, which would bind together the entire complex and fill in the gaps without destroying the patina or even the mishaps or wounds of time.[7]

Modifications to an existing building can act in an extremely intrusive manner, with new elements imposing themselves directly upon the existing structure. Being inspired by the original building, these new elements,

which can be many small changes, alterations, additions and subtractions, may often be strongly related to the original building, but the language used can be completely at odds with the host building. Franco Albini, Scarpa's contemporary, remodelled the Museo del Tesoro di San Lorenzo in Genoa, Italy between 1952 and 1956, six years before Scarpa commenced work at the Castelvecchio. He delicately remodelled the underground museum by adding three circular rooms in which to display its relics and objects. The three subterranean chambers measure just 15 x 16 metres (49 x 52 feet) and each one is top-lit by a lantern cupola.

The adaptation of large buildings can form a significant part of urban reforms and thus ensure continuity in a city – a regenerative strategy that maintains the identity of the urban fabric. In Paris, the regeneration of the Gare d'Orsay, a nineteenth-century train station built for the Paris World Fair of 1900, was one of President Mitterrand's *Grands Projets*. The station had fallen into disuse and was faced with demolition. Architect Gae Aulenti oversaw its conversion into the Musée d'Orsay

(opened 1986), with the huge train shed becoming an interior landscape of floors, galleries and rooms.

As well as becoming central to regeneration strategies, display design can become key in the narration of the stories of a city. Hans Hollein's 'Traum und Wirklichkeit Wien 1870–1930' ('Vienna: Dream and Reality') exhibition at the Kunstlerhaus in Vienna told the story of the incredible atmosphere and events of turn-of-the-century Vienna, with its group of artists, designers and architects. Hollein described the themed exhibition:

> *It is then an exhibition of tangible objects which function as metaphor for a dream which became reality, and there followed a reality which none who was there at the time ever dreamed of.*[8]

Opposite, above The vast shed that used to contain the steelworks in Rotherham before it was remodelled to accommodate the Magna Centre.

Opposite, below The water pavilion inside the Magna Centre.

Below The information benches in the Play Zone, inside the Millennium Dome, London, designed by LAND studio in 2000.

Interactivity

The displays sought to engage a type of visitor known by museum and education specialists as the kinesthetic learner. These visitors, traditionally poorly served by museums, enjoy getting involved with something – doing rather than observing.[9]

Interactivity, the act of engaging physically and intellectually with an object, along with the development of digital technology, has defined the last 60 years of display environments. In an attempt to involve visitors – particularly children – more actively in exhibitions, display methods and environments have incorporated elements that fully absorb the visitor.

The Magna Centre in Rotherham, UK, is an interactive attraction that immerses the visitor in a huge shed that was once a thriving steelworks. The processes of steel making that were used here until the steelworks closed have been brought back to life via a series of interactive pavilions.

These are named Air, Water, Earth and Fire: the four constituent components of the process. Each pavilion houses a series of interactive devices designed to invite the visitor to explore and understand the role of each element.

At the start of the twenty-first century, the Millennium Dome in London brought together 14 zones in a large tent, themed under the titles of 'Who we are', 'What we do' and 'Where we live'. The dome was conceived as a world fair-type event, incorporating a reflection of humanity's concerns at the dawn of a new century. In the 'What we do' section, Land Design Studio were commissioned to design the Play zone (the other zones were Work, Rest, Talk, Money, Journey and Learning). They designed a free-standing pavilion that had to process huge amounts of visitors whilst also leaving a lasting impression upon them.

Whether narrative, interactive or just based on the aura and power of the object alone, display design is regarded as the device that can bridge the gap between object and environment. It is a practice that creates a learning experience that can exist for any chosen period of time. The projects in this chapter exemplify the range of issues involved in the adaptation of an extant building when reused to house a display space.

1 Philip Hughes, *Exhibition Design*, Laurence King, 2010, p.10

2 Jan Lorenc, Lee Skolnick and Craig Berger, *What is Exhibition Design?*, RotoVision, 2007, p.12

3 Kenneth Powell, *Architecture Reborn: Converting Old Buildings for New Uses*, Rizzoli, 1999, p.181

4 Tulga Beyerle et al., *Friedrich Kiesler: Designer*, Hatje Cantz Publishers, 2005, p.27

5 Robert Short, *Dada And Surrealism*, Book Club Associates, 1980, p.46

6 David Littlefield and Saskia Lewes, *Architectural Voices: Listening to Old Buildings*, John Wiley & Sons, 2007, p.12

7 John Kurtich and Garret Eakin, *Interior Architecture*, Van Nostrand Reinhold, 1996, p.26

8 Hans Hollein and Catherine Cooke, 'Traum und Wirklichkeit 1870–1930' (Dream and Reality), *Architectural Design*, vol. 55 no.11/12, 1986, p.2

9 Philip Hughes, *op cit.*, p.17

PROJECT

Castelvecchio Museum

DESIGNER

Carlo Scarpa

LOCATION

Verona, Italy

DATE

1958–73

Above The first set of rooms on the ground floor are arranged as an enfilade, with paintings and statues directing the visitors' view and thus movement through the space.

Left A collage showing how Scarpa tried out the statue of Cangrande in various different positions before settling on its eventual location.

Below left The façade of the east wing after remodelling, with the statue of the Cangrande finally positioned to the left.

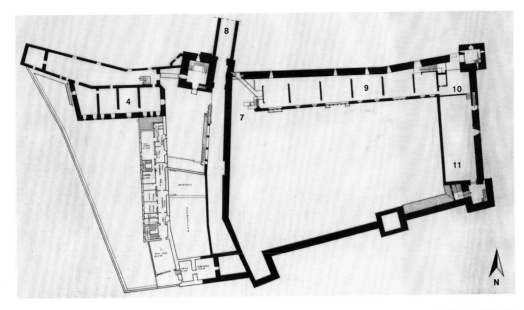

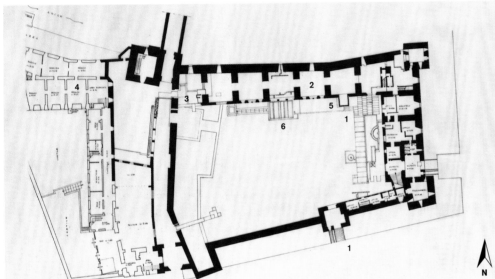

Left and above left
Ground-floor and upper-floor plans.
1 Entrance
2 East wing
3 Porta del Morbio
4 West wing
5 Sacellum (shrine)
6 Old entrance
7 Statue of Cangrande
8 Bridge over river
9 Upper east wing
10 Stair back to entrance
11 Temporary galleries

Above The ground-floor rooms under construction. Scarpa utilized large slabs of stone, extracted from the floor, and set upright into the arch, in order clearly to state the openings linking one room with the next. A matching slab was made to complete the threshold.

Context

The Castelvecchio ('old castle') was originally constructed in the fourteenth century as a fortified castle for the della Scala family. It incorporated several existing structures dating from Roman and medieval times, including the eighth-century church of San Martino in Aquaro and part of the twelfth-century city wall. The position of the building was strategically important; it assured the family's control of Verona whilst also providing them with an escape route via a fortified bridge over the River Adige. The buildings were transformed into a military garrison during Napoleon's occupation of the city. Two large barracks were constructed between 1802 and 1806, along the north and east sides of the main courtyard.

The castle was first converted into a museum by Ferdinando Forlati and Antonio Avena in the 1920s. They remodelled the barrack interiors in the manner of an early Renaissance palace. Then, in 1958, Scarpa was commissioned to undertake a new renovation that would interpret the original building and expose the changes that had happened to it over time.

Concept

With selective digs and creative demolitions, Scarpa attempted to isolate and uncover the various historical strata of the complex. He attempted to untangle the intricate remains of the various eras of construction so as to make the building itself one giant artefact or find.[1]

The approach of Carlo Scarpa to remodelling was based upon an interpretation of the meaning of the original building. He endeavoured to understand the historical and contextual qualities of the place and then to communicate this narrative by applying a new contemporary layer. The layers of the building were scraped away or exposed, in response to the three main historical periods of the building's history, until clarity was achieved. This intervention then led to a series of small and beautifully composed additions that were carefully imposed upon the building.

Organization

The main entrance to the museum was through the gate and courtyard gardens of the castle. Scarpa moved the entrance from the centre of the barracks to the north-east corner of the wing. The first set of museum rooms were arranged enfilade on the ground floor. They led to the bridge and then to the west wing, through which the visitor returned on the upper level of the museum back to the start of the journey. The simplicity of the organization belied the complexity of the approach to remodelling. The project began with a

sequence of excavations, stripping the building back to its essential elements. These exposed important junctions where historical evidence was at its most compelling. These became the sites where the placement of objects or materials could then take place. The first excavations uncovered the Porta del Morbio, an underground passageway that once linked the castle to the bridge. This site of key archaeological change led Scarpa to the placement of the most important sculpture in the museum, the

Left The desire to disrupt Forlati's fake Gothic façade resulted in a new recessed steel-and-glass screen. This is most apparent at the old entrance to the museum, at the centre of the façade of the east wing.

Far left Articulated openings between rooms in the west wing frame the paintings that are displayed on the bespoke easels.

Above Selective demolition of the end of the east wing uncovered the layers of history at this junction.

Above left and inset The Cangrande statue was placed at the junction, signifying the importance of this part of the site to the whole remodelling. Scarpa decided to set the statue on a simple concrete plinth.

Detail

Cangrande I della Scala. The statue was placed atop an external concrete plinth and formed a metaphorical 'hinge', linking both east and west wings of the museum. A new hanging bridge was constructed, affording the visitor elevated views of the statue and linking the Torre del Mastio, or castle keep, to the museum wings. The statue is seen many times during the journey around the museum. The first time is upon entering the castle grounds: it can be observed in profile in its sheltered position under the eaves of the roof of the east wing. A close-up view occurs as part of the journey through the museum from the west wing as the visitor passes through the old city wall.

In the Castelvecchio the placement of the paintings and sculptures was used to orientate the viewer and direct movement and views through the space. Scarpa also used objects and contemporary materials to illustrate narrative breaks in the building's history; their placement is often used to emphasize an important junction.

The new entrance is formed from a plane that dissects the existing Gothic arched doorway. The threshold is split by the screen wall that returns at both ends to define the journey from interior to exterior and vice versa. The screen is constructed from a steel frame with a polished plaster infill.

In the east wing Scarpa felt that the false Gothic symmetry of the Forlati renovation had to be disrupted. He achieved this by recessing new windows behind the old, as if part of another wall behind the existing one. The grid or rhythm of the new was deliberately not synchronized with that of the old façade, making it appear as though the exterior screen was scenery. Throughout the museum, the same type of screen is used as an individual backdrop for specific works of art. Coloured, polished plaster is used to highlight the details of the displayed objects. Metal and timber sculpture plinths and painting easels are carefully detailed. Protruding from the façade

and adjacent to the new entrance is the Sacellum, a small top-lit space accessed from the first room of the east wing. Its exterior is decorated with little blocks of flamed granite and Prun stone. These range in texture from smooth to rough, and from white through to pale pinks and reds. The configuration forms an abstracted pattern in the courtyard of the castle.

1 Sergio Los, Carlo Scarpa: *An Architectural Guide,* Arsenale, 1996, p.54

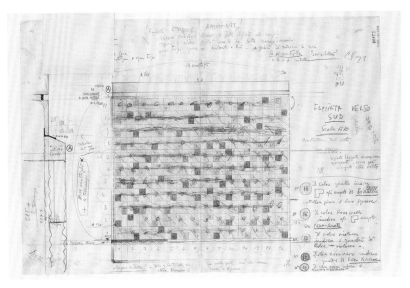

Left The Sacellum's dimensions and appearance were designed to contrast directly with the proportions of the arch and the coloured plaster of the surrounding building.

Far left The top-lit Sacellum viewed from the ground-floor exhibition rooms.

Above The pattern of the abstract grid of the flamed stone blocks of the exterior of the Sacellum was very carefully considered.

Above left A sketch of the Sacellum. Light is carefully controlled in the space.

PROJECT	**Hedmark Cathedral Museum**
DESIGNER	Sverre Fehn
LOCATION	Hamar, Norway
DATE	1967–73; interior finished 1979

Above A rough shuttered-concrete walkway soars above the ongoing archaeological dig in the medieval gallery.

Left Openings are covered with large panels of glazing bolted on to the outside of the building. While providing shelter from the elements, they do not thermally seal the interior.

Context

The Hedmark Cathedral Museum was built around the ruins of the medieval Hamar Cathedral – residence of the Bishop of Hamar (a small town north of Oslo). It also incorporated a large rural barn on the site. The location is of particular significance as it lies on the Kaupang trail, along which in 1302 the bishop made his way to Rome.

The nineteenth-century barn had been unceremoniously constructed upon sixteenth-century ruins of the bishop's manor. Initial excavations underneath the barn uncovered the remains of a tower, bakery and prison house, as well as remains of the fortress and walls that had protected the cathedral from intruders.

Concept

The main architectural concept has been to create a museum which preserves the existing remains of Hamar Bispegard and Storhamar barn and makes it possible for the archaeological excavations to function as an important part of the actual museum, in line with the exhibits.[1]

The new museum was built to display the excavated finds and communicate their meaning to the museum visitor. Fehn chose to do this by creating a 'suspended museum', a structure that hovers above the layers of earth and soil, sheltering the archaeological dig that is constantly being undertaken beneath it. The building was designed to become an integral part of the site yet it has been built to stand free of the existing walls. It does not touch the medieval ruins and its clear definition allows the visitor to clearly distinguish between old and new.

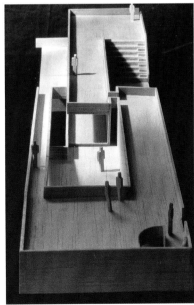

Left The entrance to the museum frames the view back across the site to the ruins of the cathedral.

Below left The model of the scheme shows the layers of the ruins of the bishop's manor underneath the U-shaped barn.

Below A model of the circulation of the ethnography wing, a journey back and forth through the two-storey space facilitated by stairs and ramps.

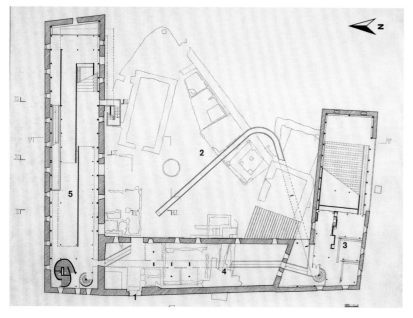

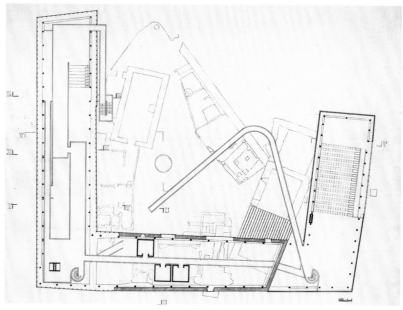

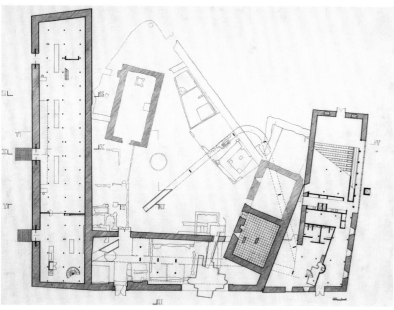

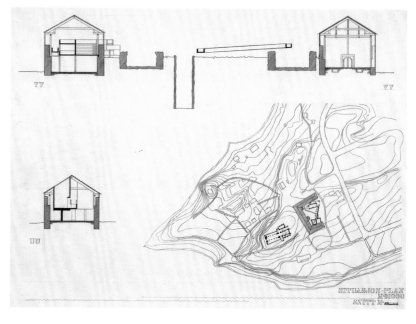

Top left and top right
Ground-floor and first-floor plans.
1 Entrance
2 Ramp
3 South wing
4 Medieval gallery
5 Ethnography wing

Above left Lower-level plan articulating the relationship between the ruins and the barn.

Above right Site plan with three short sections through the space.

Organization

The U-shaped building was divided into three parts. Each 'wing' housed the main functions of the museum, and the distribution of functions within the building related to their connection with the site.

The central wing was the medieval gallery and was dedicated to displaying the main finds from the archaeological digs carried out below it. The north-facing wing was the old barn and was designated as the ethnography gallery. The south-facing wing was situated outside of the ruined walls of the settlement, so was the space designated to house a temporary exhibition space, auditorium and offices.

A simple yet effective circulation route links all three spaces. It draws the visitor through the museum and eventually deposits them back at the courtyard, opposite the front door where they began their journey. The entrance to the museum faces the cathedral ruins and is located at the corner of the medieval and ethnography wings on the western side of the barn. The new entrance was placed at the same point where the ruined walls of the gatehouse were uncovered during excavations. A roughly shuttered concrete ramp, the beginnings of which are just noticeable from the glazed aperture opposite the front door, invites the visitor into the

courtyard. The ramp slides out across the ruins of the courtyard and bends back into the building, arriving at the second-floor south-western corner of the museum.

As well as making a dramatic gesture, the ascent into the building accommodates the significant level changes across the site. A spiral stair takes the visitor down to the first floor level and through into the medieval wing. A bridge traverses the ruins at this elevated level and spans across the archaeological dig, only lightly touching the floor in two places. Three concrete boxes are accessed from this bridge. They house precious finds excavated from the dig below. The bridge then passes above the entrance and into the ethnography wing. This consists of a two-level 'tray' of roughly shuttered concrete, which forms an inserted channel within which the museum circulation and objects are neatly contained. It appears to be independent of the existing building yet it fills the proportions of the barn without overwhelming the space. The series of ramps, steps and bridges directs the movement back and forth across this part of the museum. A small bridge punched through the wall of the barn takes the visitor back to the front door.

Detail

The main elements of the new museum were constructed in a robust fashion and designed to equal the vigour of the existing building's materiality. They were clearly articulated in order to emphasize the distinction between old and new. A new roof was built, supported by a series of thick timber columns and trusses. In the ethnography wing the new roof structure was placed clear of the old. Both structural additions lend a new proportional, rhythmic quality to the interior of the old barn. Openings in the thick stone walls of the building were clad in large, loose-fitting panels of glazing. These were bolted on to the outsides of the wall. The glass sheets, along with the roof, provide shelter from the wind and rain but little thermal protection from the harsh winter climate. (The museum is only open in summer.)

New interior elements were all fabricated from coarsely shuttered concrete. The rough, brutal qualities of these elements unify the three parts of the museum and match the vernacular of the unrefined barn structure. The objects within the museum are displayed in a sensitive manner. Elegant mild-steel brackets and thin steel rods support glass bottles, placed in the recesses of the windows. Selections of keys, excavated from the ground, are displayed in a glass-and-åsteel light box. The basic language of the rough concrete structures offsets

the delicate, refined devices used to display these precious finds.

1 Sverre Fehn, quoted in *Architecture & Urbanism*, January, 1999, p.45

PROJECT **Deutsches Architekturmuseum**

DESIGNERS Oswald Mathias Ungers

LOCATION Frankfurt, Germany

DATE 1979–84

Above The prototypical house or symbolic primitive shelter around which the museum is organized.

Left The new museum sits within the existing villa. A new ground-floor red-sandstone colonnade wraps the museum and represents the new use of the building.

Context

This project formed part of a masterplan for a series of riverside cultural attractions on the southern side of the River Main in Frankfurt. These included the Deutsches Filmmuseum by Helge Bofinger and the Museum of Applied Arts by Richard Meier; both projects reused existing buildings. By the end of the 1980s, 12 new museums had opened.

The 1901 host building for the Architekturmuseum was an elegantly proportioned four-storey mansion, located on the corner of Schweizerstrasse and Schaumainkai. The building had been unoccupied for many years. The existing floor loadings of the villa were not suitable for the new use of the building, so the interior was removed and the building was restructured, leaving just the outer shell as a symbol of its former use.

Concept

Locating the new museum in a bourgeois villa on the outskirts of Frankfurt was indicative of a new attitude towards heritage, the existing built environment and modern design in Europe in the early 1980s. The design of a museum for architecture will always ensure that each idea, gesture and act will involve the utmost scrutiny of the significance and symbolism of making space.

Unger's design utilized a number of architectonic gestures. He coordinated all of the spatial interventions into an ideal 'cube'; a three-dimensional modular form that controlled the organization and dimensions of all the interior elements. Unger's reuse of the building created a metaphorical city: the outside was wrapped by a new 'city wall' of red sandstone, while the rear of the city wall became the enclosure

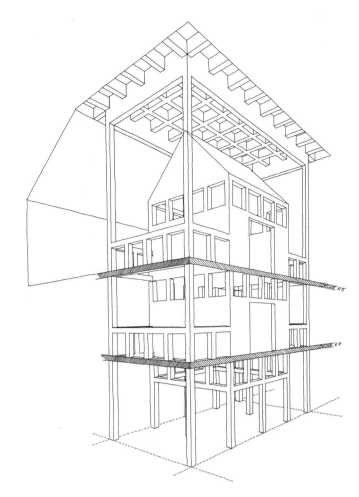

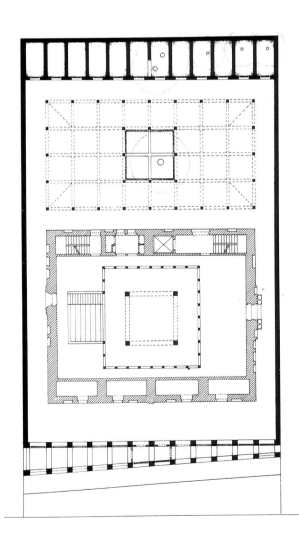

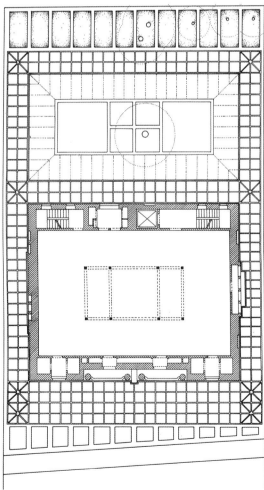

Far left The concept of the house within the house is clearly evident in the plan of the ground floor.

Left The rigorous orthogonal geometry is evident in the planning of level 4. The 'home' is at the centre whilst the tree is in the yard.

Above The development sketch of the house at the centre of the museum.

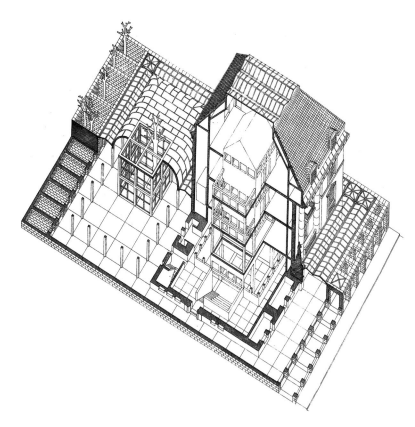

for a courtyard, incorporating nature by allowing a chestnut tree, already standing on the centre of the site, to grow unencumbered through the roof. At the centre of the building was the archetype of the built environment: the house. The building was wrapped around the abstracted box, making a house within a house. With this 'box within a box' solution, Unger celebrated the archetype of built space – the primitive hut or the shelter created by four columns holding up a roof. At the centre of the museum is an interior room from which the entire built environment is derived.

Organization

The innermost room is surrounded by a filigree-like lattice; this is surrounded by a room formed by structural framework. The next shell is the sectional wall of the existing villa, which in turn becomes an outer wall. The interlocking rooms give a three-dimensional experience of continuous alternation between inner and outer.[1]

The villa was approached from Schaumainkai. A new sandstone base was wrapped around it – an arcade that enveloped the ground floor and put the building on display, atop its own bright red pedestal. The one-storey plinth surrounded the building and filled the site, creating a colonnade at the front and a one-storey gallery space at the back. The reclaiming of what was formerly outside the building promoted a sense of ambiguity with regards to inner and outer space.

The modular system of the cube informed all aspects of the spatial organization. The proportion and dimensions of the colonnade, courtyard, circulation and rooms, as well as those of the house, were all derived from the grid system imposed upon the building. At the inner core of the museum the miniature house was set into a five-storey void, top-lit by a skylight. All levels of the building contain exhibition spaces, with a lecture theatre in the basement and offices on the top floor. This simple arrangement belies the complexity of the journey through an interior that blurs the thresholds between inside and outside space.

Detail

The house-within-a-house theme is concomitant with this journey from outside to within. The outer shell of the new pedestal is a thick, rusticated wall with niches, plinths, bays and hollow spaces – a symbol of the city wall. The wall of the existing villa is dense and thick, yet it is profiled and contains columns, windows and pilasters. Within the interior, the modular frame is a refined trellis of stone and plaster. The courtyard is a grid of brick and stone, with the tree at its heart. The inner rooms are refined filigree stone and metalwork constructions with glass inserts. The journey of the visitor through the space is symbolized by this refinement of materials, from an exterior of rusticated stone through to an interior of filigree craftsmanship. All of this is bathed in natural light that pours in from the rooftop and cascades down the five-storey prototypical house: the architectural figuration to which the museum was dedicated.

---

1 O.M. Ungers, *Die Thematisierung der Architektur* ('The Thematization of Architecture'), cited in *Architectural Review*, August 1984, p.32

Top A cut-away axonometric drawing of the museum shows the journey through the different layers of the building from the colonnade to the courtyard at the rear.

Above The grid system imposed on the building has informed everything from the proportions and sizes of the spaces to lighting and furniture.

Opposite, above The interior of the top-lit colonnade that wraps the lower level of the building.

Opposite, below The refinement of the interior's material qualities reaches its conclusion in the courtyard with its tree in the centre.

PROJECT	**Picasso Museum**
DESIGNER	Roland Simounet
LOCATION	Paris, France
DATE	1976–85

Above The top of the main stair, where the first room of the museum (left) contains the work from Picasso's Blue Period (1901–04).

Left The elegant Baroque Hotel Salé with the central main-door entrance aligned with the front gate.

Context

The Hotel Aubert de Fontenay was built from 1656–9 by Jean Bouhir. It was better known as the Hotel Salé because it was built with the proceeds from its owner's collection of salt tax. The elegant Baroque townhouse was arranged over four floors and contained a unique stone carved staircase which, along with fragments of eighteenth-century decoration, survived extensive change of use during and after the French Revolution. It had been standing empty since the 1970s.

In 1974, in accordance with a law known as *dation*, the French government obtained a substantial collection of Picasso's work, presented by his heirs in lieu of death duties. The Hotel Salé was chosen to host the new museum by the then Minister of Culture and director of the museum, who maintained that, since Picasso had always used old houses as studios, this would make a perfect setting for his work.

In 1976 a limited competition was held, and four designers – Roland Simounet, Jean Monge, Roland Castro and Carlo Scarpa – were invited to submit ideas for the new museum. Simounet won, with the only scheme that proposed to reuse the existing building in its entirety without adding an extension in the courtyard or the garden.

Concept

Historic buildings, industrial buildings, and obsolete public buildings provide exceptional opportunities to those designers who can understand them.[1]

Simounet's competition-winning design responded to the brief's demands by carefully adapting the building to house the new collection. There were several key requirements: circulation must be based upon a linear sequence and 'prosthetic' display systems were to be avoided, yet exhibition devices should be capable of modification every five to ten years without structural changes. Natural lighting was to be used where possible and display spaces were to be varied in scale and permanent in character. Simounet's understanding of the existing building resolved all of these requirements. His appraisal of the organization of the building, obscured by 150 years of accretions, alterations and decay, suggested that it could not only house the 300 paintings, 3,000 drawings and 46 sculptures, but do so with a logical route through the space.

Above right The majestic original main staircase of the entrance hall that was retained in order to tempt visitors upstairs to start the journey through the museum.

Right The top-lit sculpture court is housed in an old stable block on the north side of the courtyard.

Organization

The main house of the museum was accessed on axis from the gatehouse on the rue de Thorigny. The ticket office and bookshop were situated in the stables on the north side of the courtyard.

Beyond the entrance to the main building Simounet reiterated the axial organization of the interior. He exchanged the wooden door of the ground-floor salon, opposite the front door, with a sheet of glass. Although this transparent door offers visitors a glimpse of the final room of the museum, it does not allow entrance to the space. Instead, the majestic original

stone staircase and decoration of the hall are used to persuade visitors to ascend and begin their journey upstairs.

The chronological sequence of rooms begins in the first room at the top of the stair. This contains work from Picasso's Blue Period (dating from 1901–04). The three rooms on the west side of the house, overlooking the garden, contain work dating from 1910–24. The enfilade rooms are linked by an axis of ornately carved eighteenth-century wooden doorways. The final room contains work from 1925–9. It also contains a stair that connects to the ground-floor glass-roofed sculpture

court, inserted into the stable block. This courtyard leads to the basement, which contains work from 1930–47. An existing service stair delivers the visitor back to the ground floor and the final rooms, containing Picasso's work up to his death in 1973. These are housed in the room behind the glass door that was seen upon entering the museum. A discreet side door opens into the hallway and the main-door exit into the courtyard.

Below left First-floor plan.
1 1901–04
2 1910–24
3 1925–9
4 Stair down

Bottom left Basement plan.
1 1930–44
2 Stair to ground floor

Below right Section.

Bottom right Ground-floor plan.
1 Courtyard
2 Entrance
3 Stair up
4 View into final room
5 Sculpture courtyard
6 Final rooms

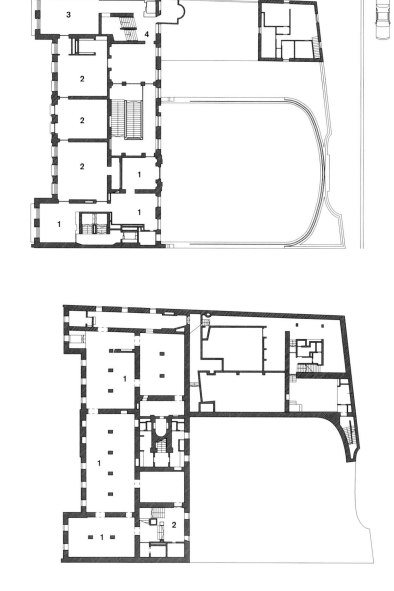

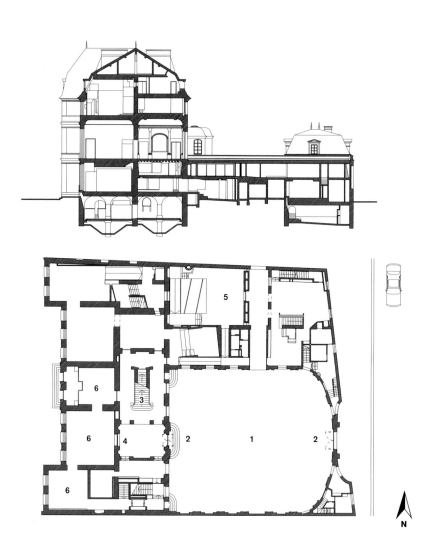

Detail

Once the circulation through the interior was organized, Simounet then set about ordering the rooms into a coherent narrative for the objects. First of all, any historic detail or decoration was preserved. Walls and ceilings were painted off-white. Simounet then introduced a Cubist-inspired tectonic interior language, one that developed the wall, floor and ceiling of each room into an independent lining against which to display and protect the objects of the collection. The insertion of a series of surfaces into each room allowed Simounet to develop a display system that was integral yet could be changed with little or no structural modification. Recessed display cases were set into the corners of the walls, drawing the eye to the object whilst encouraging movement across the room. Paintings and sketches were set into niches in the wall, which then contained concealed artificial lighting, supplementing the daylight coming in from the windows. Larger cuts and niches in the ceilings and walls allowed a general lighting scheme. Even the usual museum paraphernalia of security and environmental control devices were discreetly secreted into the hidden walls of the rooms. The floor covering was developed to stop short of the edges of each room, suggesting a barrier between the visitor and the work on the walls, avoiding an obstructive rope or chain.

The Cubist language utilized throughout the whole of the museum creates a unique fusion between view, movement and object.

---

1 Philippe Robert, 'Architecture as a Palimpsest', in *Adaptations: New Uses For Old Buildings*, Princeton Architectural Press, 1989, p.11

Above right The enfilade of rooms on the first floor during construction. The wooden mouldings of the rooms and doors were removed for renovation.

Right The Cubist-inspired geometric language of Picasso's work influenced the niche-and-recess strategy for exhibiting the objects.

Far right Even in the basement, the display strategy allows the objects to appear integral to the building, yet they can be changed with no structural modification to the space.

PROJECT	**Galleria Nazionale**
DESIGNER	Guido Canali
LOCATION	Parma, Italy
DATE	1977–87

Above The museum journey begins and ends in the wooden Farnese amphitheatre, from where a long steel-and-timber walkway leads up on to the stage.

Left The enormous edifice of the Palazzo della Pilotta, as seen from the town.

Context

This museum is housed within the Palazzo della Pilotta, a huge edifice constructed by Ranuccio I Farnese, Duke of Parma, in the seventeenth century. The *palazzo* was originally constructed to contain the barracks, stables and haylofts of the ducal residence. The building was arranged around two courtyards and faced towards the River Parma with a façade of over 200 metres (660 feet) in length. In 1618 the arms room was transformed into the horseshoe-shaped wood and stucco Farnese Theatre. In the eighteenth century Napoleon demolished the old palace and also the convent of San Pietro Martire. In 1944, heavy bombardment by American warplanes damaged the theatre.

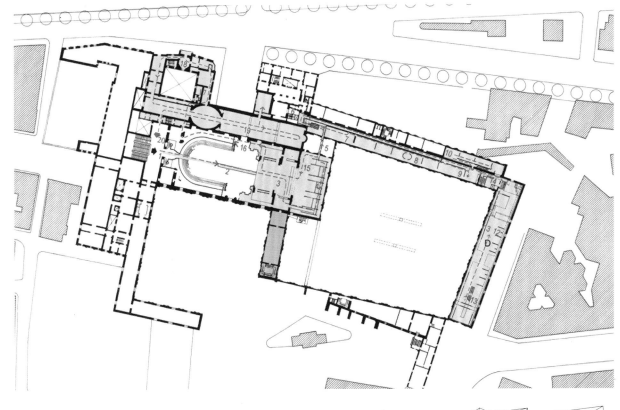

Above From the horse-shaped auditorium, the route leads through the stage and backstage areas, along the wing, into the rear stables and then back to the start.

Below Specifically positioned sculptures on a long steel beam mark the corner and turn into the upper level of the stable-block part of the museum.

Right An axonometric of the building shows the complex route back and forth through the space.

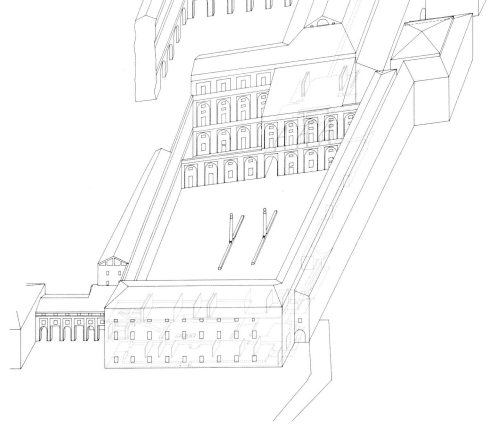

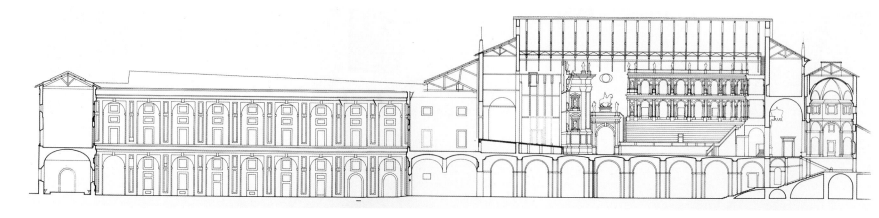

As well as the Galleria Nazionale and reconstructed theatre, the building now houses a number of important institutions, such as the Bodoni Museum of Printing, the National Museum of Antiquities and the Palatine Library. The Galleria Nazionale was constructed to accommodate the Farnese family's enormous and prestigious collection of paintings and sculptures.

Concept

The space for the museum consisted of three large, disconnected buildings: the Farnese Theatre, the 100-metre (330-foot)-long west wing, and the ex-stable block that completed the north side of the courtyard. Canali's strategy was to connect these three disparate spaces via a single route – a continuous passageway that ensured that the visitor moved through the museum without ever taking the same path.

Canali completed the design of the new interior over a period of ten years. This enabled him to respond to the various issues exposed during the renovation of the ancient building. The initial task was to strip the building to its bare essentials, removing all of the insensitive accretions added by the military and strengthening the structure, roof and some of the walls of the building. Archaeological finds were incorporated into the remodelling strategy.

Organization

Canali decided to locate both the starting and finishing points of the museum in the reconstructed Farnese Theatre. This was located conveniently close to the stone staircase entrance at the southern end of the building. Thus the timber horseshoe-shaped structure became the dramatic entrance to and exit from the journey through the museum. To reinforce the drama of this journey, Canali placed a long, slender steel ramp in the centre of the theatre, leading up to the stage.

Walking through the proscenium arch initiates the journey into the museum and conflates the relationship between audience and actor.

The large backstage volume is traversed by a raised walkway connecting to the side of the stage. This passes westwards across the space towards the long, thin wing. The journey is punctuated by a series of packing cases, irreverently displaying statues and sculptures as though only partially unloaded. A bridge through to the west wing precludes a sharp turn to the right and a view down the 100-metre (330-foot)-long corridor. At the end of this journey another stair

Far left A framework of scaffolding columns and beams supports the stable block. Paintings and sculptures are displayed on and within the structural system.

Below far left The adaptable trellised steel beams support the floors and walls of the museum (upper image). The lower wing is on two levels; the raised walkway on the left is the route back to the start (lower image).

Left The lower level of the backstage walkway allows visitors a freer space in which to view the paintings.

Below left The new structure of the rear block places no extra loading on the delicate vaulted ceiling of the ground-floor stables below.

Below The final part of the journey back to the theatre takes place under the stage and then out into the main auditorium.

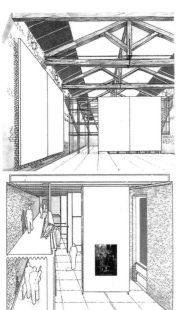

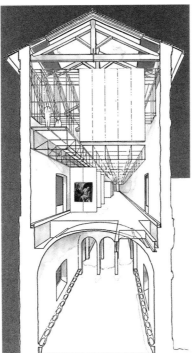

junction turns the visitor right into the north wing and into the lower level of the old stables.

Canali restructured the fragile stable walls and ceilings with a temporary scaffold structure. The floors of the stables were exposed to show the vaulted stable roofs and a system of ingenious brick shafts, thought to have been either channels for ventilation or for horse food in the stables below. The journey back through the museum is via an upper level in the long corridor, looking down upon the previously passed-through gallery. The final sequence is through the lower level of the backstage area and then

underneath the stage, where the visitor enters the theatre auditorium stage left, thus completing the cyclical journey without ever retracing their footsteps.

Detail

By treating the Pilotta as an archeological object, Canali has respected and, theoretically, enhanced the historic structure through opposition. The geometric severity of the ancient buildings is underscored by the flexibility and impermanence of the new interior.[1]

The Farnese Theatre and the long west wing were difficult to alter radically because of their historical importance

(theatre) and their distinct dimensions (wing). The stables, however, could be significantly altered without diminishing their archaeological and historical significance. Canali used a system of adaptable trellised beams here. This framework of scaffolding was used to hold the floors and walls as well as paintings and sculptures. The system could be adapted, when required, to host new configurations of objects whilst still fulfilling its structural role. The off-the-peg quality of new elements was also utilized in the backstage area, where the raised walkways appear temporal, constructed from steel poles and with a wooden decked floor. Tension wires brace the

structure and are reminiscent of the backstage fly-tower machinery that the theatre once housed. The west wing is a more solid affair, with sandstone floors, polished stucco walls and elegant steel and encaustic panel display systems set against the rough masonry of the existing building. The materials throughout the space were chosen in order to clearly distinguish the new from the historic fabric of the building.

1 Jeanne Marie Teutonico, 'Pristine Intervention', *Progressive Architecture*, April 1988, p.124

PROJECT **Grande Galerie de l'Évolution**

DESIGNERS Paul Chemetov and Borja Huidobro; René Allio (lighting and sound design); Roberto Benavente (display case and exhibit layout)

LOCATION Paris, France

DATE 1994

Top A cavalcade of animals roaming a metaphorical ground-floor 'savannah' greets visitors as they enter the museum.

Above The designer inspects a model of the layout of the space.

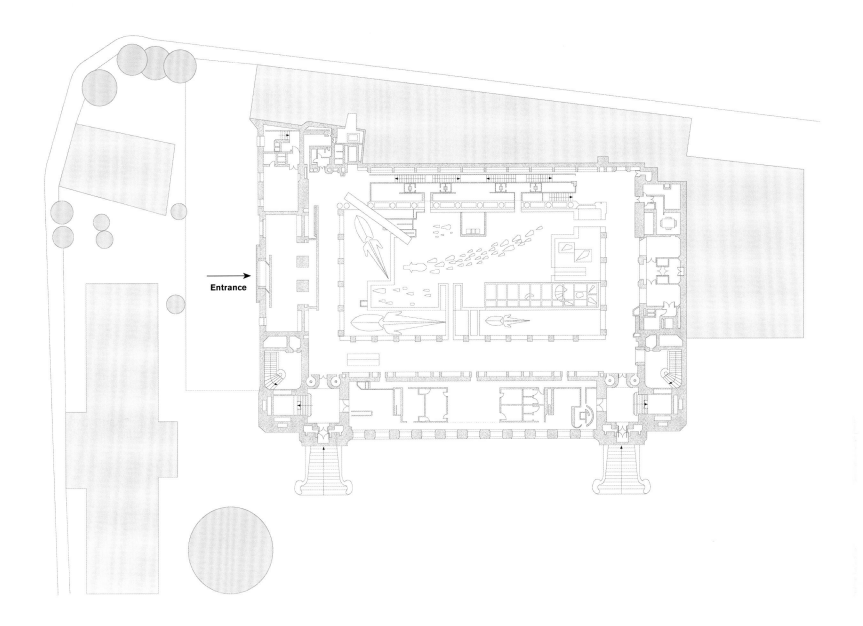

Entrance

Context

Along with the remodelling of the Louvre and the Musée d'Orsay, the transformation of the Natural History Museum into the Galerie de l'Évolution was one of President Mitterrand's Grands Projets. The original building, designed by Jules André, had opened in 1889. The building entrance was a grand portico facing the Jardin des Plantes. The interior consisted of a three-storey grand hall with a glass skylight. Slender cast-iron columns held up a series of galleries.

The host building had sat unoccupied since 1965, but since remodelling its popularity has soared; the building celebrated its ten millionth visitor in November 2010.

Concept

Our intention was not to try and preserve the building as a valued antique, we wanted to transform it whilst acknowledging its past, breaking down the frontiers between the old and the new.[1]

The elegance of the existing space and the restricted budget ensured that the designers exercised the utmost imagination in their proposal for the new gallery. The educational remit of the new exhibition space also required a gallery that captured the imagination of young minds. The raw material with which to achieve these goals was an extensive collection of taxidermy and a spectacular host building.

The designers chose to utilize the drama of the grand hall and treat it as an allegorical spectacle. The ground floor became a symbolic 'savannah', a plane across which a cavalcade of animals marched in a long sweep across the floor. The sea, underneath this plane, was filled with fish, sharks and even a whale, enigmatically displayed against blue-lit screens. Animals that live on both land and sea were placed upon floating sheets of sandblasted glass, imitating the ice sheets upon which they roam. Birds and other flying creatures were arranged on the upper-floor galleries, and climbing animals were mounted on the balustrades, ascending the walls of the hall.

Above As well as allowing the museum to stay open once the adjacent gardens have closed, the new axial entrance to the gallery reinforces the drama of the ground-floor spectacle as the visitor enters the space.

Top Blue-tinged glazing panels provide the metaphorical backdrop for the sea animals in the basement.

Above The section shows the dynamic interplay between the existing building and the arrangements of exhibits within the space.

Organization

A new entrance was opened on the side of the museum. This affords a closer connection to the street and allows the museum to remain open after the garden closes. It also reinforces the full spectacle of the massive central hall, as the visitor enters on axis.

The permanent exhibition created display space for 1,000 invertebrates, 450 birds, 350 mammals and 100 fish, amphibians and reptiles; just a fraction of the overall collection. Educational, administrative and ancillary spaces, such as a café, bookshop and conservation area, were located at the edges of the building, allowing them to operate in natural light.

Whilst the visitor is free to move amongst the displays, the designers proposed that the best route through the space was a reversal of the chronological theory of evolution. Lifts and stairs ascend to the top floor from where the visitor starts with an overview of the 'landscape', as though a bird looking down from the sky. The descent through the side galleries and towards the savannah is analogous to the descent from the trees to earth. Finally, locating the sea-life display in the basement, at the end of the route, is a new interpretation of the theory that human life evolved from creatures emerging from the sea.

Detail

Natural history museums tend to be associated with dusty relics and yellowing labels of information. This gallery was designed to demonstrate that music, film, light and sound stimulate the imagination and bring exhibits to life.

Lighting and sound were designed to perform three tasks: emphasize the scientific aspect of the displays, provide information such as the names of the species, and highlight the circulation through the building. The vast number of species to be displayed meant that there were 11,000 lighting points. The existing display cases were adapted during their renovation in order to incorporate integrated fibre-optic lighting systems. The glass roof was screened and supplemented with artificial light with which to animate the space.

The acoustics of the space are carefully managed. Sound zones were created in which rain, wind and birdsong could be broadcast at different times of the day. To avoid a cacophony, visitors are treated to a specific sound as they approach a particular specimen; as they move away again this is replaced with the ambient sounds of the natural environment.

Where possible the smaller side galleries where retained and restored. The former Galerie des Oiseaux (Bird Gallery) is a long, thin, double-height corridor gallery adjacent to the main hall. Its elegant interior is lined on both the ground and upper gallery levels with refined wooden display cabinets topped by a vaulted ceiling. The original display cases were restored and reused to house a poignant exhibition on extinct animals – ironically a condition that this museum once contributed towards. The gallery is exceptionally dark, with the animals picked out in sharp, crisp LED lighting. The atmosphere is reverent and gloomy, especially when visitors realize that this gallery is full of animals that have vanished from the planet.

1 Paul Chemetov, quoted in *Architecture Intérieure – Créé*, June 1994, p.35

Far left Collections of small but colourful creatures such as butterflies are grouped in display cases.

Left Natural habitats are reflected in the exhibition strategy. The basement is the sea and the ground floor is the earth, for example.

Far left The lighting is carefully controlled to animate the exhibits to their full potential.

Left The sombre former Galerie des Oiseaux, which contains a display of extinct animals.

PROJECT	**Great Expectations**
DESIGNERS	Roger Mann, Dinah Casson and Craig Riley
LOCATION	New York, NY, USA
DATE	2001

Above The long display table was split into two by a canopy that looked like a tablecloth blown up in the air by the draught from the passing commuters.

Left The raised canopy allowed the travellers to pass underneath and through the table.

Context

Commissioned in 2001 by the Design Council for the month-long festival of 'UKinNY', *Great Expectations* was an installation designed to showcase the best of contemporary British design. It featured 100 exhibits drawn from a broad range of creative disciplines, such as furniture and graphic design. Casson Mann was responsible for the selection, curation and design of the installation.

The installation was housed in the imposing surroundings of Vanderbilt Hall, in New York's Grand Central Station. (The 1913 station was owned by the Vanderbilt family, who had a 12,000-square-metre/129,000-square-foot hall, adjacent to the main concourse, named after them.) This distinguished space is 16 metres (52 feet) high and is lined with 'Tennessee pink' marble. Five large, ornate golden chandeliers, suspended from a richly detailed ceiling, illuminate it. Approximately 500,000 commuters pass through the terminal each day.

Concept

The perfect setting for a banquet, an internationally acknowledged space where communication happens and deals are struck.[1]

Installation is a strategy that can be used to describe the temporal inhabitation of a space. A building may be used to contain a display element for just a short period of time. The temporal dimension of this type of approach means that the existing structure is left relatively untouched and that no permanent alterations are made. Any changes made are corrected after the exhibition is over.

Great Expectations was designed to inhabit the hall for just one month. It was intended to slow down and catch the eye of the bustling, busy commuters as they passed through the station. It was also designed to provoke reflection upon the displayed objects. Casson Mann positioned a large free-standing table centrally in the space — it was hoped that around this table, and amongst the loose arrangement of chairs and exhibits, an informal dialogue could begin, which in turn would trigger a renewal of interest in British design.

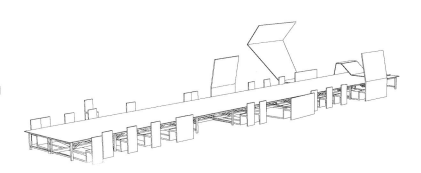

Above The informality of the seating and the folds of the canopy are shown in these two axonometric sketches of the scheme.

Below A computer rendering of the table in the space.

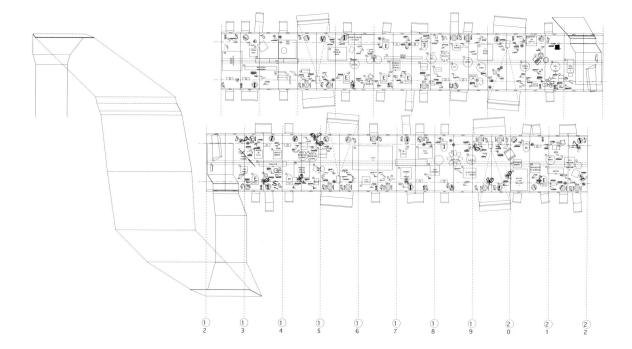

Organization

The installation took the form of a 60-metre (200-foot)-long light box, styled as a banqueting table, placed on axis within the hall. It was separated into two parts to ensure that it did not impede circulation and the flow of commuters as they hurried through the space. The break in the table was announced by a canopy that flowed from the top of the light box and folded up and over the top of the passageway between the two table ends. This was shaped to represent a tablecloth, one that had been blown upwards in the current of air caused by the throng of travellers as they rushed through the hall. The title *Great Expectations* was projected on to the canopy's folded surface so that it could be seen by passers-by.

The 100 exhibits were laid out on the table like different courses of food drawn from an exquisite menu. The exhibits ranged in scale from a chair and a bike to the graphics of an album cover. Placing them on a static plinth unified the exhibits and presented them to the public with a narrative that was continuous. No matter what size or shape, each exhibit was considered to be the best of British creative products.

Above The plan of the table in its context in the hall.

Top The plan of the table and its contents.

Detail

The lighting of the majestic hall was adapted in order to accentuate the standout qualities of the exhibition. The large windows of the space were blacked out. Tinted lights were installed that washed the marble walls with colour, accentuating their elaborate hues and texture. The reveals of the windows facing 42nd Street were also lit, in order to announce that something exciting was happening within the space. The stark white light of the table stood out in the colourful room. In order to capture the after-dinner atmosphere, one that was convivial to informal chat and conversation, the designers configured the chairs around the table and in front of the objects in a loose and unceremonious manner. To stimulate conversation the exhibits were accompanied by audio-visual accounts of the design process. These were relayed via monitors set into the table. Speakers were secreted within the chairs. Stories of innovation and excellence in design were filtered into the ears of the seated guest, informing their understanding of the exhibit's qualities.

After one month the table was taken down, the lighting was returned to its normal colours and the hall was returned back to its original condition. It was as though the table had never been there.

1 Roger Mann, quoted in *Frame*, January/February 2002, p.12

Above left The light-box table made a strong impact against the pink-tinged walls and floor of the main hall.

Above The wide light-filled display table unified the disparate collection of objects.

PROJECT **British Music Experience**

DESIGNERS Land Design Studio

LOCATION London, UK

DATE 2009

Above The 'core', a central space organized around one of the 12 columns of the dome.

Left The Millennium Dome on the Greenwich Peninsula in south-east London.

Context

The Millennium Dome was built upon derelict wasteland on the Greenwich Peninsula. It sits on the Prime Meridian, the line of longitude that passes through Greenwich. Twelve 100-metre (328-foot)-high yellow columns support the 365-metre (1,198-foot)-wide dome, representing a clock face when seen from the air. The roof canopy is elevated 52 metres (170 feet) from the ground,

symbolizing each week of the year. The Millennium Dome originally housed an exhibition consisting of 14 zones, each named after various elements of human existence, such as Faith, Work, Body, Mind, Rest and Play. This *Millennium Experience* was open for exactly one year. The Dome then became the O₂, housing the O₂ Arena – a large multi-purpose venue.

The British Music Experience (BME) is an exhibition mapping the 60 or so years that British pop music has existed. It features music created in the British Isles as well as international artists who have found their inspiration or audience within the UK. The exhibition opened in March 2009 and is located on an upper level of the O₂.

Concept

It's a sort of comprehensive, conceptually flamboyant Wikipedia history of British pop music in shape-shifting multi-dimensional interactive form, a Disney Epcot ride designed by minds who have comprehensively digested every issue of Q magazine and quite a few Mojos.[1]

The relationship between audience and displayed object is an important consideration in exhibition design. In recent years this connection has entailed less instruction and much more participation. This evolution is personified by interactive exhibition display methods. Interactive exhibitions have been around since the early 1960s and were adopted in order to involve visitors who enjoy 'doing' rather than just observing. The notion that a museum or exhibition experience no longer needed to be didactic also coincided with the evolution of sophisticated digital equipment and software. Visitors were no longer content to stand back and just look; they wanted to interact with objects and experience them by touching, examining and interpreting them in their own particular way.

The BME is the spatial embodiment of an exciting, interactive, encyclopedic digital music environment. Annual visitor numbers were expected to be in the hundreds of thousands. Therefore the spatial modelling of the complicated site into a logical exhibition with a clearly defined route was of paramount importance. The collection of physical objects had yet to be established, so the curation and compilation of exhibits was started from scratch. The exit area of the exhibition had to be able to host corporate events for up to 300 guests. These complex and exacting requirements led the designers to conceive an interior that was a free-flowing mechanism, one that was carefully choreographed with a five-minute 'pulsed' entry sequence and was ordered around a central hub to which everything connected.

Below A sequential series of spaces and objects was carefully orchestrated to control the complex ebb and flow of the anticipated large crowds of visitors.

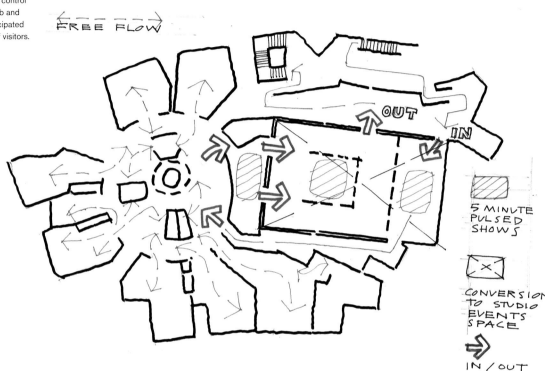

Below Beyond the entrance and pre-show area, visitors entered the 'core'. The seven 'edge zones' fanned out from the central structural member.

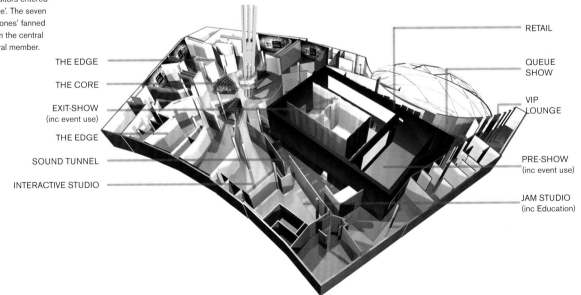

THE EDGE

THE CORE

EXIT-SHOW
(inc event use)

THE EDGE

SOUND TUNNEL

INTERACTIVE STUDIO

RETAIL

QUEUE SHOW

VIP LOUNGE

PRE-SHOW
(inc event use)

JAM STUDIO
(inc Education)

Above The edge zones representing (from top to bottom) the 1960s, the 1970s and the 1990s.

Opposite The exhibition included interactive displays that people could revisit through the internet and their own smart card. It culminated in an immersive live show, during which famous concerts were projected on to large screens surrounding the visitors.

Organization

The BME was allocated an irregular-shaped space on an upper level of the dome. Visitors had to arrive at and depart from a fixed point via the stairs and lifts. This required careful choreography of the entrance and exit sequences of the experience, and the time that the visitor was expected to spend within them. A careful mapping of the proposed exhibition concluded that an average visit would last about 90 minutes. This duration was ordered within a combination of events, activities and exhibits – a sequence that would allow the large numbers of visitors to flow easily and comfortably through the space.

The 500 visitors per hour enter the space with a timed smart ticket. This can be clicked at a number of sensors around the exhibition so that the visitor can build up a personal archive of favourite moments. These can be accessed later via the website. Visitors travel from the entrance pre-show through the sound tunnel into the 'Core'. This is a large central space that is organized around one of the O_2's 12 yellow structural columns, which have been incorporated into the design of the interior. The Core contains a series of interactive exhibits displaying artists' backgrounds and contextualizing British music. Seven rooms, known as the 'Edge Zones', fan out from the Core. They are ordered chronologically from 1945 through to the present and contain 'timeline' exhibits such as guitars and outfits worn by the stars

of each era. There are also interactive elements such as 'Table Talk', hosting interviews with the stars. The final spaces of the experience consist of an immersive film environment, replaying iconic concerts from the last 60 years, and an interactive studio, where visitors can play instruments and receive digital tutorials from current stars.

Detail

The interior of the space is contained in one large, blacked-out box built within the interior of the dome. The various spaces are formed from subdivisions within the box. Because of the theatrical and immersive scenography of the experience, the surfaces of the interior were designed to ensure that lighting and projections are shown in

optimal conditions. Interactive furniture is all hard-wearing. Rooms, such as the interactive studio, where noisy 'events' and music making take place, are extremely well insulated to avoid any sound transferral.

1 Paul Morley, *Observer Music Monthly*, March 2009

The position that an epoch occupies in the historical process can be determined more strikingly from an analysis of its inconspicuous surface-level expression. The surface level expressions, however, by virtue of their unconscious nature, provide unmediated access to the fundamental substance of the state of things.[1]

In *Capitalism and Leisure Theory*, published in 1985, Chris Rojek identified four key features, or spatial types, of contemporary leisure.[2] He suggests, firstly, that spaces used for leisure must reflect the secure and personal space of the home rather than the public sphere. Secondly, leisure spaces are personalized and therefore must deliver menus of options for their users. Thirdly, leisure is a major commercialized industry, incorporating brands, food, tourism and advertising. Finally, Rojek suggests that leisure is more regulated and formalized than ever before, that it has been 'pacified'; in other words, it generally involves activities that require learning, mastery and practice, such as dance lessons, learning to cook or sampling

a new cuisine. Rojek concludes that as work patterns have diversified and become more varied, so has leisure time. As time gets squeezed and compartmentalized, especially in parts of the industrialized world where work is prevalent and patterns of working are fluid, leisure has adapted accordingly. Whatever type of leisure activity is undertaken, the space in which it is contained is of paramount importance. It needs to act as a stimulant, a facilitator and a secure environment that puts its occupants at ease.

In the *Oxford English Dictionary*, leisure is described as 'the freedom or opportunity to do something'.[3] Its etymology is rooted in the French *leisir*, to be permitted, and the Latin *licere*, which has its roots in licence. Freedom, and permission to be free, are therefore central concerns. Traditionally, the spaces that encourage and facilitate leisure have revolved around forms of relaxation, often involving socializing, eating and drinking. Latterly, 'leisure' has been used to describe time spent in a range of pursuits entailing contact with a variety of environments, such as branded and themed spaces, where shopping and entertainment may

take place. Whichever form of leisure is chosen, it is obvious that this time and space affords the freedom and opportunity for people to indulge. Leisure spaces that have been created within an existing building offer a multiplicity of spatial experiences that provide an antidote to a homogeneous interior. Spatial atmospheres can differ radically when activities are housed inside a building that has been built for a very different previous function. The embedded values of an existing building, as well as the wider cultural landscape, offer the designer a different set of possible responses. This introduction will explore the general patterns of these developments in the creation of new leisure spaces.

The coffeehouse and the public house

Sociologists have identified the seventeenth-century coffeehouse as one of the birthplaces of the modern public realm. This was an accessible space where people from a range of social backgrounds could meet, and unfettered social interaction could take place. The organization and forms of the interior, along with its spatial arrangements, were relatively

CHAPTER 5 **Leisure**

Opposite One of the early models of the modern public realm, Vienna's *Kaffeehaus* was vitally important to the life of the city.

Above Liverpool's Philharmonic Hotel. The central bar served various rooms, each of which attracted a different clientele.

Above The dynamic shapes and surface treatment of the Café l'Aubette were designed to simulate dancers' movements.

straightforward. Fundamentally, it would generally consist of two types of space: a service area and a place to consume. The service space would include counters, serveries, bars, storage and maybe a preparation area. The space for the consumer would include places to sit and eat and drink.

As the popularity of the coffeehouse grew, its design became more sophisticated and its importance to the commerce of the city increased. The Viennese *Kaffeehaus* played a central role in the organization of the city as well as the working day. It not only provided space to socialize and drink but the variety of rooms – some private, some public – and the connection to various services such as telephones also facilitated business meetings and transactions. As the *Kaffeehaus* became central to the public and private life of the city, other functions such as games rooms (containing billiards, dominoes and card tables), a ladies' room and even bowling alleys were added. The *Kaffeehaus* provided breakfast, morning and afternoon tea and sociability in the evening, ensuring that it played a central role in the leisure and business time of the inhabitants of the city.

In the UK the emergence of the late-nineteenth-century Victorian public house, or 'pub', followed some of the ideas and organizing principles of the coffeehouse. Like a miniature city, the rooms of the pub would reflect the various uses required by the city's inhabitants: there would often be multiple entrances to a public bar, a saloon, a smoke or 'news' room, all of which were usually served by one central circular bar, a spatial device that would link all of the rooms together. The interior of the Philharmonic Hotel in Liverpool was organized around a central radial bar that served the billiards, smoking, lounge and news rooms. Its interior was aspirational in that it signified a time when public houses and coffee bars designed their interiors in order to appeal to their clientele.

The combination of innovative layout and particular decorative treatment suggests that the brewer and architect were attempting to propose a pub interior more like a gentlemen's club than a nineteenth-century gin palace.[4]

In the early twentieth century the development of the 'fluid' modern

interior was exemplified by the Aubette leisure centre (or Café l'Aubette), located in Strasbourg, France. Theo van Doesburg, Hans Arp and Sophie Taeuber-Arp were commissioned to design an entertainment complex that consisted of a series of large rooms where various forms of entertainment such as dancing, dining, films and music could take place – all contained within a nineteenth-century barrack building that had previously burned down and been reconstructed. The new interior space was dynamic and colourful. This was realized with a geometric surface pattern that covered the walls, floor and ceiling. The pattern was designed to simulate the dynamism of the whirling forms of dancers inside the space, and the planes of colour appeared to continue infinitely across the rooms. The organization of the interior was more straightforward, with seats and counters arranged orthogonally. Although designed to express the dynamism of modern life in form and colour, the citizens of Strasbourg found the new interior disconcerting – the diagonally arranged colour planes on the walls, floor and ceiling caused confusion with the real dimensions of the space. After the opening in 1928, the interior was radically altered; ten

years later the entire interior was replaced and nothing of the iconic space remained.

Themed environments

Postmodernism cultivates a conception of the urban fabric as necessarily fragmented, a 'palimpsest' of past forms superimposed upon each other, and a collage of current uses, many of which may be ephemeral.[5]

In the recent past, leisure environments have become more sophisticated in their methods of appealing to particular groups of customers. The development of the model of these environments can be seen in the early 1980s, when postmodern design strategies promulgated the reworking of the urban fabric as a series of fragments, containing vernacular traditions, historicized forms, eclectic styles and often including spectacular spaces. The redesign of existing spaces was, and is, in part, predisposed to the spectacular, in that part of its appealing nature is that it can be ephemeral and not always have to conform to traditional structural requirements. 'Themed' environments, where the new interior treatment of an existing building shell might wilfully,

and often surreally, juxtapose with the building envelope and its context, gained currency, and treated the city as a plaything where the existing could be recombined, reworked and reused to spectacular effect.

Much of this spectacularization of the city began in the Far East. In the 1980s, much of the new design work in this part of the world expressed the desire to recombine existing aesthetics, ideas and language to form something new. In 1986, designer Nigel Coates described one of his own Japanese projects:

> *Situated on Tokyo's busiest crossroads, Caffé Bongo's dramatic entrance was an arresting pop-classical collage. Bursting with vocabulary from the worlds of music and fashion, the café's aircraft-wing-meets-Piranesian-Rome aesthetic expressed the fundamental design currents of the late twentieth century.*[6]

The lower floor of a nondescript tower block was radically transformed with an aeroplane wing that swept into the building and terminated in a Rococo interior. The stage-set qualities of the project meant

that it could all be removed without compromising the structural integrity of the existing building. This type of exotic scenographic interior, a surreal spectacle, was the pioneer of the themed environment – a space that is designed to take on the appearance of somewhere else. Themed environments revel in the surreal juxtaposition of elements to create fantastic scenery, where appearances are often quite deceptive.

Modern entertainment and leisure facilities, usually in out-of-town locations, utilize scenographic effects and stage-set strategies to create an atmosphere that is conducive to suspending reality, even if just for a fleeting moment in time. Described as an urban entertainment centre, Printworks in Manchester, UK, is a place where cinemas, shopping, sports, eating, drinking and socializing take place under one large roof. Printworks is housed in the stripped-out shell of a redundant printing factory, adjacent to the Urbis exhibition centre – both buildings formed part of a regeneration of this part of the city after the 1996 IRA bombing. Printworks is organized around an internal street that was designed to look like a New York City

avenue, complete with walkways and cranes. It also includes an old railway turntable set into the new floor – a remnant of the old printworks' internal railway. At night the street comes alive with revellers, who venture along the thoroughfare, sampling the 20 or so bars and restaurants, such as Café Rouge and Wagamama, that line the street. The concept of the Printworks is a palimpsest, a compacted layering of eclectic forms and places from another space and time.

Above left The exterior of Caffé Bongo is announced to the city by a gigantic aircraft wing that appears to have crashed into the building's lower floor.

Above The aircraft wing is supported by steel columns and then terminates inside the interior to become a canopy sheltering the tables and chairs in the Rococo interior.

Below The interior of the printworks, once an old printing factory in central Manchester, now contains a new internal street that is conceived as a collage of fragments of parts of cities and places from across the world.

Far left The luxurious Cathay Pacific lounge in Hong Kong is symbolic of how travel hubs such as airports have become an extension of leisure spaces across the world.

Left The foyer of the Hempel Hotel in London was formed from the ground floor of five terraced houses. The space provides a relaxing destination for world-weary travellers.

Destinations

Tourism, human circulation considered as consumption, a by-product of the circulation of commodities, is fundamentally nothing more than going to see what has become banal.[7]

Tourism and increasingly cost-effective forms of travel have influenced new types of leisure space. As tourism grows, transport hubs and hotels are required to provide more than just a mode of transport or a bed. In the twenty-first century, many airports, train stations and other transport hubs have been transformed so that visitors can spend more leisure time in increasingly sophisticated environments and amongst a wider range of amenities.

These spaces are now as much about shopping, eating and socializing as they are about travel. John Pawson's Cathay Pacific lounges at Hong Kong International Airport have been designed with all of the luxury of a five-star hotel.

Key was preservation of the spectacular views – both of Foster's architecture and of the comings and goings of planes outside – whilst creating sheltered enclaves for drinking, dining, working, bathing or relaxing. Etched glass screens provide privacy whilst not entirely blocking the view of the double-height departure lounge below. Water – and particularly the effect of light on water – is used to foster a sense of tranquillity.[8]

Hotels are often described as destinations that strive hard to simulate the visitor's own domestic environment, from which they may have travelled a long way. The Hempel Hotel in London is constructed from five Georgian terraced townhouses. The foyer is one large and open space – a minimalist, abstracted cube created from the lower floors of the houses being knocked into one space, where no trace of the previous small rooms of the terraces can be seen. Its qualities as a destination are extolled thus:

The ambitious atrium lobby – awash in shifting shadows and light throughout the day – features a Portland stone floor and sunken seating areas with Indonesian ox cart tables, warmly offset by two glowing fireplaces. This is a place to relax in style. Contemporary world music sets a tranquil mood, whilst scented candles delight the senses. Upstairs, each of the rooms, suites, and private apartments are a reflection of our signature minimalist style, yet no luxury amenity has been spared.[9]

Throughout history the development of leisure spaces within existing buildings has entailed the incorporation of scenography; the creation of a new surface that acts as a backdrop to occupation. The stage-set quality of a new interior inside an existing building provides a lining that is created by rooms, furniture and surfaces, all designed to encourage their use. The case studies in this chapter provide examples of the changing nature of leisure space and its requirements.

1 Siegfried Kracauer, *The Mass Ornament: Weimar Essays*, translated by Thomas Y. Levin, Harvard University Press, 1995, p.75

2 Chris Rojek, *Capitalism and Leisure Theory*, Tavistock Publications, 1985

3 C.T. Onions *et al.* (editors), *Shorter Oxford English Dictionary on Historical Principles*, third edition, Oxford University Press, 1972

4 Christopher Woodward, *Cafés and Bars: The Architecture of Public Display*, Routledge, 2007, p.126

5 David Harvey, *The Condition of Postmodernity*, Blackwell Publishing, 1990, p.66

6 Nigel Coates website: www.nigelcoates.com/project/caffe_bongo

7 Guy Debord, *Society of the Spectacle*, Black & Red, 1983, p.168

8 John Pawson website: www.johnpawson.com/architecture/commercial/cathaypacificlounges

9 Hempel Hotel website: www.the-hempel.co.uk

PROJECT	**Willow Tea Rooms**
DESIGNERS	Charles Rennie Mackintosh and Margaret MacDonald Mackintosh
LOCATION	Glasgow, UK
DATE	1904

Above The Salon de Luxe, or ladies' room, on the first floor of the Willow Tea Rooms. The upper frieze of the room was leaded mirror-glass and the chairs were silver with purple glass inserts.

Left The façade of the tea rooms was rendered white in order to make it stand out amongst its neighbours on the street.

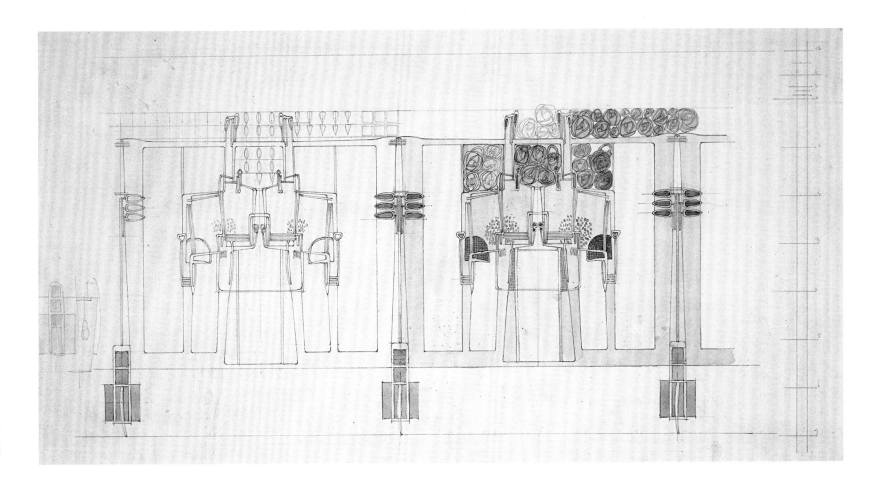

Context

The Willow Tea Rooms are located at 217 Sauchiehall Street, in the centre of Glasgow. The original building was a four-storey tenement house. Commissioned by the client and tenant, Catherine Cranston, Mackintosh reworked the existing building and the ground floor of the adjacent house. He remodelled the façade and interior and added a new double-height back salon studio to the existing building. This was the fourth and final tea room that Mackintosh designed for Cranston. A recent partial restoration has returned the tea rooms back to a version of the original.

Concept

Until the opening of Miss Cranston's new establishment in Sauchiehall Street today, the acme of originality had not been reached. Her 'Salon De Luxe' on the first floor is simply a marvel of the art of the upholsterer and decorator.[1]

Often referred to as the 'Cranston Tea Rooms', Sauchiehall Street was the last and most elegant of a series of interiors commissioned over a period of 20 years by Mackintosh's main patron. In response to her brother's tea-importing business, and the belief that the tasting rooms could be presented in a different, more inviting manner, Cranston established a chain of tea rooms across Glasgow. As a result of the Temperance Movement, the popularity of the tea room had increased enormously in the late nineteenth century, offering as it did an alternative to alcohol and a respite from the long working day. In Gaelic 'Sauchiehall' meant 'the Alley of Willows'. This not only gave the tea rooms their name, but it also translated into a recurring motif for the design of the interior. The Willow Tea Rooms were designed to cater for a cross-section of Glaswegian society, with business lunchrooms, billiards and smoking rooms, and a women-only space, where ladies could escape their chaperones for a period of time. Sauchiehall Street was chosen for its close proximity to the new and fashionable department stores that were opening, catering for the new middle classes and their spare income and leisure time.

Top The designs for the plaster relief friezes that lined the upper level of the front saloon. The starting point is an abstracted willow tree.

Above The front door of the Salon de Luxe.

Organization

The site consisted of an existing four-storey building along with a basement. Mackintosh added a rear double-height extension, at the same time extending the basement. He remodelled the façade by creating a large shop window that ran virtually the entire width of the building. Both the upper and lower parts of the window were formed from small square panes of glazing. Above, at the first-floor level of the tea rooms, a wide, slightly bowed strip window was inserted into the façade. A new entrance was created to the side of the ground-floor window and the whole façade was rendered in white stucco, ensuring that it stood apart from its neighbours. Mackintosh arranged three tea rooms on the ground floor: one in the front, one in the back and one in the gallery. The Salon de Luxe, predominantly a ladies' room, was on the first floor in the front building, and the smoking and billiards rooms were located on the second and third floors.

Detail

Mackintosh's wife, the artist Margaret MacDonald, worked extensively with her husband on the project, particularly on the design of the Salon de Luxe (or, as it was labelled by the journalists of the day, the 'Room of Looks'). From the first-floor strip window the salon overlooked Sauchiehall Street. This room was the most precious interior of the tearoom. The walls were clad in panels of silver and purple silk, stretched and stitched with beaded seams. Above the panels ran a frieze of leaded mirror-glass sheets. Fixed seating against the walls was upholstered in purple silk, and the loose, high-backed chairs, arranged in the middle of the space, were painted silver, while their backs were inset with purple glass.

The ceiling was vaulted and from it hung an elaborate chandelier, with balls, ovals and tear drops of semi-precious glass, reflecting light around the room. A gesso, or plaster panel, painted by MacDonald was set into the wall and was based upon the poem by Rossetti, 'O Ye, All Ye that Walk in Willow Wood'. The front room on the ground floor was painted brilliant white. The only colour in the space was the purple upholstery and the dark oak ladder-back chairs. Positioned between the fireplace and the entrance was an oak frame that incorporated two tables positioned below a wrought-iron cage. This frame supported a large glass bowl, from which tubes were suspended, each one holding a long-stemmed flower. The 5.5-metre (18-foot)-high room was accentuated by a white panelled frieze that contained a stylized willow tree and leaf motif and lined the upper level of the walls of the space.

In contrast to the light and airy quality of the front room, the backspace of the salon was dark and low ceilinged, with stained wood panels and dark ladder-back chairs. Above this salon, the mezzanine gallery was arranged around a series of columns that supported the roof structure. The floor beams spanned the entire width of the salon, keeping the ground floor clear of structure. The top-lit mezzanine space was painted white in order to contrast with the dark lower floor of the salon.

1 Author unknown, *Glasgow Evening News*, 29 October 1903, p.7; cited in Alan Crawford, *Charles Rennie Mackintosh,* Thames and Hudson, 1995, p.70

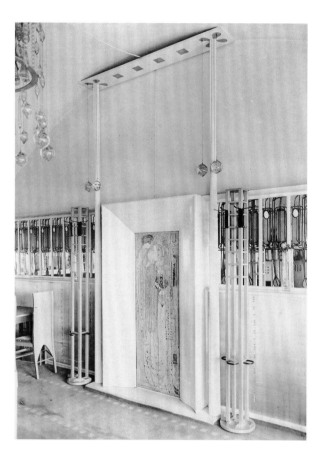

Left The framed painting of Rossetti's poem by Margaret MacDonald situated in the Salon de Luxe.

Left The front salon was illuminated by light pouring in from the new large window on the front façade.

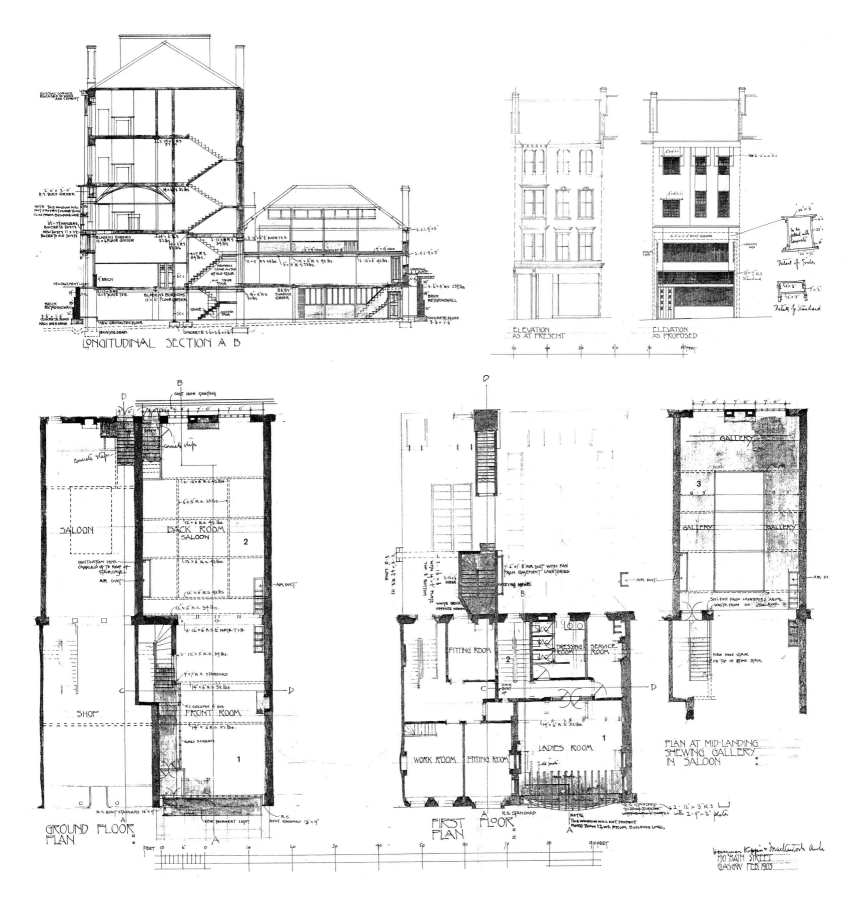

ELEVATION
AS AT PRESENT

ELEVATION
AS PROPOSED

LONGITUDINAL SECTION A B

GROUND FLOOR
PLAN

FIRST FLOOR
PLAN

PLAN AT MID-LANDING
SHEWING GALLERY
IN SALOON

Top left Long section
through the tea rooms.
The double-height
extension is on the right.

Top right The existing
elevation on the left
was transformed
with new openings
and a covering of
white render.

Above left Ground-
floor plan.
1 Front room (double
height)
2 Saloon

Above right First-floor
plan.
1 Salon de Luxe
2 Stairs
3 Mezzanine gallery

PROJECT	**American Bar**	
DESIGNER	Adolf Loos	
LOCATION	Vienna, Austria	
DATE	1908	

Above The entrance to the bar is across a deep threshold that is curtained off from the street, increasing the separation between interior and exterior.

Left The gaudy backlit mosaic sign leans towards passers-by at an acute and awkward angle. Four marble columns frame the doors and windows.

Context

Also known as the Kärntner Bar due to its location off the street of the same name, this project was completed in the same year as the publication of Loos' controversial essay 'Ornament and Crime'. As a young man Loos spent three years in America, therefore this commission coincided with his cultural sympathies; the bar was formulated to introduce American-style drinking, and drinks such as cocktails, to Viennese café society.

The bar is housed in a quiet side street of shops just near the Stephansplatz, the central cathedral square in Vienna. The one-storey bar, with a small basement, occupies the street level of a nondescript block of buildings. It is announced to the street by a gaudy, backlit mosaic sign that lurches at an ungainly angle towards the pedestrianized street.

Concept

The spaces that Loos created often expressed his uncompromising character. He published articles throughout his life, in newspapers and in journals, on topics as diverse as gentlemen's hats and plumbing. The ideas promulgated in his writing were often themes that were also expressed in his buildings and interiors. In particular, Loos developed the *Raumplan* (space plan), a complex ordering of space and materials to facilitate occupation. *Raumplan* interiors were often complex domestic entities. They were characterized by a series of differing levels, sophisticated circulation patterns and a series of views that conflated the relationship between the occupants and the space. The rooms of the space were then finished off with elaborate materials.

The American Bar demonstrated some of the themes of the *Raumplan*. The bar was a skilful manipulation of classical materials such as marble, onyx, mahogany, brass, leather and mirror, all used entirely in their natural state. Loos derided ornament as a mask, one that overlaid the properties of an original material, and which then compelled it to lie. The intimacy and atmosphere of the American Bar, due partly to its very small size, was fractured by an upper-level frieze; a mirrored wall that projected the image of a series of further spaces beyond the bar. The endless reflected marble ceiling counterpointed the constrained and formal straightjacket of the lower-level room.

The prominence of the American flag on the sign outside was a gesture that Loos saw as an attempt to liberate Austria from its nostalgic attachment to the ornaments of the past and an urge to look to the future, which Loos believed was American.

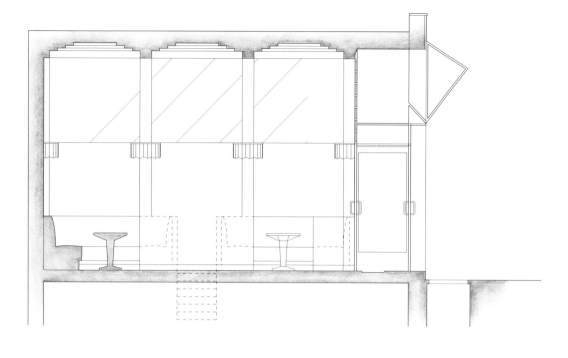

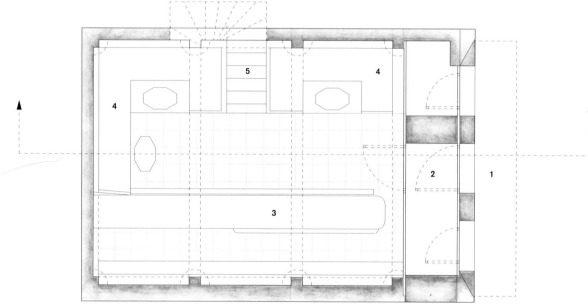

Organization

The bar was designed within a very restricted space, measuring just 6.15 x 4.45 metres (20 feet 2 inches x 14 feet). Originally the venue was intended for men only, but because of its popularity this soon changed. From the outside the contrast between the exterior and interior of the bar was pronounced. The striking façade was divided by four colourful columns of yellow Skyros marble framing two glass windows and a glazed central door. Curtains, in both the door and the windows, obscured the interior from any curious passers-by. A 1-metre (3-foot)-deep interior threshold, which acted as a buffer between inside and outside whilst doubling up as a cloakroom, supplemented this veiled entrance sequence. Even though the space was incredibly restricted, Loos considered the compression of the entrance, and the subsequent relief as it was traversed, important enough to incorporate into the interior.

The bar ran the length of the room from front to back, and was configured at just over 1 metre (around 3 feet) high so that, like an American bar, it would feel natural to stand at. Opposite was a banquette of low seating, separated in two by a stair that led to the basement toilets. Three lozenge-shaped tables, with frosted glass under-lit tops, were fixed in front of the seats, completing the simple arrangement of the room.

Top Section. The intimacy of the small bar is counterpointed by the tall ceilings and the endlessly reflected spaces in the upper-level mirror frieze.

Above The space is organized around the long bar and a series of banquette seats. A stair leads to the basement toilets. The deep threshold entrance sequence contains the cloakroom as well as acting as a buffer zone between the city and the bar.

1 Entrance
2 Cloakroom
3 Bar
4 Banquette seating
5 Stairs down to basement toilet/office

Detail

In short the subtle play of the Kärntner Bar moves between two opposite poles: optical deception and technical certainty.[1]

The dark and atmospheric interior was ordered on a strict pattern. The chequered floor tiles, the square panels of onyx on the upper part of the entrance hall, and the elegant coffered marble ceiling were reinforced by the marble pilasters dividing the room into three bays. The walls of the room were panelled in mahogany to the height of the entrance door, a line that followed the room around to the back of the bar in order to create shelves to house the glasses and bottles of drink. The bar was fashioned from the same dark mahogany as the wall panels. To deal with the limited size of the space, a deceit was introduced with the placement of mirrors at the upper level of the walls, with which to endlessly reflect the coffered marble ceiling. Yet the taut, technical structure of the interior was anything but uncertain. It was these two polarities that created the tension of the interior.

It is significant that Loos dedicated the bar to his friend the poet Peter Altenberg, a portrait of whom was placed in the bar, and whose poetry relied on a strict structural certainty that was then infused with elaborate and florid prose.

Above The coffered marble ceiling is reflected endlessly in the mirrored frieze.

1 Benedetto Gravagnuolo, *Adolf Loos: Theory and Works*, Idea Books, 1982, p.117

PROJECT	**Haçienda**
DESIGNER	Ben Kelly
LOCATION	Manchester, UK
DATE	1982

Above The main space containing the dance floor edged with traffic bollards.

Left and below The discreet roller-shutter-door front of the Haçienda and the inset plaque were the only hints that the club existed at this location.

Context

The Haçienda nightclub was built inside a large warehouse on Whitworth Street West in central Manchester. The clients were the independent record label Factory Records and one of the bands they represented, New Order.

The run-down canal-side warehouse was a former yacht showroom. It comprised two co-joined elements: a cavernous top-lit main shed and a four-storey masonry building that provided the street frontage of the space.

Concept

The design was essentially a direct response to the building. It was never our intention to lose the scale or proportions offered but to enhance and capitalize on it. A formal 'disco' environment was out of the question … The most memorable moment was when the sound system was finally switched on and the whole point became obvious; no pretension, no fuss, no glamour – just as intended.[1]

Utilizing an existing building requires the designer to recognize what is already on site. It is a process that enables them to make judgements about a place and reinforce a process of accentuating or editing what is extant. The design of the Haçienda was a process of uncovering and responding to what the existing building already offered and then accentuating those qualities with the addition of the requirements of the new interior. This type of strategy calls for flexibility, as the reworking of existing buildings suggests an acceptance that the new use is just one part of the story of a building's life. The designers of the Haçienda understood this and, in response, created a space that allowed the owners and users to dramatically alter the mood and atmosphere of the interior with temporary installations and lighting. These events ranged from swimming pools to fairgrounds, sculptures and even a circus with a trapeze artist, all within the main space.

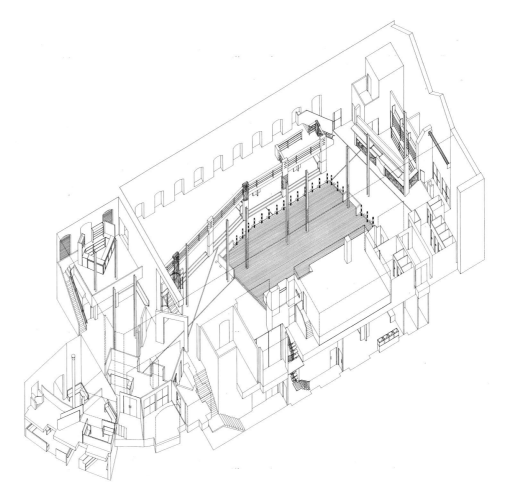

Left Axonometric showing the main space with the dance floor and the four-storey masonry building on the front that contained the entrance.

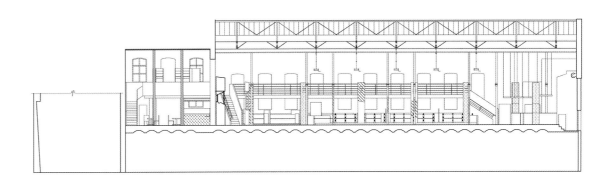

Above The long section through the space reveals the upper balcony and bar, as well as the lower-level dance floor and bar to the right.

Left The short section looking back towards the front door. The stage is on the left.

Organization

Working to a perfunctory brief – 'big bar, small bar, food, stage, dance floor, balcony, and a cocktail bar in the basement' – Ben Kelly was expected to realize the spatial equivalent of the innovative and pioneering Factory Records identity. The enigmatic nature of the client started at the front door, where the only visible sign of the club was a small granite plaque imprinted with the name in silver leaf and red enamel. This was set into the brickwork alongside the galvanized steel roller doors. The designers were well aware of the constant movement of club-goers within the interior, as they travelled from the front door to the dance floor, from the bar to the restaurant and from the balcony to the basement cocktail bar. They therefore choreographed the interior so that this circulation would be enjoyed as a series of distinct environments, a journey that passed through a sequence of varied interior 'rooms'. Much like an enfilade of rooms, each threshold was marked and distinguished by its spatial and material qualities.

The low-ceilinged metallic entrance lobby, which contained the ticket office, pre-empted the vast shed space and the dance floor. This junction was demarcated with an archway, clad in industrial plastic sheets that muffled the sound of the club and ruffled the hair of clubbers as they passed through them. A promenade through the interior, alongside the dance floor, edged with traffic bollards, and past the columns supporting the balcony, was required in order to get a drink at the bar situated at the far end of the main room. A stair that was framed by an abstract 'ruined' classical masonry and steel arch aggrandized the journey to the upper balcony. This level offered a view across the dance floor as well as access to the bar that overlooked the entrance lobby. A journey to the subterranean Gay Traitor bar meant a voyage through the club, back to the lobby and then down the narrow stairs past a hidden landing to a different nocturnal atmosphere altogether.

Detail

The vigorous test to which the interior would be put, in combination with the industrial quality of the warehouse, provided the influences for the chosen aesthetic of the space. A series of tough and robust materials were chosen to reinforce the collage-like effect of the spatial experience of the interior. These consisted of a number of 'off-the-peg' found materials and objects, which added to the resolutely urban quality of the space. Traffic bollards, cat's eyes, painted chevrons and hazard stripes, painted on the steel frame of the building and the edges of the dance floor, denoted an urban 'found' aesthetic that placed them firmly out of context within the interior.

Rubber flooring, perforated sheet steel, Douglas fir ply and Alvar Aalto stools, all set into a painted pigeon-blue interior, completed the effect.

1 Sandra Douglas, quoted in Catherine McDermott (editor), *Plans and Elevations: Ben Kelly Design*, Architecture Design and Technology, 1990

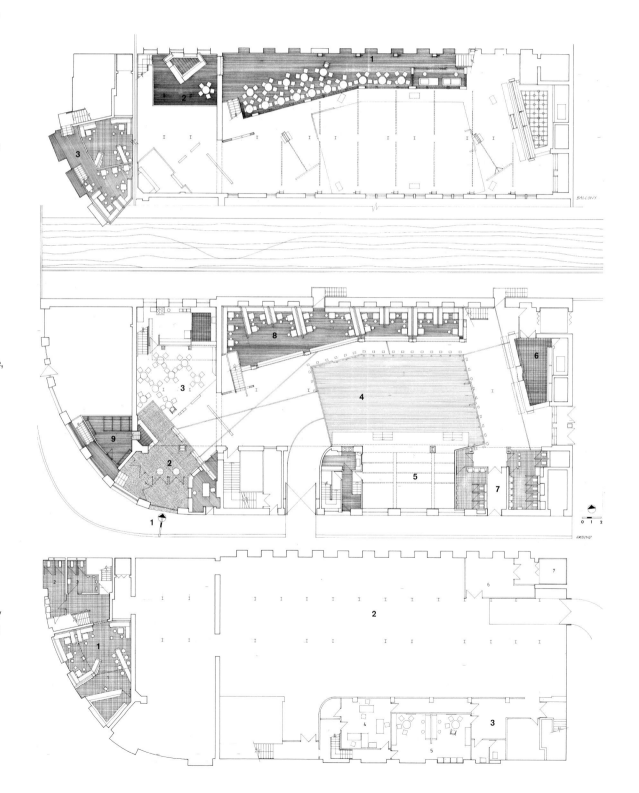

Opposite, top A bar and seating on the upper-level mezzanine offered a good view as well as respite from the frenetic activities on the dance floor below.
1 Mezzanine
2 Bar
3 Lower-level landing before basement bar

Opposite, middle The club interior was based on a sequence of spaces that culminated in a journey via the dance floor to the bar at the end of the main hall.
1 Entrance
2 Ticket office and lobby
3 Café and restaurant
4 Dance floor
5 Stage
6 Bar
7 Toilets
8 Seating
10 Stairs to basement

Opposite, bottom The subterranean Gay Traitor bar occupied the tip of the basement.
1 Gay Traitor bar
2 Basement
3 Backstage and changing rooms

Top left The journey from the front door to the dance floor took the clubber through a concrete frame replete with plastic sheets.

Top centre The metallic entrance lobby with the Factory Records catalogue number of the Haçienda '51' (Fac 51) cut into the doors.

Top right The bar at the far end of the main space.

Above left A 'ruined' classical arch framed the stairway that led to the balcony and the upper bar.

Above centre The robust palette of materials – such as steel, rubber and concrete – included Alvar Aalto stools, exposed Douglas fir and neon lights.

Above right The subterranean Gay Traitor bar was atmospherically lit and offered a very different opportunity to get away from the noise of the upper-level dance floor.

Royalton Hotel

PROJECT	**Royalton Hotel**
DESIGNERS	Philippe Starck; Gruzen Samton Steinglass (executive architects)
LOCATION	New York, NY, USA
DATE	1988

Above The long and dramatic catwalk required guests to promenade through the space until they arrived at the reception.

Left A new bright-red door, extravagant lighting and the uniformed attendant were the only elements announcing the new hotel to the street.

Context

The Royalton Hotel, at 44 West 44th Street, in Manhattan, New York, was the second project by entertainment entrepreneurs and hotel developers Ian Schrager, Steve Rubell and Philip Pilevsky. The first, the Hudson Hotel, contained a restrained and tasteful interior designed by Andrée Putman. For this second project the designers decided to let themselves loose and create a hotel that would become a meeting place to attract fashionable New Yorkers and astute world-travelling connoisseurs.

The architects Rossiter and Wright had designed the original 1897 building as the residential Hotel Royalton, exclusively for bachelors. The 12-storey building had apartments at either end of each floor slab, with servants' rooms in the middle facing the central light well. Since the 1930s the hotel had declined into a second-rate hostelry, until the developers bought the derelict building in 1985.

Above Rhinoceros-horn-shaped glass sconces illuminate the gently curved mahogany-and-steel wall guiding guests to the reception.

Right Ground-floor plan.
1 Entrance
2 Library
3 Bar
4 Reception
5 Lifts
6 Toilets
7 Sunken lounge
8 Restaurant

Far right Indicative floor plan of hotel. The rooms were carefully planned around the requirements of the existing structure and the need for maximum natural light.

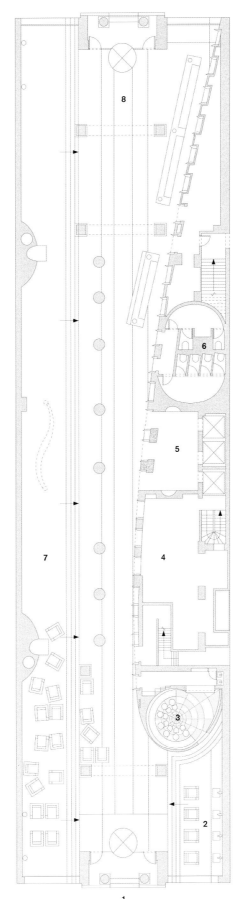

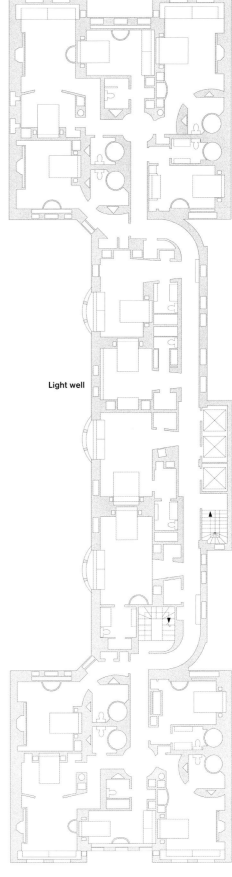

Light well

Concept

Let's start by remembering why Starck's design for the Royalton was so great. It's hard to understate its impact back in 1988, at least for people who (like me) were among its target market of globetrotting 20-somethings. We were bored with checking into hotels that looked as though they were designed for our (great-grand) parents, but didn't have an alternative. Not until Ian Schrager and the late Steve Rubell, who'd made their name by running the discotastic 1970s New York nightclub, Studio 54, commissioned Starck to redesign the Royalton, a dowdy late-nineteenth-century flophouse in midtown Manhattan.[1]

The Royalton hotel and lobby was intended to be a modern update of its neighbour, the Algonquin, and, like the 1920s' infamous round-table events across the road, host a fashionable and infamous gathering of international society. Schrager, Rubell and Pilevsky envisioned the hotel lobby as the primary social environment of the 1990s, following on from the disco in the 1970s and the restaurant in the 1980s. After seeing some of his bathroom-fitting designs, Schrager was impressed enough to commission Starck to deliver the luxurious contemporary interior that they thought their guests would require. The strategy for the interior relied upon an acute understanding of the requirements of its patrons, and ideas for creating a backdrop in which they could relax. Starck, himself an international design celebrity and itinerant traveller, was uniquely positioned to deliver this.

Organization

The 'performance' started outside the hotel as you arrived in the street. Doormen, dressed in Mao-jacketed outfits – also designed by Starck – greeted you and whisked your luggage away to your room. New mahogany doors, a balustrade and extravagant lighting were the only changes to the outside of the building. The restraint of the exterior modifications did not prepare the visitor for the interior.

The theatrical and luxurious lobby was a richly decorated, dramatic statement, all of which was carefully organized. All of the services, including the reception, toilets, emergency stairs and storage, were gathered around the existing lift core and were tucked away behind a tapering mahogany wall. This allowed the rest of the lobby to be open plan. The 55-metre (180-foot)-long lobby was organized into several distinct yet overlapping spaces, manifested in the form of a sunken lounge that ran from the front to the back of the foyer and which continued at the end of the space into an exclusive restaurant.

The lounge was edged by a series of exaggerated columns. It was populated with an assortment of Starck-designed furniture, including large mirrors and a 6-metre (20-foot)-long desk, inviting guests to form their own literary round table. The front desk was positioned deep into the lobby space. A blue-carpeted catwalk invited guests to promenade through the lobby whilst guiding them straight to the reception. An intimate circular cocktail bar was positioned by the front entrance and was entered via the front library through a discreet doorway, positioned by the wall, that only those in the know were able to find.

Detail

The theatrical and atmospheric lobby of the hotel was counterpointed by the restrained elegance of the rooms. All of the 205 rooms contained custom-designed furniture and light fixtures. The penthouses were decorated with mahogany, grey carpeting and slate fireplaces that, if requested, would contain a roaring fire when you returned to your room. The bathrooms were less restrained, with round bathtubs, mirrored showers and glass-topped vanity units. Instead of commissioning permanent artwork, each room had a candle stand that held a postcard that was changed every day. Controversially, the Royalton interior was remodelled in 2007 and the space was radically altered.

---

1 Alice Rawsthorn, 'The Risks of Playing with a Brand's "Look"', *New York Times,* 4 November 2007

Opposite, above The open-plan lobby was organized around the journey to the reception on the blue carpet. The sunken lounge was separated from the circulation space by oversized columns that announced steps down to the lower 'room'.

Opposite, below left Extravagant bespoke furniture, mirrors and lighting designed by Starck populated the foyer and the sunken lounge.

Opposite, below right The library consisted of a long table filled with books, inviting guests to sit, read and socialize.

Above left The circular shape of the small and intimate cocktail bar was exaggerated by the monochromatic, geometric tiled floor.

Above A large slate fireplace dominated the more restrained guest rooms on the upper floor of the hotel.

PROJECT	**MAK Café**
DESIGNER	Hermann Czech
LOCATION	Vienna, Austria
DATE	1993

Above The imposingly ornate high ceiling has influenced the organization of the wide, open-plan café space.

Left The new entrance to the café is located in the linking passage between the museum and the neighbouring art school.

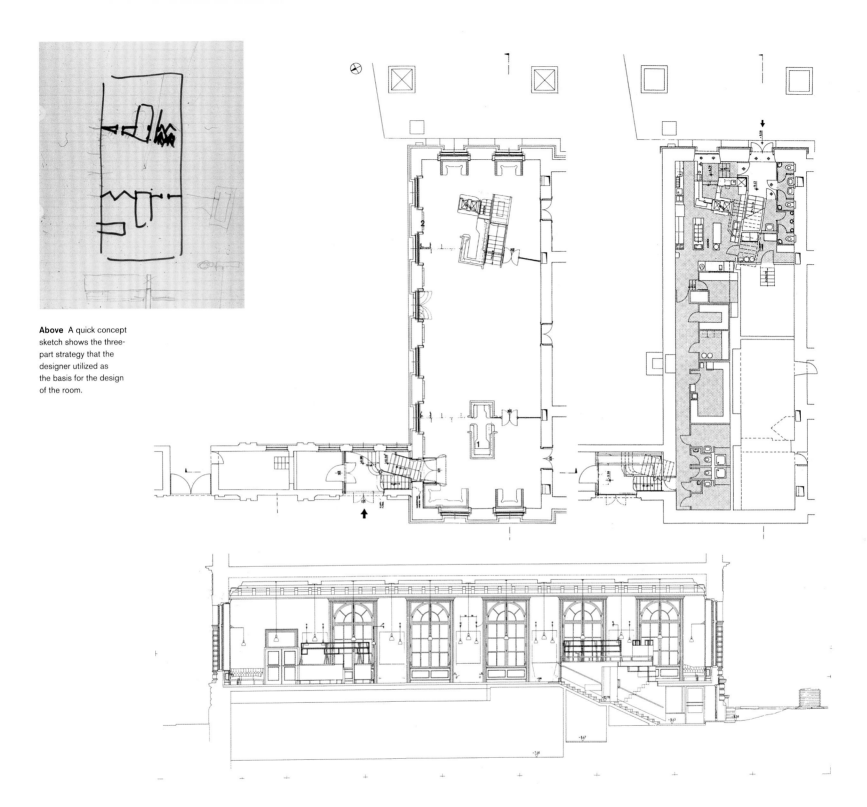

Above A quick concept sketch shows the three-part strategy that the designer utilized as the basis for the design of the room.

Context

The MAK Café was part of the Museum fur Angewandte Kunst (MAK) – or Museum of Applied Arts – located on Vienna's Ringstrasse. It was housed in a large room, which had once been an exhibition hall and a part of the museum's display space.

Heinrich von Ferstel, the noted Viennese architect, completed the museum building in 1871. (He was also responsible for the city's Austrian-Hungarian National Bank of 1859 and the University of Vienna of 1884). The neo-Renaissance building was conceived as the Austrian response to the 1851 Great Exhibition in London (see p.130), and the equivalent of that city's Victoria and Albert Museum. The Österreichischen Museum für Kunst und Industrie, as it was first known, had the task of showcasing the quality of industrial production in Austria by presenting good design to artists and industrialists in the city.

Top Ground-floor plan (left) and basement plan. The entrance from the street is to the left (arrow). The three 'sections' of the space are organized by the positioning of the two serveries (1, 2).

Above Section through the space. The stair to the basement is on the right.

Right The café's
ornate ceiling pattern
influenced the placing
of the new lighting.

Far right The serveries
are given presence in
the space with glazed
display cabinets for
drinks and glasses set
on top of tripod legs.

Below right The café
is connected to the
adjacent museum by
two circular viewing
windows.

Concept

A museum – an institution that collects and then presents artefacts to the public – is always closely associated with the city in which it is located, although this relationship, especially with the increased digitalization of environments, is increasingly fluid. The removal of boundaries can be reflected in the physical presence of the built fabric of the museum and its context. The erosion of the MAK's boundaries started in 1993 with James Wines/SITE's 'Gate to the Ring' – a slice of building removed from the façade that created a new entrance to the interior bookshop from the Ringstrasse.

Much later, James Turrell's permanent *MAKlite* installation lit all of the windows and doorways of the front façade with pale blue lighting, announcing the museum, particularly at night, to the city. This project had the same intentions: to invite the city into its interior. The development of the exhibition hall into a new café would reconnect a previously interior room, one that was part of the museum's circulation of exhibition spaces, to the city, by creating a public space in which to eat, drink and socialize.

Organization

The existing hall was a large, well-proportioned rectangular room that measured 10 metres (33 feet) wide and 30 metres (100 feet) long. Its most striking feature was a 6-metre (20-foot)-high ceiling that had a panelled neo-Renaissance painted coffered soffit. The room was lined with tall arched windows facing the Ringstrasse at the front, the courtyard at the side and the garden to the rear of the building.

Czech made a new entrance to the café from the Ringstrasse by using a linking passage between the museum and the neighbouring art school. Resembling James Wines/SITE's new bookshop door, Czech cut away the rusticated plinth on the front of the passage and removed the front wall. A porch was made that had a series of exterior qualities. These extended the atmosphere and feel of the street from the city into the interior of the entrance. These included a new polychromatic stone floor, a large circular light, similar to ones used on the Reichsbrücke, a bridge that crosses the Danube, and a large circular mirror that reflected the city back to the viewer. A set of stone stairs led up to the café, which was 2 metres (6 feet) above street level.

Detail

Inside the café a series of subtle installations articulated the spaces of the room. Two free-standing serveries, placed on axis and with the rear one twisted at an angle, ordered the room into three overlapping spaces.

At the front of the space was an informal café, the rear was a dining space, and the middle could be both. A series of moveable partitions could be pulled across to connect to the serveries and enclose each area when necessary. The kitchens and toilets were in the basement and accessed by a stair at the rear of the space and complemented by a pair of service elevators.

The result is not demonstrative, the architecture remains a background to the life it contains, but it is there, as if to step in when conversation dries up or if your thoughts should falter: a winter sky and the bare twigs of trees, reflected in black glass, beautiful beneath your dinner plate.[1]

Both the original parquet floor and the ceiling were cleaned and preserved. All of the new elements, such as the serveries, furniture, lighting and air-movement features, were carefully considered in order to establish their own subtle design language within the interior. The two serveries were constructed from maple. Glazed cabinets were projected from the bar top upon tripods of cylindrical timber legs and held glasses and bottles of drink. These tall punctuation marks in the room were counterpointed by a series of thin cables dropped from the ceiling and supporting a series of spun-metal pendant lights, which lit the tables below.

The front café seating and far end of the room consisted of deep leather banquettes, fixed in front of the large windows overlooking the Ringstrasse and the rear courtyard; the atmosphere in the front was similar to a traditional Viennese café. The main dining space contained remodelled versions of the classic bentwood chair, originally produced by the furniture maker Thonet. Czech reworked the traditional chair by adjusting the back to recline at a much more acute angle. The chairs were then dipped in white gloss, but with the bottoms of the legs left bare to show the beech in its raw condition. When in place, this made them appear to float. Small round tables with highly polished surfaces reflected the ornate ceiling directly in front of the diner. A pair of circular windows, similar in proportion to the mirror in the entrance porch, was set into the wall. and both offered views into the adjacent museum hall and exhibition. Industrial details such as wall-mounted air vents and brushed-steel brackets for the wall lights provided an informal contrast to the grandeur of the vast room.

---

1 Ingerid Helsing Almaas, *Vienna: Objects and Rituals*, Ellipsis Publishers, 1997, p.27

Left Spun-steel pendant lights hung from white-gloss brackets and brushed-metal air-movement ducts express a subtle but persuasive language amongst the maple partition screens and beech, gloss-painted Thonet chairs.

Above The highly polished black glass surfaces of the tables reflect the ceiling and view through the large arched windows surrounding three of the four sides of the café.

Georges Restaurant

PROJECT **Georges Restaurant**

DESIGNERS Dominique Jakob and Brendan MacFarlane

LOCATION Paris, France

DATE 2000

Above Four organically shaped elements lined with coloured rubber stand out in the interior of the restaurant.

Left The Pompidou Centre, a large shed-like cultural space, has most of its service elements hung on the outside, creating an open, flexible interior.

Context

An icon of the twentieth century, the Pompidou Centre was designed by Richard Rogers and Renzo Piano and opened in 1977. It was named after the French prime minister, Georges Pompidou, who commissioned it. The radical building was designed to be the antithesis of normal cultural monuments. Instead it was to be an open, flexible, democratic space for people of all ages to use and be a part of. This resulted in the design of what is essentially a large seven-storey shed, albeit one that has all of its services and structure placed on the outside of the building. This allowed the design of large, free, flexible interior floor spaces for exhibitions, with the proviso that the services could be easily updated when obsolete.

The Georges restaurant is housed on the 6th floor of the centre. The design for the restaurant won first prize in a 1997 competition. It was installed during a two-year renovation of the building, directed by one of its original architects, Renzo Piano.

Concept

Working with such an important and well-known building required the designers to consider carefully how to intervene in such a distinct environment. They decided that rather than imposing an abstract solution, the idea needed to come from the properties of the host building. The iconic status of the building in fact meant that much of the interior could be not touched in any case. The trademark coloured air, water and electrical service pipes on the ceiling were listed. The balcony and the exterior glass walls could not be moved. The only site or surface where they could effect most change was the floor. After a rigorous analysis of the building the designers found that the whole construction, from the primary supporting structure right down to the floor tiles, was divisible by an 800 x 800 millimetre (31 x 31 inch) grid. By using this grid they could form a dialogue with the original building's 'systems', yet they could do so without compromising them. The building's

structure was engineered to such a high level that the thickness of the concrete floors was only 100 millimetres (4 inches). This meant that any additional loading to the floor had to be light and evenly distributed. The designers used the floor as a 'mask' and, as though peeling back the surface, they digitally manipulated the grid, distorting and deforming it until it formed four ruptures; a series of 'skins' that would house the functions of the restaurant.

Organization

The 750-square-metre (8,100-square-foot) space was transformed by the addition of four large aluminium-clad shells. These ranged in size from 8 to 21 metres (26 to 68 feet) in length. Each shell housed a function of the restaurant; one was a reception with cloakroom and toilets, another a bar. There was a VIP and private dining space in another and the largest element housed the kitchens. Outside the enclosures, and arranged in an ordered pattern, was a landscape of tables and chairs. Each shell was lined with coloured rubber; lime green for the reception/cloakroom and bathrooms, yellow for the bar, red for the VIP lounge and grey for the kitchen.

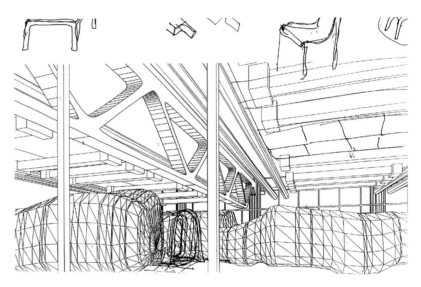

Top right and above right Concept sketches showing the contrast between the new forms of the space erupting from the floor plate, and the beams, columns and services of the existing building.

Right The dramatically lit interior comes alive at night.

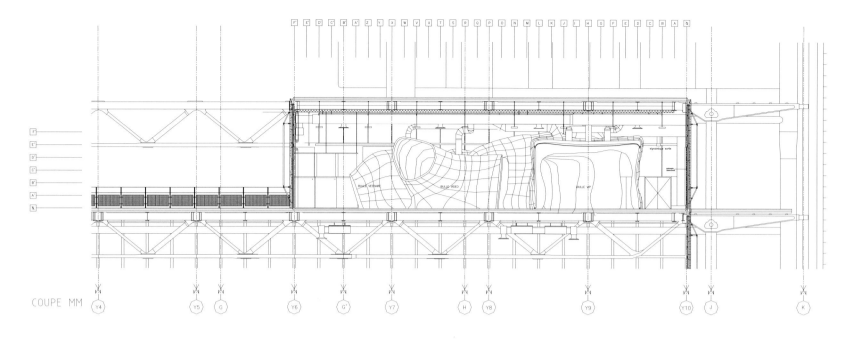

COUPE MM Y4 Y5 G Y6 G' Y7 H Y8 Y9 Y10 J K

Above In section, the organic forms of the elements provide a counterpoint to the restricting grid of the existing structure.

Right The interior of the reception, cloakroom and bathroom element was clad in lime-green rubber.

Below right Sophisticated software modelling was used in order to be able to detail and fabricate the elements off site before transporting them and installing them in the space.

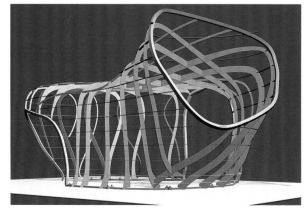

Detail

We went through a fantastic process as if we were building four large yachts. The digital models we developed were very important, because they articulated the tectonic relationships between the skin, the primary structure, the secondary lateral structure and the structure that would hold the volumes down to the floor.[1]

The designers chose a 'monocoque' solution for the design of the shells. This is a technology prevalent in the design of boats. It is a method in which the skin and frame of a building are united as one. Jakob and MacFarlane employed a team of boat builders who produced their own models and drawings for the space and prefabricated the units, then constructed them on site. The four enclosures were constructed from 80 small fragments, which could be carefully disassembled and transported to the site, yet were small enough to fit into the Pompidou's lift. The shells were clad in 4-millimetre (1/6-inch)-thick sheets of aluminium. This was the same material as the floor tiles, which were laid using the same 800-millimetre (31-inch) grid of the original building. The tiles were brushed and waxed and blended seamlessly with the shells as they erupted from the floor plate. A new 100-millimetre (4-inch) raised floor was

floated on the existing one in order to house plumbing and electricity, and to hide the servicing that was on show all around the space.

The static loads of each enclosure were evenly distributed with the use of up to 27 spring connections, which were attached to steel plates and secured to the original concrete floor. Whilst the surrounding context was happy to display its prefabricated inner workings, Jakob and MacFarlane utilized digital technology in order to craft a seamless and camouflaged invader, one that bore no traces of its innards and which seamlessly blended skin with services and structure.

---

1 Dominique Jakob and Brendan MacFarlane, quoted in *L'Architecture d'Aujourd'hui*, May/June 2003, p.69

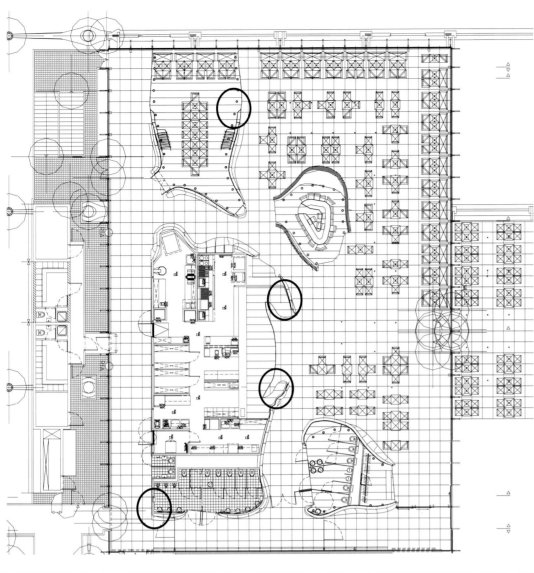

Left The plan of the restaurant with the four new elements arranged inside the grid of the space.

Below left The sinuous curves of the forms and the openings into them frame very particular views.

Below centre The brushed-steel skin of the shells was designed to emerge seamlessly from the floor and contrast with the brightly coloured and untouchable service pipes of the interior.

Below In recognition of the qualities and status of the context, the plumbing of the bathrooms was artfully deconstructed and exposed.

PROJECT	**Brasserie**
DESIGNERS	Elizabeth Diller and Ricardo Scofidio (Diller + Scofidio)
LOCATION	New York, NY, USA
DATE	2000

Top The main entrance to the dining space is via a dramatic steel-and-glass staircase.

Above The entrance to the brasserie is on a side street at the back of the Seagram Tower.

Context

The Seagram Building is a 38-storey tower designed for the distilling family of the same name. Designed by Ludwig Mies van der Rohe in 1958, in conjunction with Philip Johnson, the bronze and smoked-glass tower is regarded as one of the seminal architectural moments of Modernism and it defined the design and image of the prestigious office block for a generation. In a city where land prices are exorbitant, the decision for the Seagram tower to occupy only half of its plot was a move that was regarded as highly unusual. The resultant development of a new public square in front of the building was a strategy that not only demonstrated the wealth of the company but also allowed the building to stand out from its immediate neighbours.

Phyllis Lambert, the daughter of the Seagram president who commissioned Mies and Johnson, appointed Diller + Scofidio to remodel the basement brasserie. (Johnson had designed two restaurants for the building – the Four Seasons and the original Brasserie – but the latter had been damaged in a fire in 1995.)

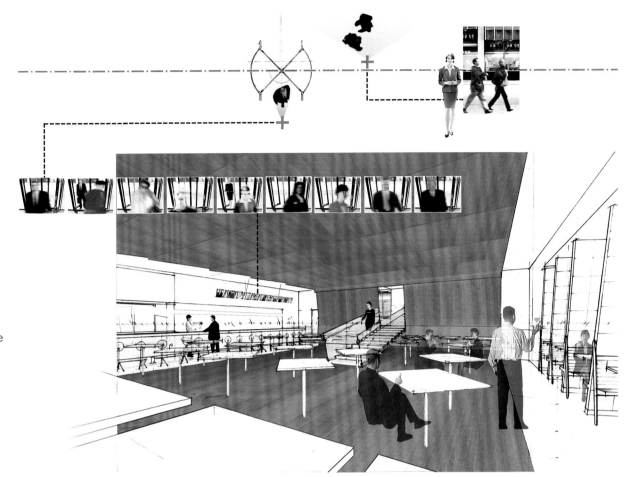

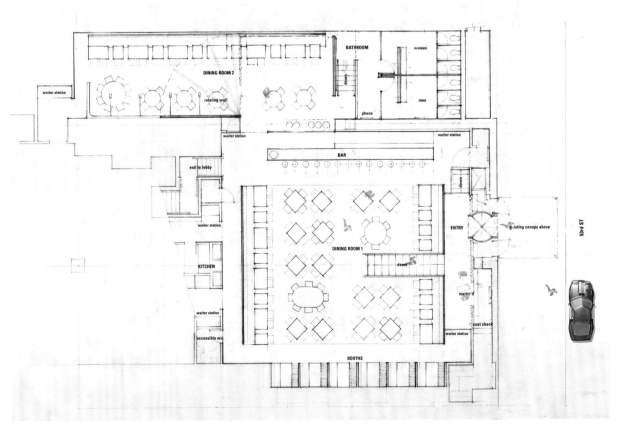

Above right A concept sketch that shows guests being filmed as they enter the interior – images that are then relayed to the row of screens above the bar.

Right The main dining hall is shown in the centre of the plan. The smaller, private eating space is located next to the toilets, behind the bar.

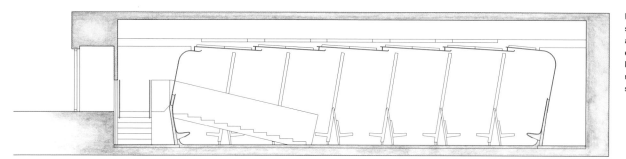

Left The grandiose statement staircase at the entrance is expressed in the section looking towards the recessed banquette seating.

Below A series of private booths are set into a wall adjacent to the main dining space and enclosed with exaggerated backrests, enclosing diners in a towering wall of green upholstery.

Concept

The prospect of redesigning one of New York's legendary restaurants in one of the world's most distinguished Modernist buildings was as inviting as it was daunting. The architecture of the new restaurant respectfully challenges many of the tenets of Modernism.[1]

The Seagram Building is a symbol of the Modern fascination with transparency. The concrete reinforced shell of the building is clad in a diaphanous steel-and-glass skin, with non-structural bronze I-beams articulating the edges of the large window panels. Mies wanted the building to appear light and almost see-through, so much so that window blinds were specified that could only operate in three positions: open, half-open or fully closed. The location of the new brasserie in the basement, however, meant that it would have no view to the outside. This contradiction was not lost on the designers, and the irony prompted a series of contemplations about glass and transparency. Diller + Scofidio made use of this contradiction with a series of ideas that explored the voyeuristic thrill of viewing and watching visitors enter and use the restaurant. The visitor is filmed as they enter the Brasserie. The image is then relayed to one of a line of 15 monitors positioned above the bar inside the restaurant. The street entrance and the reception are both monitored by cameras and a screen relays images of the activity within the space to those just arriving. The main entrance to the dining space is via a long, shallow stair, creating a dramatic physical entry for the guest. They are aware that their arrival has already been observed on the monitors, so this entrance has greater impact as the performer enters. The restaurant can be likened to a theatre set: the space is the stage, the elements are the backdrop and the diners are the actors.

Organization

The substantial structure of the existing building meant that the restaurant naturally divided into two parts – a large area that became the main dining space, and a smaller side gallery with a private dining room. The entrance, to the side of the Seagram Building, was about a metre higher than the floor level of the restaurant, meaning a change of level as diners enter the space.

A number of elements were placed within the restaurant to define and control the room. The main dining room is contained within an enormous timber sleeve that wraps around the space. This pear-veneered plywood tube is expressed as both the horizontal plane of the soffit and the vertical plane of the wall. Its ceiling conceals lighting and its base provides bench seating. A glass staircase supported on stainless steel stringers sliced through this element to link the raised entrance with the dining area. The bar was positioned against the side wall of the space opposite a series of private booths, which were separated from each other by tilting panels of green vinyl, and were set into the opposite wall.

Detail

The huge timber 'wrap' contains the main dining area. It is not a single continuous sheet, but was formed from a series of overlapping panels, each one supported by the hidden steel frame. The basic nature of the loop is consistent, but the detail changes in order to conform to a specific function, such as lighting, as it moves through the space. It is supported upon a steel frame at the sides and is folded at the base to provide seating. The sheet above the seat is positioned slightly behind it, to conceal the lighting as it curved upwards, to then be supported by the ceiling of the building. The floor of the element appears to be continuous, whilst the edges curl up to join the folded seating and thus progress the movement of the loop.

The back bar area consists of a long counter, above which is a glazed wall of bottles on display. Its brightness is achieved by backlighting the cupboards that contain the bottles. Lenticular glass obscures the view of the bottles from one angle and clarifies it from another as visitors take up different seats at the bar.

1 Diller + Scofidio, quoted on Arcspace.com

Above The main dining space features a pearwood veneered screen that wraps around the space.

Far left The 'wrap' conceals lighting in the ceiling and then folds down to provide bench seating at the edges of the room.

Left The back wall of the bar consists of a display of bottles behind large panels of lenticular glass. The bar stools are filled with medical gel, creating a comfortable spot from which to watch the screen images of arriving visitors.

PROJECT **Town Hall Hotel and Apartments**

DESIGNERS Michel da Costa Gonçalves and Nathalie Rozencwajg (Rare)

LOCATION London, UK

DATE 2010

Above The high-ceilinged De Montford suite, one of the previous council chambers.

Left The orignal Edwardian building facing Cambridge Heath Road.

Context

In 2010, Rare architects remodelled a listed 1910 town hall and its 1937 extension in Bethnal Green, east London, to house a new 98-room hotel and apartments. Both hotel and apartments use the same services and share a common entrance.

The town hall, facing the main road, had been designed in a robust Edwardian style, with a rusticated plinth and a short, but elegant, tower. Its 1930s addition was much larger, and had been built in a classical style, yet with an Art Deco interior. Both were brick constructions faced with a cladding of Portland stone. The extension duplicated the ceremonial rooms and council chambers contained in the original building and which it had outgrown. By the mid-nineties the building was closed, only being used as a period location for films such as *Atonement* and *Lock, Stock and Two Smoking Barrels*.

Concept

The idea was to edit the surroundings.[1]

In order to unify the disparate elements on the site and to reverse the clearly defined front and back aspects, with their combination of different styles, the designers reworked the building with a bold addition. They clad the side and top of the town hall and extension under one new skin of laser-cut, powder-coated, perforated aluminium, creating a distinct and unique covering. This addition also created a new roof level on top of the four-storey building, which gained the hotel an extra floor of accommodation space – adding 1,500 square metres (16,000 square feet) to the existing 7,500 (80,700). The veil has a modulated pattern that filters light, frames views and provides privacy for the occupants. A careful and delicate reworking of the existing rooms and furniture of the building, creating a very close connection between the period detail of the host and the new additions of the interior, complemented this bold addition to the exterior.

Organization

The building was organized in a pragmatic fashion, with a layout that echoed the plan of the original. Both the town hall and extension adopted a central corridor plan that allowed rooms to be placed towards the windows so that they received natural light. The 98 hotel rooms and apartments are all bespoke, responding to the variation in size and scale of the building's existing rooms. In addition, there is a bar and restaurant in the hotel, facing the main street, and a 14-metre (45-foot) swimming pool in the basement. The hotel also contains the usual meeting room and conference facilities. These are located in the restored Art Deco council chambers, the period rooms that had been used as film sets. The

Below left The laser-cut, powder-coated, perforated aluminium skin that connects the two buildings.

Below Axonometric drawing of the new skin covering the side of the Edwardian building and folded over and on to the roof of the extension.

Bottom The new skin brings together the two stylistically and chronologically disparate parts of the hotel.

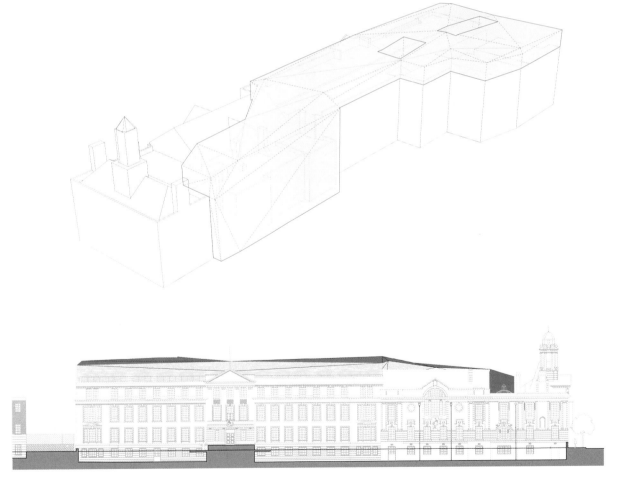

Above left
The restored 1930s
council chamber.

Above A 'found'
1930s Art Deco grille
became the inspiration
for a series of features
such as the perforated
patterns on the new
exterior skin and the
detailing of metal wall
surfaces around the
new basement pool.

Above left First-floor
plan. A central corridor
organization allows
each room to have
the maximum amount
of natural light.

Left Ground-floor plan.
The main access to the
hotel and apartments
is through the 1930s
building entrance,
facing Patriot Square.

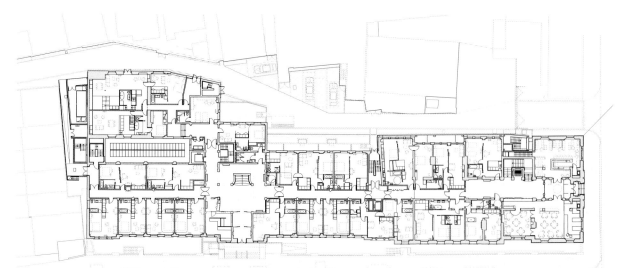

main entrance was located on Patriot Square, utilizing the original entrance to the 1930s extension. The grandeur of the reception, with its marble staircase and columns, corresponds to the well-appointed rooms.

Detail

A recurring theme of the reuse is the visual and material language of the additions and their relationship to the period detail of the host. From their research the designers formulated a 'pattern book' of details, which contained images of materials and furniture from the originals. These formed the basis of the new additions.

Inspiration was drawn from an existing Art Deco ventilation grille, which was abstracted to become the pattern for the exterior 'veil'. It was also used in the interior as CNC-routed MDF walls for enclosing the kitchens, wardrobes and services in the apartments. The designers also retained furniture found in the derelict building. They restored it and used it in communal areas such as the reception and breakfast room. The larger rooms of the hotel, such as the De Montford Suite (the previous council chamber), are triple height and were considered too elegant to subdivide and partition. These rooms were reused by installing a series of

elemental furniture 'objects', boxes that contained bedrooms and bathroom. These installations were raised on platforms and were intended to maintain a clear distinction between the room and its new use. So much so that in the future they could be removed without compromising the integrity of the rooms in which they are placed.

---

1 Michel da Costa Gonçalves, quoted in *Frame*, November/December 2010, p.124

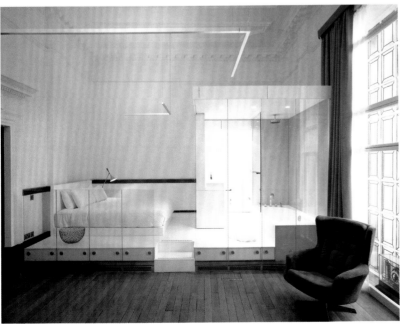

Above left Free-standing platforms containing bathrooms and beds are inserted into the existing rooms of the building.

Left Showers and baths are enclosed in white Corian and glass 'rooms' that appear to be independent of the existing rooms and can be removed when they become obsolete.

Above When the details of the old and new came into contact with each other, the designers ensured that each was clearly expressed and that one did not compromise the other.

PROJECT	**The Waterhouse at South Bund**	
DESIGNERS	Neri&Hu Design and Research Office (Neri&Hu)	
LOCATION	Shanghai, China	
DATE	2010	

Above The bathrooms are given prominent positions in each of the hotel rooms.

Left The building is located on a busy main road facing the Huangpu river.

Context

The Waterhouse is a 19-room boutique hotel on the South Bund in Shanghai. It has been inserted into the decaying shell of a three-storey 1930s warehouse.

The reused building lies on the edge of the Huangpu River, across from the skyscrapers of Pudong. The retention and reworking of the building, in a city that is changing rapidly, is unusual, not just because of its previous life as the headquarters of the Japanese Army, but also because land prices, in this fast-expanding city, ensure that space is developed to its maximum value.

Concept

In any hotel the boundaries between private and public space are clearly delineated – public spaces, such as the lobby, are usually kept well away from the private realm of the guest room. In the Waterhouse hotel NHDRO drew inspiration from a local housing type that was rapidly being eradicated from the city, but which in their view offered an interesting precedent for dealing with the relationship between private and public spaces.

Shikumen, or 'stone gate', is a style of housing that appeared at the end of the nineteenth century in Shanghai. Like a Western terrace, or townhouse, it consisted of a series of joined houses sharing communal space. These houses were often characterized by a wall separating them from a communal alleyway. Behind the wall was a courtyard that offered a public space in which residents could congregate, make a garden, hang the washing out and so on. Drawing inspiration from the *nong tang*, or 'alley' houses, the designers created a vertical courtyard inside the hotel, a place where public and private overlap in a series of carefully choreographed moves.

Top left The entrance is announced with a new Corten-steel screen cut into the façade of the building.

Top right A concrete slab has been formed into a reception desk in the triple-height lobby. A window cut into the upper part of the space offers views directly into one of the rooms.

Above The internal courtyard is animated by the continuously moving shutters that reflect light and also views into the hotel rooms.

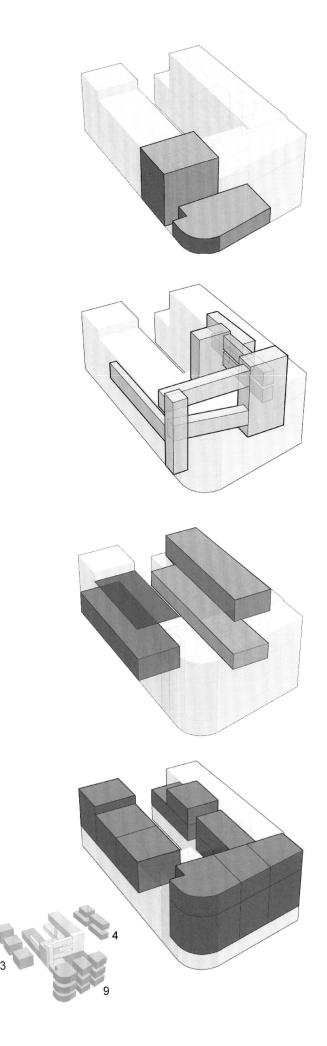

Top left The arrival areas, consisting of bar, reception and lounge.

Above left Public circulation: corridors inside and outside the hotel.

Left The public areas comprise a library, a restaurant, a lounge and a rooftop bar.

Bottom left There are 16 hotel rooms, nine with river views and seven with views of the courtyard.

Above The top of the new Corten steel addition on the roof contains the garden and a bar.

Organization

You constantly see other people. There are sightlines from bathroom to bathroom, bathroom to balcony, balcony to restaurant and so forth. The view of Pudong melts into the garden. That intermingling, that blurriness is what defines Shanghai today.[1]

The U-shaped plan of the existing building contained a central open square that the designers utilized as an intimate courtyard, protected from the noisy main road. Reminiscent of the typology of the *nong tang*, many of the rooms open on to the courtyard, recreating the tightly packed urban texture of the city. The public spaces of the hotel – the lobby, lounge, restaurant and their associated services, such as

the kitchens – are arranged around the courtyard on the ground floor. A bar and garden inhabit the roof. Three blocks of hotel rooms are arranged on the upper floors, seven with courtyard views and nine with views across the river. The intimate relationship formed through views in the space contextualizes the hotel interior and makes it feel like an extension of the city in which it resides.

The entrance to the hotel is tucked down a side street and is announced by a tall Corten steel screen. The lobby is a double-height concrete box, with the cracks and scars of the building's life etched into the interior and on full view to the visitor. The erosion of private and public spaces starts here. One of

the hotel room interiors is on view to the lobby, via a glazed slot cut into the concrete wall. Views directly into or from the bedroom make it a room for exhibitionists only.

In the restaurant, a pair of long and deep slices in the ceiling bring in light from the guest rooms above. The narrow slot ensures that the guests cannot be viewed but the connection makes the relationship between private and public space just a little bit more ambiguous. In a city where the lift is an everyday fact of life, the stairs of the building were retained and promoted as the main methods of moving though the interior. The courtyard was finished in a white rendered plaster, with timber shutters for the windows, allowing

residents to either join or shut out the action below. Their insides are covered with mirrored steel, continuing the voyeuristic games of the interior.

Top left and above left During construction the eroding fabric of the building was celebrated and retained, and used as a backdrop against which the new, crisp, modern interventions could be installed.

Above The original concrete stair was retained and incorporated into the main circulation routes through the space.

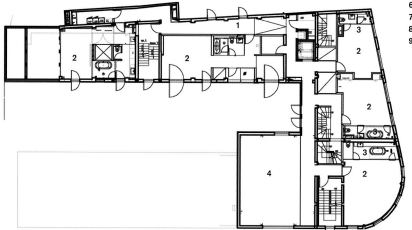

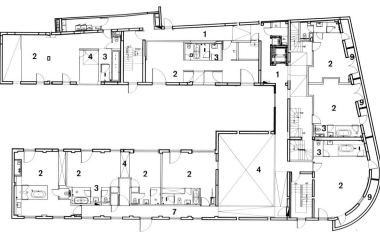

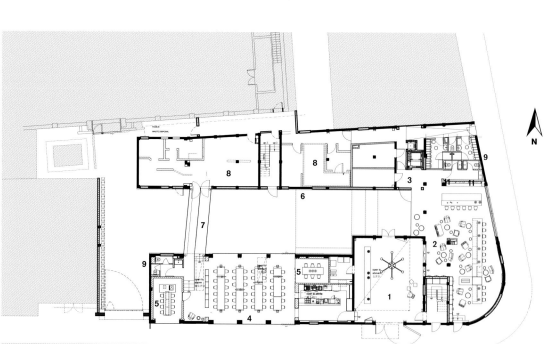

Bottom Ground-floor plan.
1 Reception
2 Lounge
3 Lift
4 Restaurant
5 Private dining room
6 Courtyard
7 Corridor
8 Kitchen
9 Toilets

Below right First-floor plan.
1 Circulation
2 Rooms
3 Bathrooms
4 Voids

Below left Second-floor plan.
1 Circulation
2 Rooms
3 Bathrooms
4 Voids
5 Terrace

Left Third-floor plan.
1 Circulation
2 Rooms
3 Bathrooms
4 Voids

Detail

The endurance of the original building inspired the designers to celebrate its survivor status by leaving its decaying and gritty condition intact. They then utilized the eroding fabric, the peeling walls and flaking plaster, as a backdrop for the new. Instead of 'making good', they distinguished the decaying charm of the space by applying new interventions directly upon and into it. The resulting interior is a patchwork of both new and old. In the lobby, 'ghosted' outlines of removed floor slabs have been retained. A remnant of green tiling, from a previous use of the space, has been kept. The designers also blurred the distinction between what has been retained and what is new by using new bricks with old floor pavers and recycling the old timber roof to create large tabletops for the ground-floor restaurant.

New interventions were fabricated from materials such as Corten steel, glass, brick and concrete, and were juxtaposed with recycled materials such as oak for the floors and shutters. A new Corten steel extension to the roof is articulated with two large, glazed apertures, allowing light into the rooms and framing the view across the river. None of the 16 guest rooms has the same layout as any other. The rooms range from 28 to 60 square metres (300 to 650 square feet) in size. They all share a material palette that consists of different configurations of exposed building walls, concrete, Corian, and wide-plank oak floors and bed furniture. To complete the voyeuristic qualities of the hotel, the bathrooms are contained in tinted-glass enclosures and are often placed in a prominent position in the room. On the top floor, the bath is placed in the newly formed Corten slot in the roof, affording the bather a glorious view.

1 Lyndon Neri, quoted in *Frame*, November/ December 2010, p.111

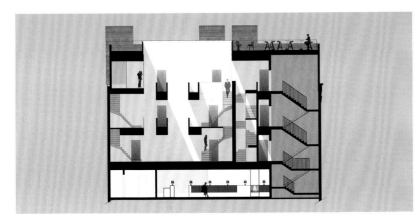

Above left The short section through the courtyard.

Left The longitudinal section shows the intimate relationship between public and private, emphasized by the foyer and the slots cut into the floors above the restaurant.

Above The restaurant, with its recycled timber tables and views from the rooms above.

Top Selected spaces in the hotel rooms offer very special viewpoints across the river.

Middle The elegant rooms are furnished with a mixture of contemporary and vintage furniture.

Function creates form, but what is to be done with the form once the function has disappeared? Can the existing form accommodate the new function? The whole business of working with existing buildings turns upon the form/function dialectic: a conversion only succeeds when there is a good match between new function and existing form.[1]

The built fabric of our cities, created by humans over thousands of years, is constantly changing. Recycling buildings to adapt them to new uses is a process that requires the reconstitution and recombination of potentially disparate elements into something new. The new use of an existing building means not just working with the volume and fabric of the space, but also with less physical entities, such as history, atmosphere, materiality and former uses. Transforming existing spaces and bringing them back into life, with a

new occupation, is a process that not only turns on the intended new use of the space but which also involves the careful choice and selection of a building to be adapted. As Philippe Robert suggests above, the form/function dialect is a significant element of the transformation.

Cultural spaces

Cultural areas include galleries, libraries, theatres and archives, spaces where information is sought and knowledge is cultivated, whether through acquisition, via an object such as a book, or through a performative type of art, such as contemporary dance or a play. The discovery of knowledge is a process that can be promulgated via space as well through objects. In other words, the building may well form part of the narrative of the occupation that is taking place within it. Whichever way culture, knowledge and information are imparted, the role of the space in which they are delivered is of great importance.

Building reuse for a cultural occupation has a long and illustrious history. In the sixteenth century, in Vicenza in northern Italy, a permanent theatre was constructed within an old fortress, the Castello del Territorio, which itself had been converted into a prison before falling into disuse. The architect Andrea Palladio had been asked to produce a design for a theatre and, despite the awkward shape of the old fortress, he decided to use this space to create an adaptation of the Roman theatres that he had studied so closely. In order to fit the theatre into the wide, shallow space, Palladio had to flatten the semicircular seating area of the Roman theatre, forming it into an ellipse. The *trompe l'oeil* stage set, with its seven street scenes modelled in an acute perspectival style, was credited to Palladio but was in fact executed by his protégé Vincenzo Scamozzi, after Palladio died at the start of the project's construction. The theatre was installed in 1585 for the first play and then retained. The stage set and the building in which it was housed was to become part of the city and its rich expression of cultural spaces for over 500 years, and is still in working order today.

Cultural spaces can be temporary as well as permanent and can be used to impart knowledge for a short time. This is a defining characteristic that can also entail the exchange of knowledge through museum and exhibition design. In the early twentieth century, Lily Reich (a pioneer of modern interior design in Stuttgart and Berlin in the 1920s and 1930s), created the Velvet and Silk Café in partnership with Ludwig Mies van der Rohe. Designed in the autumn of 1927 for the exhibition 'Die Mode der Dame' ('Women's Fashion') in Berlin, the space was conceived as a salon for discussion and a platform for the display of Bauhaus Modernist furniture to the exhibition visitors, with a series of curtains enclosing the exhibits and the discussion spaces. In this temporary exhibition space, installed in a large show hall exhibiting women's fashions, Reich designed a group of small spaces that flowed into one another with the use of black and yellow silk draperies, suspended from

CHAPTER 6

Culture

Right An exaggerated perspective of one of the seven streets of the Teatro Olimpico, Vicenza, Italy, by Andrea Palladio and Vincenzo Scamozzi.

curved metal rods. The colourful design of the space stood out in the large, anonymous exhibition hall.

Cultural spaces and the city

Working with existing buildings has long ceased to be only a question of preserving the city image and historic monuments; it has become an economic and ecological imperative.[2]

The retention of the composition of the city is nowhere more apparent than in the city of Venice, where the urban fabric, and arguably its culture, has been gently reordered and inscribed over many centuries. The ecological imperative mentioned by Schittich above – in this case protecting the city both from sinking and the rising waters of the lagoon that surround it – is also crucial. The fabric of Venice is pervaded by this perilous battle between water and history – a factor incorporated by one of its most well-known designers into a project in the city.

The Fondazione Querini Stampalia was established by Giovanni Querini Stampalia in a sixteenth-century palace in 1868. The Fondazione contains a library of almost half a million volumes, a museum and a temporary exhibition space on the ground floor. In the early 1960s Carlo Scarpa remodelled the ground floor and garden of the Fondazione in order to meet the needs of the library's scholars and other users.

The lower ground floor of the building was liable to flooding from the adjacent canal and its existing entrance was problematic. Water would enter the building at high tide through the front façade of the building, through the gates of the portico, where it would enter the ground floor gallery. Scarpa created a new bridge across the canal that entered the gallery space directly and alleviated the problem of access. He also reordered the interior around a recess that formed a conduit around the perimeter of the room, which would retain any floodwaters that entered the building. This stone channel dispersed the water back to the canal via a series of Istrian stone steps, and back into the lapping waters of the lagoon. The

Querini Stampalia unites both city and culture through the reuse of an existing building in a unique context.

The transformation of run-down areas of a city generally follows a particular pattern of colonization. 'Pioneer' occupants, usually looking for cheap rent, start the process, followed by work and social spaces, which attract new inhabitants, and ultimately gentrification. This cyclical process is often characterized by the reinhabiting of buildings that were previously unused, dilapidated and considered ready for demolition.

Many of the great cities around the world, from New York to London to

Paris, have experienced this process of transformation. Tate Modern in London exemplifies the regeneration of parts of this city through the reuse of existing buildings turned into cultural edifices. The remodelling of the Bankside power station, a much-loved but redundant monument in the city, into an art gallery, set in motion a regeneration strategy for this previously foreboding part of south London. Today the area is full of homes, offices and social spaces, and has become a thriving and expanding community.

Knowledge and performative spaces

In the 'performative' world of digital architecture, one assesses an architectural object or component not just for its beauty or its utility, but for its capacity to allow – and even encourage – change.[3]

Archives and libraries are the cultural storehouses of generations of knowledge and history. Housing them in adapted buildings, themselves receptacles of layers of history, can lead to a rich and complex dialogue between information and space. A performative occupation of an existing building can be configured to be either permanent or temporary. Whichever way it is constituted, the essence of the space lies in its ability to unify the body, whether performer or audience, and its environment. The elements of performance share a common language with design, and particularly the creation of interior space through building reuse. Occupation of a space through the placement and organization of a body or bodies, the way in which rhythm, sequence and form are manipulated in order to construct narrative, either through movement in dance or through acting in a play, are also central concerns in the making of space. This relationship can be heightened by the use of unusual spaces as backdrops or scenographic elements of a performance.

The designers Haworth Tompkins worked on a series of theatre projects where the relationship between the building, its occupants and the very fabric of the space was given paramount importance. In London's Royal Court Theatre this manifested itself in a 'stripping back' strategy,

Above A disused petrol station in London has been restored to become the Cineroleum, a cinema housed under the roof of the garage forecourt.

Above right The curtain of the cinema is constructed from recycled damp-proof membrane material. It is lifted up when the film is finished.

Right The reception and social spaces of the Young Vic theatre in London are housed in a collage of new and existing spaces, adjacent to the main auditorium building.

where the layers of years of accretions, applied to spaces and surfaces of the theatre, were exposed, as if to turn the theatre itself into an actor in a play. In another London theatre – the Young Vic – a similar approach was pursued. For 30 years after its construction in 1970, this theatre happily occupied a 'temporary' home designed by Bill Howell. It was much loved by audiences and artists, but by 2004 most of the building was at the end of its useful life. Haworth Tompkins were commissioned to replace the building with a larger, more flexible theatre. Early on in the process it was decided to retain the architectural heart of the Young Vic – the auditorium and its adjacent fragment of pre-war building fabric – rather than demolish them. New theatre and social spaces were arranged around them to form a 'conglomerate', rather than a single compositional statement. The aim was to create a theatre that would continue to be knocked around, painted over and treated with healthy disrespect by designers, directors and actors.

The creation of spaces in which performance, and in particular dance, can take place requires a certain sensibility. For the Siobhan Davies Studios, the designer Sarah Wigglesworth took a formal building – a turn-of-the-century former Victorian schoolhouse – and turned it into an informal space, where

performance, practice, body and space are combined. The dancer and client Siobhan Davies stated:

[Wigglesworth] loves the idea of balancing from a dancer's perspective – not being rigid, not being uptight but being sinuous. I was certainly conscious I wanted enough focus to concentrate but with a sense of place. We were always talking about movement in the body.[4]

The building itself is a solid masonry brick construction but the new intervention imbues it with a sense of fun, with bright colours, playful materials and witty detailing. A new performance space is configured on top of the building, which rises out of the Victorian masonry as a light-filled timber box with a ridged roof.

Temporary inhabitation

Despite definitions, bodies of knowledge and business and professional practice, interior design is also about the intangible aspects of interior spaces such as atmosphere and performance.[5]

Transforming derelict spaces, even for a very short period of time, is an implicit aspect of interior architecture and design and the reuse of existing buildings. Films, theatre performances and dance are cultural 'events' that

take place in an environment that can accentuate their qualities. The finite resources of the world ensure that existing buildings, and the new occupations that take place in them, are part of the endless recycling of spaces, materials and ideas.

In London, a disused petrol station (of which there are currently 4,000 in the UK) was transformed into a temporary cinema. Primarily constructed using donated and found materials, the Cineroleum was organized under the sheltering roof of the petrol station forecourt. It was enclosed by an ornate shiny silver curtain hung from the roof – a nod to the golden days of cinema spaces. The curtain was fashioned from recycled DuPont AirGuard, essentially a damp-proof membrane. The screen itself had been rescued from a skip outside the National Theatre and the chairs and main structure were built from cheap scrap-board that would otherwise have been thrown away. The seating was arranged as a tiered bank of temporary terraces. The silver curtain framed the tiered theatre within and managed to protect the audience from the rain and wind and occasional loud noises and smelly exhaust fumes from the traffic on the adjacent Clerkenwell Road. At the end of each performance, the curtain was pulled up to reveal the packed hidden theatre to the street beyond, much to the bemusement of unsuspecting passers-by.

This chapter examines a series of cultural spaces that have been created by colonizing existing buildings to form places for the acquisition of information and knowledge.

1 Philippe Robert, *Adaptations: New Uses For Old Buildings*, Princeton Architectural Press, 1989, p.9

2 Christian Schittich, 'Creative Conversions', in Schittich (editor), *Building in Existing Fabric*, Birkhäuser, 2003, p.9

3 Reed Kroloff, 'Architecture by the Numbers: Winka Dubbeldam and the Mathematics of Performance Design', in Winka Dubbeldam,. *AT-INndex*, Princeton Architectural Press, 2006, p.15

4 Hugh Pearman, 'The Dancing Building: Siobhan Davies Dance Gets its London Base', *Sunday Times*, 12 March 2006

5 Clive Edwards, *Interior Design: A Critical Introduction*, BERG, 2010, p.5

Above left The curve of the new attic dance space of the Siobhan Davies dance centre provides a counterpoint to the formal qualities of the former Victorian schoolhouse.

Above Light pours into the timber-lined space via a series of glazed clerestories inserted between the ridges of the roof.

PROJECT	**Glasgow School of Art Library**
DESIGNERS	Charles Rennie Mackintosh | Honeyman and Keppie
LOCATION	Glasgow, Scotland, UK
DATE	1897–9 | 1907–9

Above left The view of the library from the entrance. The facing windows are set into the west façade, animating the interior with light in the afternoon.

Above The double-height room is a carefully considered composition of columns, beams and surfaces that have been arranged to create a room within a room.

Left The library is located behind the tall, narrow windows on the west side of the building, where the road falls away sharply from the school's hilltop location.

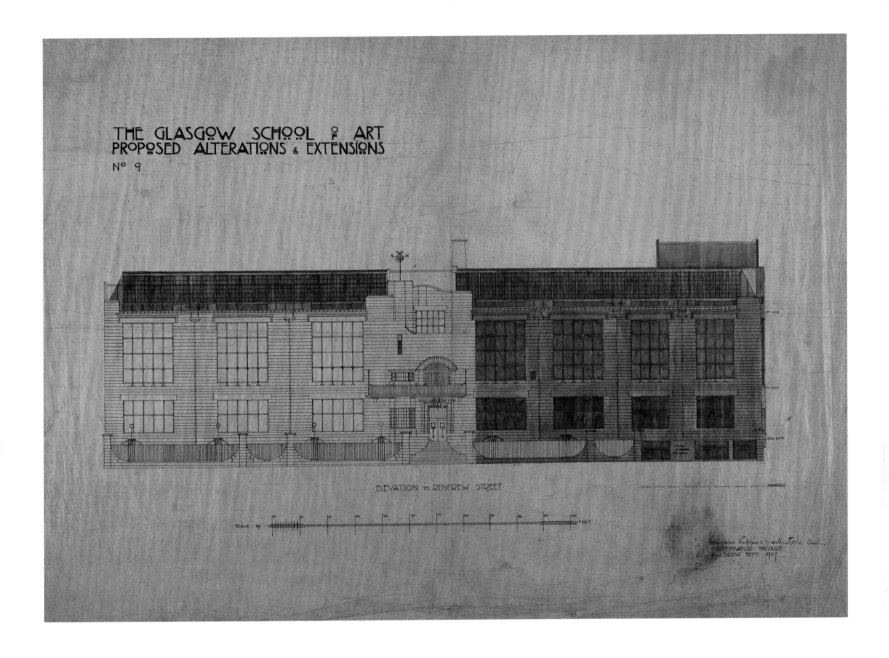

THE GLASGOW SCHOOL of ART
PROPOSED ALTERATIONS & EXTENSIONS
Nº 9

ELEVATION to RENFREW STREET

Context

Attributed to the Scottish architects Honeyman and Keppie, the Glasgow School of Art was designed in 1897 by Charles Rennie Mackintosh, a relatively new employee of the firm. In a perceptive move, Mackintosh, an ex-student of the school, was handed the brief by the partners of the practice for the project competition, in which they took first prize.

The grey granite school building, located on an awkward hill site, was completed in two phases: the first phase completed half of the building up to and including the central director's room. The second phase, started in 1907, included a radical redesign of the project and involved the insertion of new circulation elements such as corridors and stairs. It also included the design of the library in the new west wing. The redesign of the project, and in particular the library, demonstrated how Mackintosh's ideas had matured since his work on the first competition-winning project.

Concept

In the library there is an extraordinary air of frozen excitement. The lines are dynamic and everywhere the stress is on the manipulation and control of space. The structural form is revealed and emphasized; the timber itself speaks. Post, brackets, rafters organized within recognizable modules of measurement, speak of timeless space, of a place of assembly which would be appropriate to any age.[1]

In the library project Mackintosh reworked the extant space significantly in order to reflect his growing maturity and his increasingly sophisticated spatial and material preoccupations. Whilst the first phase of the building explored an expressive, solid, Gothic Revivalist language, also evident in the 1897 Queen's Cross Church, the spatial manipulation of the library interior demonstrated a wider and more eclectic range of influences. These varied from Japanese symbolism to Art Nouveau abstraction.

Above The elevation of the school, with the proposed later extension to the right.

Organization

The library was attached to the main east–west corridor of the school and was entered at its north-east corner. Thus, the visitor was placed on the diagonal as they crossed the threshold. This increased the visual complexity of the space, with the angled view through the columns of the interior towards the windows.

The redesigned west façade of the building was designed in conjunction with the positioning of the new library. This enabled Mackintosh to puncture the exterior wall with a series of three-storey-high windows, which allowed light to pour into the library in the afternoon, and reinforced the idea that the library's timber structure was analogous to a row of trees – a metaphor that, some commentators

have suggested, reflected Mackintosh's interests in natural symbolism.

The walls of both the upper gallery and lower library housed cabinets of books whilst tables and chairs for reading the material were placed in the aisles. The central space contained a magazine rack and table that was illuminated by a series of decorative lamps suspended from the roof of the room. These completed the vertical articulation of the interior composition. Mackintosh elected for an interior strategy that created a room within the existing room of the double-height space of the building shell. The result was a double-height room with a central nave surrounded by four aisles.
An upper gallery, set back from the edges of the supporting columns,

themselves aligned on floor beams, created the lower aisles below. The gallery encircled the room, yet it was set back from the column edges to ensure that the main space was not oppressive or compressed by the low soffit of the landing above. This masterful stroke allowed Mackintosh to express the balcony and supporting beam and column composition as a clearly defined element, one that reinforced the height and articulation of the room. This move placed an emphasis on the balustrade, which was formed from a series of solid panels with carved and pierced dropped ends, giving them the appearance of boards of textiles. These were alternated with scalloped balusters painted in red, green and white, which connected the main columns to the gallery edge.

Above left The gallery balustrade was designed to resemble a hanging textile, while the scalloped balusters were painted and put on top of the beams connecting the columns to the set-back edges of the upper level.

Above The central table with carefully detailed seats that stack underneath is illuminated by the collection of hanging black-and-silver glass-and-steel lights.

Right The library is in the south-west corner of the first floor of the building, with its mezzanine in this plan of the building.

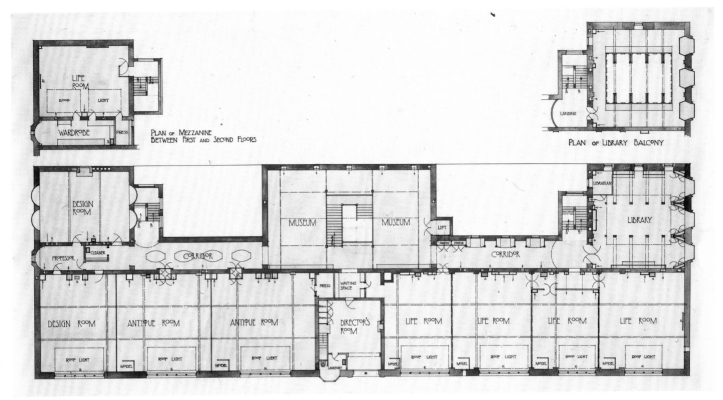

PLAN OF MEZZANINE
BETWEEN FIRST AND SECOND FLOORS

PLAN OF LIBRARY BALCONY

N

Right Section through the library. An elaborate frame was used in order to hang the structure from the roof trusses of the school above and ensure that the loading on the first floor of the library was as light as possible.

Detail

The generally dark and earthy space was punctuated by moments of colour. The vivid balusters and the central lights suspended from long chains and hanging over the central table were black and silver and had glass inserts of purple and heliotrope. Oak chairs, along with other bespoke pieces of furniture, were designed to fit the space exactly and slide below the table in order to harmonize with it and maximize the small space. Their spindly forms and legs were designed to reinforce the tree-like canopy effect of the surrounding gallery structure.

1 Denys Lasdun, 'Charles Rennie Mackintosh: A Personal View', in Patrick Nuttgens (editor), *Mackintosh and his Contemporaries in Europe and America*, John Murray, 1988, p.120

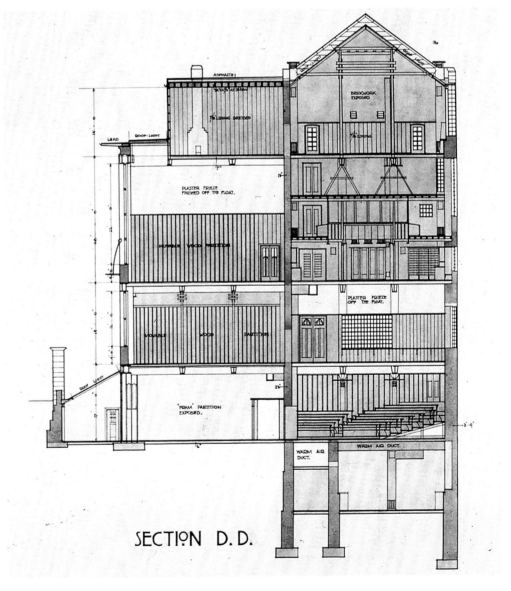

SECTION D.D.

Royal Exchange Theatre

Above The new theatre was designed to ensure maximum contrast between old and new.

Left The old exchange building built by Bradshaw, Gass & Hope.

PROJECT **Royal Exchange Theatre**

DESIGNERS Levitt Bernstein in association with Richard Negri (architects); Ove Arup and Partners (structural engineers)

LOCATION Manchester, UK

DATE 1976

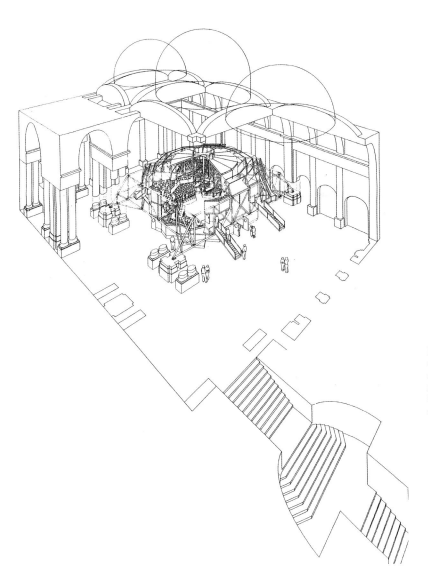

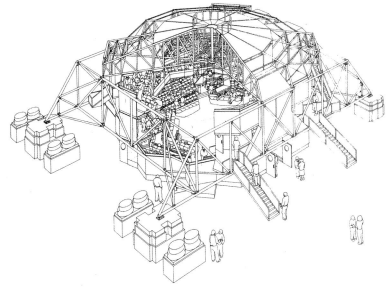

Left The new theatre enclosure was placed directly under the main dome and was influenced by its formal qualities.

Above The main structure of the theatre took the form of two trusses 4.7 metres (15 feet) deep and 30 metres (98 feet) long connected to the main columns of the hall. The remainder of the enclosure was connected to these beams, ensuring the lightest loading possible for the existing hall floor.

Context

The Manchester Royal Exchange Hall, or Cotton Exchange, was designed and built between 1914 and 1921 by Bradshaw, Gass & Hope, and was an extension to the third cotton exchange built on this site since 1792. When in operation, the Edwardian building was the largest trading hall in England, capable of accommodating thousands of people. The exchange ceased trading in December 1968 and remained empty for five years.

In 1973, the Royal Exchange Theatre Company – formed from a group of actors and performers who were temporarily based at Manchester University – obtained a lease from the Prudential Assurance Company, the owners of the empty exchange, and created a temporary auditorium in the vast halls of the Grade II listed building. The new Royal Exchange Theatre opened in September 1976.

Concept

A theatrical experience … a bejewelled lunar module set in sombre Edwardian splendour.[1]

The theatre company's initial temporary occupation of the exchange gave them an understanding of the capacity and character of the existing building. When the funding for the project became available, this then enabled them to form a very particular brief for their new theatre. The company rejected the traditional 'upstage' and 'downstage' arrangements of a theatre, along with the proscenium arch, with its clear distinction between stage and spectators. Instead they chose a 'theatre in the round', for its associated close and vibrant connections between the performers and the audience. Actors had to be allowed to gather outside the theatre in the hall, and be able to enter the stage at several points around the perimeter of the space. The audience was to be seated never more than 10 metres (30 feet) away from the action. Scenery was to be adaptable and flown in when required.

The company wanted to retain the great hall's character, yet they needed some form of acoustic enclosure that would deal with the large space's 7.5-second reverberation time. They also needed to control the natural light that poured in through the three glass domes. Therefore the strategy for the theatre, initially devised by Richard Negri, was to insert a new enclosed concentric auditorium under the main dome of the great hall. It was to have a form that would be contemporary and appear lightweight, precisely the opposite of the masonry and steel construction of the exchange. The new theatre was not only designed to contrast with the character of the existing building but it was also expected to reinvigorate it and make it a part of the daily life of the city, with new bars and restaurants open outside normal performance hours. It was hoped that this would help draw in people who had never previously been to the theatre.

Far left The mixture of clear and opaque cladding materials highlights the contrast between the theatre and the old building, as well as responding to the fire-evacuation strategy.

Left The audience ascends the stair to get to the upper level of the auditorium, while the lower levels are accessed through ground-floor doors that also allow the actors to enter anywhere on the stage during the performance.

Below A new section through the hall shows how the theatre was positioned to achieve maximum contrast with the proportions of the host building.

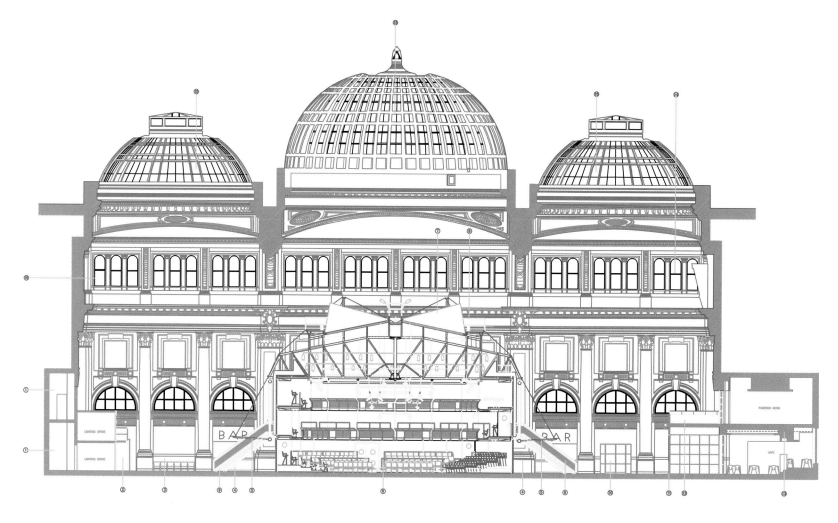

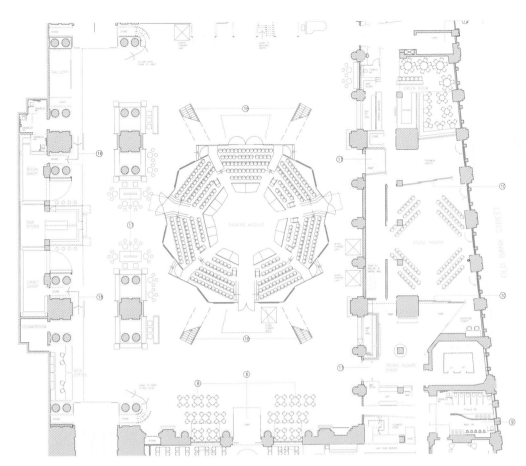

Organization

The new theatre was conceived as a large, self-sufficient, enclosed unit, seven-sided in plan, inserted into the cavernous volume of the great hall. The brief called for an auditorium that could accommodate 700 people seated concentrically within the hall, but a structural analysis revealed that the load capacity of the existing floor could only carry the extra weight of a 450-seat structure. The same survey also concluded that the masonry columns supporting the large domed roof were capable of taking a far greater load than they were currently undertaking.

The structural determinants of the existing building, and the resultant form of the hall, determined the exact location for the new insertion. The auditorium was located under the largest of the three domes, the biggest space between the columns; 450 seats could be positioned on the floor, with a further 300 located in two tiers of galleries above. These were accommodated by a primary structure that took the form of two huge 4.7-metre (15-foot)-deep trusses

that spanned the 30 metres (98 feet) between the brick piers of the hall. Secondary trusses, of the same depth, formed a 21-metre (69-foot) square, which enclosed the auditorium. Seven radial trusses carried the roof of the theatre and were supported by the primary and secondary structures. These carried the seating and lighting galleries and thus placed no extra load on the floor of the hall. All of the structural load of the upper part of the theatre was diverted to the existing columns. The complex geometry of the building was completed by a series of smaller structural elements spanning the main structure, which carried the glass and steel cladding and completed the enclosure. Ancillary functions, such as the box office, bar, restaurant, dressing rooms, rehearsal studios and storage, were dispersed around the edges of the building.

Detail

Utilizing tubular steel, glass and sheet-metal cladding achieved the maximum contrast between the new structure and the old building. These particular materials were also chosen because of their resistance to fire, an important consideration for the building. Possible patterns of fire and smoke were analysed and from this research a material strategy was put in place. The clear views through the glass cladding of the auditorium and towards the numerous entrances and exits ensured efficient evacuation in the event of a fire. Low-flammable upholstery and materials were used in the inner auditorium. All of this meant that cladding the steel structure in a fire-resistant material became unnecessary, leaving the clarity of the design language visible to all.

1 The second-stage jury report for the North West RIBA Awards, cited in the *RIBA Journal,* August 1977, p.334

Above left The theatre was conceived in the round and took the form of an enclosure that would allow public facilities, such as bars and restaurants, to continue to function when the main theatre was not in use. Along with a small studio theatre, these were located around the building's periphery.

Above The internal street of the building with new services and lighting – added when the theatre was remodelled after a terrorist bomb struck Manchester in 1996.

PROJECT	**Trust Theater**
DESIGNER	Francine Houben (Mecanoo Architects)
LOCATION	Amsterdam, The Netherlands
DATE	1996

Above The ground-floor bar inside the colonnade of wooden columns.

Left The Lutheran church was designed to look like a large house on the outside.

Context

This project was the creation of a new home for independent theatre company, Trust, in a late-eighteenth-century Lutheran church on the edge of Amsterdam's red-light district. Trust is known for staging avant-garde productions of work as diverse as Werner Schwab and Chekhov. Their previous home had been a disused swimming pool.

The church had been erected in 1792. Due to a city council decree regarding reformed religious buildings, the Evangelical Lutheran Church had not been allowed to make their building look like a church. Instead it was styled as a sober, classical building which, from the exterior, simply looked like a large house. The building was sold in 1952 to a bank that used it as their archive. The remarkable organ at the end of the nave was donated to a church in Arnhem and the pulpit to a church in Elst. The building was then abandoned in the 1980s.

Concept

Old and new do not come into contact, that is the principle of the details. We do nothing to the old building except what is technically necessary, but the piece of furniture must be expressive and decorative.[1]

The constraints of the existing building and a restricted budget required the invention of a new interior language for the company. The previous occupants had stripped out the decaying building, exposing a central void framed by a row of wooden columns. Houben also noted the removal of the imposing, highly decorative, three-storey church organ – this influenced her reflections on the life of the building, a rumination that in turn underpinned the key strategy of the reuse, and also the 'afterlife' of the new inhabitation.

Houben decided to reinvigorate the interior by placing a new free-standing furniture element into the void. It would not touch the existing wooden

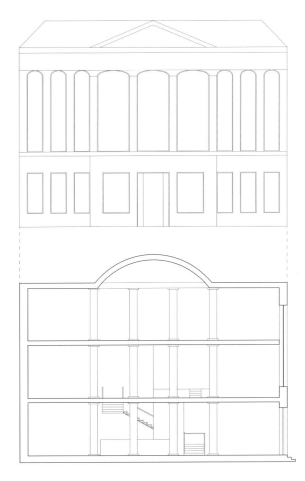

Right The new theatre occupies the central void of the old church, surrounded by a colonnade of columns. The church's simple façade acts as a mask and screens the interior from the city.

Right The church on the edge of the canal.

Below right The designers reworked the interior by inserting a new three-storey piece of furniture that contained a bar, circulation and services such as a sound and lighting booth into the central void.

Far right A three-storey organ dominated the far end of the nave of the building.

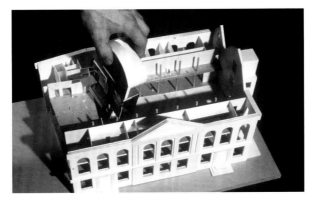

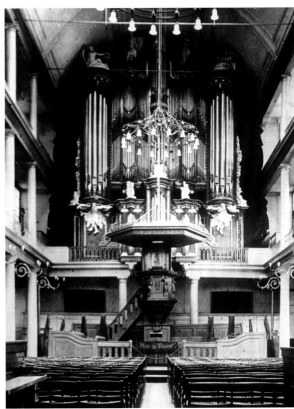

colonnade but instead it would service the new use on each floor of the theatre. It would house circulation, a bar, a kitchen and, at the top, facilitate the workings of the theatre with a sound and light desk. The idea was that the new and the old would not touch and yet their close proximity would generate a dynamic charge that infused the theatre with energy.

Organization

The new organization of the interior was wholly dictated by the form and structure of the existing space. A new 300-person auditorium was inserted into the void at the centre of the building in the form of a carefully angled plane of seats. The 14-metre (46-foot)-wide space between the columns was just enough to accept adequate seating, with the stage traditionally placed at the far end of the hall. If required the colonnade could be used as a side stage. A black curtain, draped between the wooden columns, ensured that the theatre could be blacked out for performances or, when pulled back, be naturally lit during the day for rehearsals and routine maintenance – an unusual condition in what is usually a closely controlled, artificially lit environment.

Rehearsal spaces, foyer, bar and offices were arranged around the central auditorium and located over the three floors of the building. The new furniture element was placed prominently in the entrance to the theatre, occupying the opposite end of the space where the organ once stood.

Detail

The material language reflected the restricted budget. The outside walls of the building were left bare and merely lit with a spotlight. The bare brick of the interior walls was left exposed. Furniture, such as the chairs for the foyer, was bought from a demolished school in Belgium. Timber columns and floor and ceiling joists were sanded and left exposed. The raw simplicity of the interior was used to great effect, transmitting the identity of the theatre company. The timber and plasterboard 'furniture' element was painted blood red on the outside and gold on the interior. The director of Trust insisted, against the designer's wishes, that three chandeliers were hung within the new piece of furniture. These add a touch of theatricality to the space. The details of the new interior were considered temporary in that they could be removed in the future without interfering with the structural integrity of the original building. Just like the organ before it, Houben envisaged that the new furniture element could well be removed in 50 years' time and the building returned back to its ecclesiastical origins.

1 Francine Houben, *Composition, Contrast, Complexity*, Birkhäuser, 2001, p.104

Top The central void of the building during construction.

Middle The new circulation before it was enclosed in the main furniture element.

Bottom The raked seating of the auditorium fits neatly inside the central space.

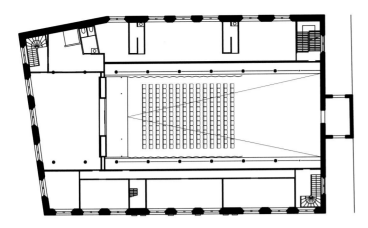

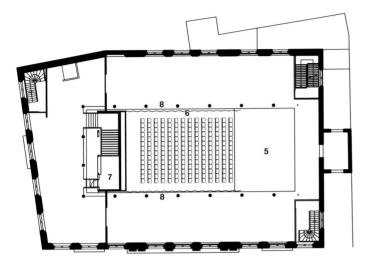

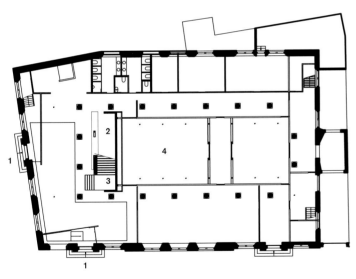

Above (top to bottom)
Second-, first- and ground-floor plans. The circulation, bar and auditorium are all contained within the structure of the building.

1 Entrance
2 Bar
3 Stair
4 Rehearsal rooms
5 Stage
6 Seating
7 Sound box
8 Curtain and foyer

Top right The colonnade could either be blacked out during performances or the curtains could be drawn back to fill the space with light.

Middle right Exposed ceiling joists and second-hand furniture emphasized the raw simplicity of the existing space. This contrasted with the colourful finish of the new insertion.

Right The theatrical language of the interior was highlighted by the use of the curtain as a temporal screen.

Far right The stair in the element was rendered in gold leaf.

PROJECT **Müncheberg Church and Library**

DESIGNER Klaus Block

LOCATION Müncheberg, Germany

DATE 1997

Above left The new library and offices are housed in a four-storey vessel, positioned in the nave of the old church.

Above In various places the ash cladding has been turned on edge to allow light into and views out of the vessel.

Left In the early nineteenth century Karl Freiderich Schinkel made additions to the building, such as new entrance porches and a Gothic campanile (left).

Context

Klaus Block remodelled the Church of St Mary in the town of Müncheberg, approximately 30 kilometres (19 miles) east of Berlin, so that it could better accommodate its religious requirements, and also incorporate the inclusion of a municipal library.

There had been a church on this site, a small hill at the centre of the town, since the thirteenth century. Between 1817 and 1829 the church underwent a series of alterations, designed by the German architect Karl Friedrich Schinkel. These consisted of the addition of a Gothic campanile and new entrance porches. The strategic importance of Müncheberg, between the Polish border and Berlin, meant that in 1945 the town was overwhelmed by advancing and retreating armies, a situation that left the church roofless and in ruins. It stayed this way until a post-reunification competition was organized in 1991 for its renovation.

Left Services such as storage and toilets are located on the ground floor and accessed via vertically lifting doors. A new lift, located in a tower, and clad in grey steel mesh, appears to counterpoint the outward bow of the new element.

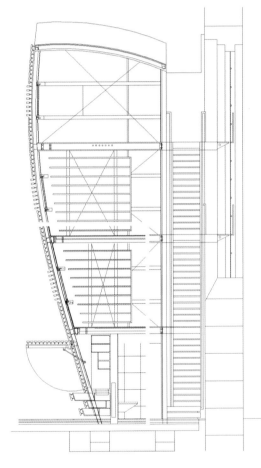

Above left To separate old and new, the stairs are positioned between the vessel and the old building. Above the stairs, reading rooms connect back to the windows of the church.

Above Structural elements such as the steel frame, bracing and connections back to the existing church between the stairs are exposed in a short section through the vessel.

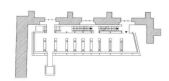

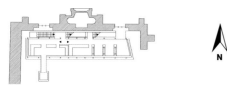

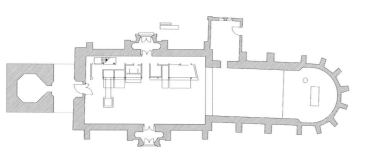

N

Concept

A pragmatic solution to the existing building and its new requirements won the competition. Block understood that the small parish church was no longer used to its full capacity, except on special occasions and during festivals. Therefore, the notion of sharing the space with the new library meant that a symbiotic relationship between the two functions needed to be established. Their independence from each other was required, yet their existence in the same space needed mutual reciprocation in order to make the building become, once more, the centre of the community.

Block decided to house the new library in an independent 'element', one that occupied the tall nave of the church. In German the word *Schiff* ('nave') also means 'ship', and Block derived the formal language of the new library with a play on words; the new element is like a ship moored within the building.

Organization

The new 'vessel', situated in the nave, was given four storeys. The ground floor, from the chancel to the base of the library in the nave, was designated for the church. The congregation numbers could grow or contract throughout the space as was necessary. The lower level of the library contained the services, such as toilets and storage, that supported both the church and the library. It also allowed visitors through and into the space as they entered from the north porch. The first and second floors held the library and community office, and the third floor housed the new council chamber: a room for meetings. Vertical circulation took the form of a stair that was inserted into the void between the library and the old north wall of the church. It connected the ground to the top floor and neatly separated the old building from the new element. A new free-standing lift tower, connected by bridges to the library on each level, acted as a counterpoint to the outwards-bowing wall of the library. The tower 'quoted' Schinkel's campanile by reiterating the independent qualities of this later addition to the church.

Above (top to bottom) Section through the church showing the steel-framed structure and circulation of the new element; third floor, containing the council chamber; second floor, containing the library; first floor, containing reception, community office and library; ground-floor plan showing the north and south entrance porches added by Schinkel.

Right The enigmatic vessel was formulated using the German word for 'nave'. The 'ship' is 'moored' in the church and appears to be supported by the tower containing the lift. The altar table is to the right in the apse.

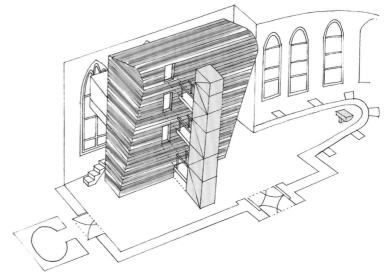

Detail

The new interior insertion was conceived as a large, continuous object rising up through the space of the church and forcefully expressing its independence from the host building. Block kept the library distinct by constructing it from modern materials, and by allowing sufficient space around the insertion for it to be read as an autonomous entity. The primary structural system for the element was a steel frame. The frame was clad with horizontal ash slats that can be turned on edge when required to let light in and allow a view out of the inner glass skin of the structure.

Concrete floors and steel bracing, concealed by the library bookshelves, stiffen the construction. The lift shaft was clad in perforated grey steel mesh. The leaning library façade appears to be steadied by the tower. The vertical supports of the balustrade were deliberately positioned off centre and towards the lift tower in order to provide the lightest of touches between walkway and library. Situated within the circulation void are special alcoves that connect the existing windows to the main floor levels of the library. These provide places for reading or private contemplation.

The restoration of the fabric of the church led to an unusual patchwork quality on the surface of the host; on both the exterior and the interior, building repairs were made with no attempt at concealment or amelioration. This unusual patchwork effect is also discernible in the upper levels of the building. Originally the church had an elegantly ribbed vaulted brick roof. This was too expensive to replicate so it was replaced with a timber and slate structure. However, the pilasters of the vaults of the original roof ribs have been retained, and these have become sculptural reminders of the old structure.

Top right The first-floor library reception.

Above right The quiet reading rooms that connect directly back to the Gothic windows of the north side of the church above the stairs.

Above far right The patchwork quality of the repairs to the church has been emphasized by the retained pilasters and the masonry piers from which the vaults of the ribbed roof once sprang.

Right In a subtle attempt to link the two functions of the space, a section through the new altar table is reminiscent of the form of the new library element.

PROJECT

San Marcos Cultural Centre

DESIGNER Ignacio Mendaro Corsini

LOCATION Toledo, Spain

DATE 2002

Above The partly raked seating of the new auditorium is installed in the pale white church interior.

Left The lower level of the site is taken up by the archive, the outside wall of which forms the edge of Toledo's civic square.

Context

The seventeenth-century church of San Marcos was located alongside a thirteenth-century monastery on top of the highest point of the city of Toledo. In 1985 the Madrilène designer Ignacio Corsini won first prize in a national ideas competition with his design for a cultural centre and civic archive, both of which were to be housed in the existing buildings.

The monastery had been founded in 1220, was later destroyed, then subsequently rebuilt in the middle of the sixteenth century. The church, which belonged to the Trinitarian order, was added to the monastery in 1628, and was built in an early Spanish Baroque style. The monastery and church were then used as a barracks in the early nineteenth century, hastening their demise and ensuring the monastery's almost total demolition in the 1960s. The site then remained derelict and run-down until the government obtained it in 1980 and set about planning a renovation. Due to funding issues, however, the project was not fully realized until 2002.

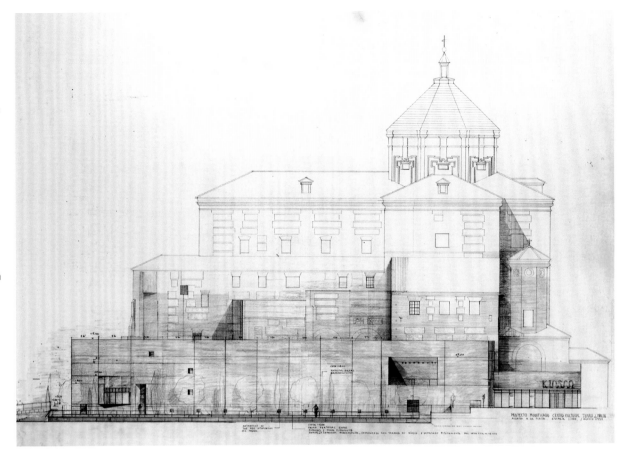

Top The multi-layered history and the many levels of the site made for a demanding project. The San Marcos church stands on the top of the hill and the archive is located much lower down the slope.

Above The entrance to the archive was floated over the ruined walls of the monastery.

Above The raw and uncompromising shuttered-concrete wall, adjacent to the square, was deemed appropriate because of the Roman origins of concrete.

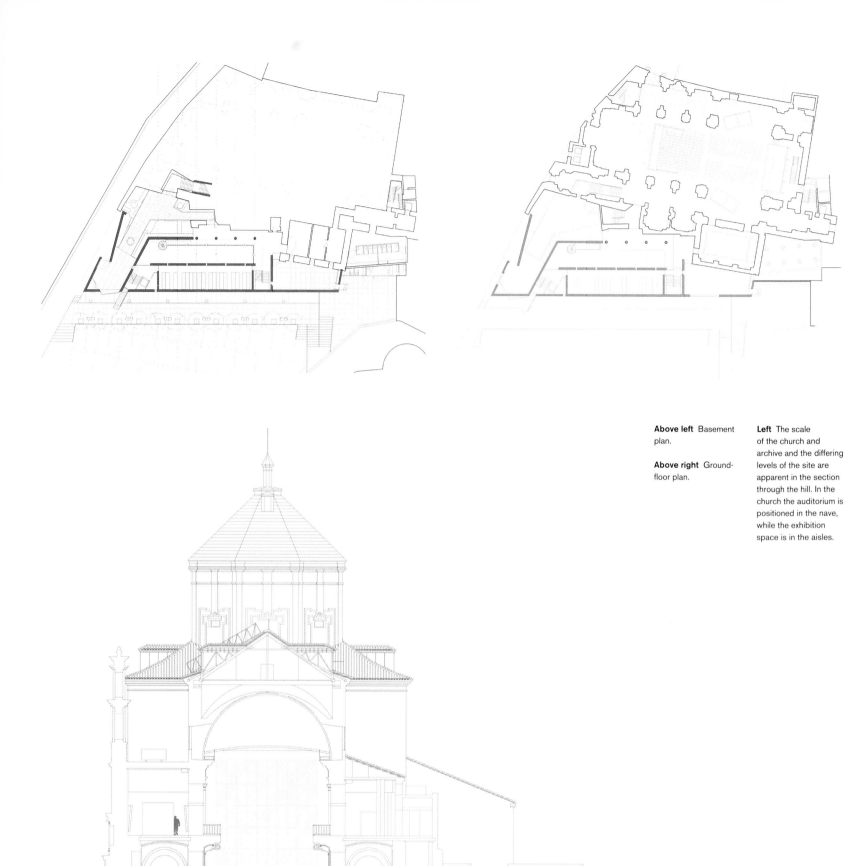

Above left Basement plan.

Above right Ground-floor plan.

Left The scale of the church and archive and the differing levels of the site are apparent in the section through the hill. In the church the auditorium is positioned in the nave, while the exhibition space is in the aisles.

Concept

The new cultural centre and civic archive were to be located within a complicated site that consisted of the historic remains of buildings from early Jewish, Christian and Islamic settlers. As is usual with a site that is loaded with layers of history, the strategy for the reuse focused on consolidating what already existed with the careful integration of any new additions. Corsini formulated a three-part urban plan. Firstly the church, which was by the start of the project almost a ruin, needed to be structurally reinforced. Secondly, the adjacent site of the former monastery, further down the hill and on the south-west flank of the church, needed to be excavated, analysed and secured. Thirdly, Corsini decided that the church would house the cultural centre – consisting of an auditorium and temporary exhibition space – whilst the monastery site would become the location for the new archive. Because of the sensitivity of the site, any excavated traces of history that were deemed important were to be preserved and then integrated into the project. On the other hand, any new additions were to be clearly contemporary and distinguished by dramatically different materials.

Organization

The church has two entrances, one in the north through its original door and the other in the south. The church was adapted to house the new auditorium, and a bank of partly raked fixed seating was placed in the nave. The exhibition space was located in the surrounding aisles.

The lower-level archive was housed in a new build adjoining the church. This consolidated the monastery

Top The rough shuttered concrete of the interior is contrasted with steel, brass and timber to offset the raw qualities of the space.

Above A new steel skin announces the entrance to the archive.

Detail

site and formed a new edge to the adjacent square. The archive and the church were linked through a series of connecting walkways, bridges and ramps, some of which passed through open courtyards. The new archive was realized behind a solid retaining wall, formed from poured concrete, that created the new edge to the lower level of the site and the square. The controversial and brutal appearance of the wall was deemed appropriate because of the history of the material and its Roman origins. The archive was entered through a courtyard on the south-west corner of the building via a bridge that was floated over the medieval foundations of the monastery. The visitor enters the archive on the gallery floor, an intermediary level that overlooks the four-storey reading room. The three-storey archive was set into the adjacent wall. An elegant spiral stair, clad in a steel drum, accesses the reading room and archive.

With simple, restrained means, the new architecture has been carefully integrated into the existing fabric. Old and new are nevertheless distinguished through the choice of materials.[1]

The church interior was restored and painted white. New means of circulation, in the form of bridges and stairs, were constructed from oxidized and polished steel sections, maintaining the connection to the archive, whilst contrasting with the crisp, meditative space of the pale white church interior.

Careful to preserve any traces of the history of the site, Corsini distinguished between the new and old by utilizing sharply contrasting materials. Where possible, archaeological remains were also incorporated into the site. Fragments of walls and floors imposed changes on some aspects of the project as they were uncovered

during excavations. A remnant of the old monastery wall was incorporated into the lower-level reading room wall and the floors of the old building were maintained for the archive entrance. Inside the archive, the roughly shuttered concrete was counterpointed by steel and brass details, such as the spiral stair drum and balustrades. The interior was completed with timber flooring.

1 Christian Schittich (editor), *Building in Existing Fabric*, Birkhäuser, 2003, p.42

Below left Surviving parts of the monastery walls are exposed and incorporated into the side wall of the main stair connecting the archive to the church.

Below The archive's spiral stair is clad in steel. Remnants of the ruins were uncovered during construction and incorporated into the building.

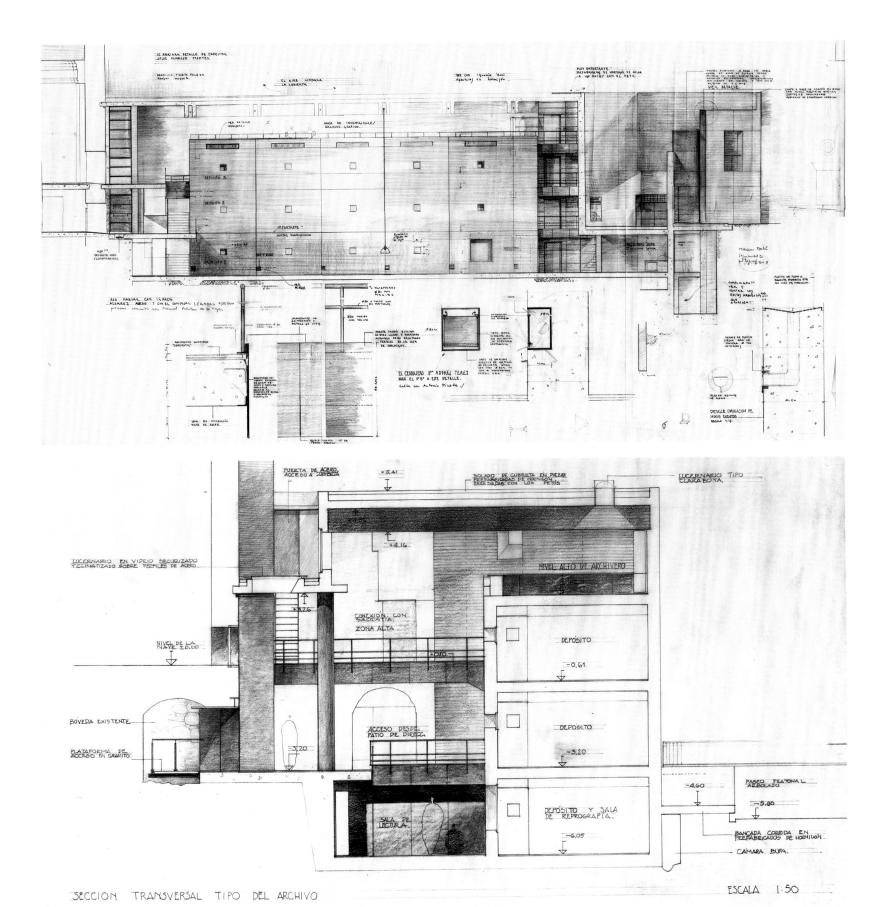

SECCION TRANSVERSAL TIPO DEL ARCHIVO

ESCALA 1:50

Top The elevation of the concrete interior wall of the archive. Small apertures admit light into the space.

Above Short section through the archive.

Maison de l'Architecture

PROJECT	**Maison de l'Architecture**
DESIGNERS	Chartier-Corbasson
LOCATION	Paris, France
DATE	2003

Above The new auditorium of the centre is housed in the chapel of the old Capuchin monastery. It can be configured with raked seating.

Left and opposite, above left The new auditorium floor can be raised by 1 metre (3 feet) to be a stage for performances or it can be lowered flush with the ground, providing totally flexible space. Audio-visual and sound equipment is housed in apertures high up in the walls.

Context

The existing building was once a Capuchin monastery, founded in the seventeenth century. Between 1973 and 1990 the large host space was used as a school of architecture but was vacated and left empty until 2000, when a plan to remodel it into a centre for culture, art and architecture was approved. The designers were commissioned to reconfigure a 930-square-metre (10,000-square-foot) section of the existing building space to house a library, auditorium, café and administrative offices.

Concept

The present building displays a succession of strata laid down at different points in the past. We are convinced that our proposal should be in the form of an operation to be carried out on the existing building in such a way as to be easily legible by everyone, a logical consequence of the history of the site.[1]

Archives and libraries are the cultural storehouses of generations of knowledge and histories. Housing them in adapted buildings, themselves receptacles of layers of history can lead to a rich and complex dialogue between information and space.

A seventeenth-century Capuchin-Franciscan monastery in Paris was converted from a school of architecture into a cultural centre with multi-purpose flexible spaces set against the fixed, focused rooms of the library. Chartier-

Corbasson decided that the layers of history of the existing building could allow them to formulate a strategy for the remodelling of the existing space. They began by scraping back the various layers of the building, noting where accretions and surfaces were at their most dense and most enduring. This resulted in a process of architectural sedimentation, a solidification of the surfaces and atmosphere of the old space, in order to fix it as a backdrop for a series of contemporary insertions.

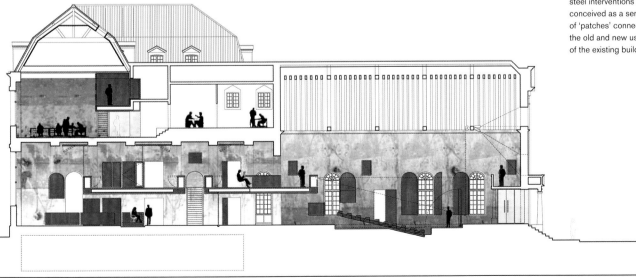

Left The new Corten steel interventions are conceived as a series of 'patches' connecting the old and new uses of the existing building.

Above The sloping rake of seating on the steel platform is accessed by stepping off from the floor of the auditorium.

Organization

The interior is organized around the main chapel, positioned at the back of the L-shaped building towards the street. The entrance to the centre is from the Jardin Villemin, itself entered from Rue des Recollets, a street just in front of the Gare du Nord train station. The entrance is off-axis and requires the visitor to step from the corridor into an adjacent double-height room developed as an extension to the chapel with a set of large steel doors opened to the chapel. The reception and study spaces flow into the bar area that itself spills into the garden. Cellular spaces such as meeting rooms and services, along with a lift, are tucked behind the reception. A wide mezzanine floor above links circulation and can be used as exhibition and/or study space.

What was once the chapel is now a flexible auditorium space. Lectures or performances can take place in the chapel either formally or informally. The room is transformed via the use of a ingenious floor-plane that can be utilized in any one of three ways. It can be set up as a simple, stage-like platform, raised about 1 metre (3 feet) from the floor. It can be adjusted to become a rake of seating or, when not in use, can be recessed into the ground, leaving the space free and flexible for any use. A mezzanine at the back of the room provides a space for projectionists and sound and visual engineers.

The library is situated on the second floor and is housed in a double-height space that runs the full width of the front of the building facing the garden.

Top right
Second-floor plan.
1 Library reading room
2 Mezzanine level

Middle right
First-floor plan.
1 Mezzanine bridge
2 Library meeting rooms

Right
Ground-floor plan.
1 Entrance
2 Reception
3 Chapel
4 Bar/café
5 Meeting rooms

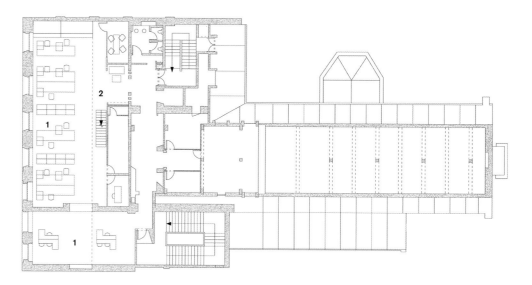

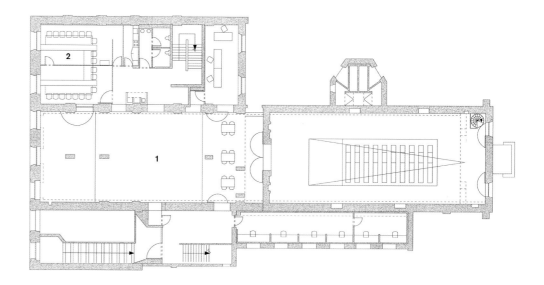

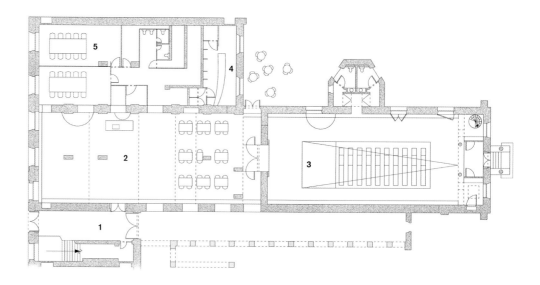

Detail

Layers of history are etched into the walls of the building, an aesthetic the designers have retained and utilized as a backdrop to the crisp new insertions in concrete, steel and glass. They have described the new additions to the space as 'patches', elements that are intended to be links between the history of the building and its new use.

The designers used Corten, a pre-rusted steel that connects the past with the present yet which stands out against the scraped-back existing surfaces of the building. It was used to form the reception desk and bar, doors and window shutters for all rooms including the chapel, and as a screen for the mezzanine level of the second-floor library.

The problems presented by the weight of the material prompted the designers to design a set of overscaled hinges that allow the shutters and doors to be moved easily. Steel panels cover apertures in the walls of the chapel that house projection and sound equipment. These can be easily reconfigured depending on which type of event is taking place in the auditorium.

1 Chartier-Corbasson explaining the concept behind the building, cited at http://www.archdaily.com/66716/maison-de-l'architecture-chartier-corbasson

Top The Corten steel of the bar contrasts with the rough finish of the entrance-room walls. It is located in a small space off the main hall that opens out to a terrace.

Above The deliberately ruinous look of the interiors is exemplified by the reception space with the wide upper-level mezzanine.

Top A Corten steel screen runs the length of the mezzanine in the library. The artfully distressed walls of the space contrast with the contemporary furniture systems.

Above The entrance to the chapel flows from the reception through a large opening screened by tall steel doors.

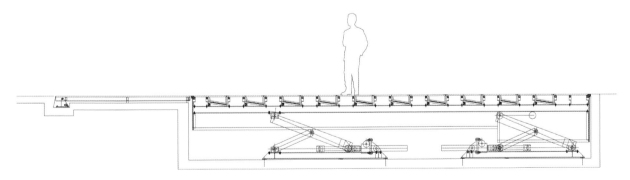

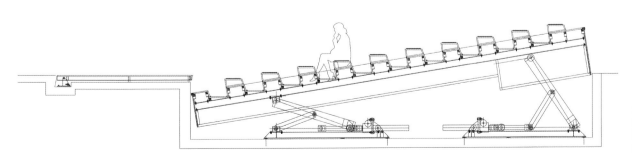

Left The auditorium floor is operated by hydraulics, much like a platform lift.

PROJECT	**Architectural Documentation Centre and Lecture Hall**
DESIGNERS	Jesús Aparicio Guisado and Hector Fernández Elorza (Aparicio + Fernández Elorza)
LOCATION	Madrid, Spain
DATE	2004

Above The auditorium is located in a concrete channel, set into the basement of the long, thin space.

Left The street entrance to the lecture space is via a new steel-and-glass door inserted into the archway of the colonnade on Paseo de la Castellana.

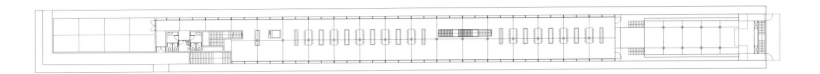

Context

This project was located in an existing one-storey neoclassical arcade in the centre of Madrid. The arcade was connected to the Nuevos Ministerios, the Spanish Ministry of Public Works and Urbanism. The new occupation also extended into a disused subway tunnel that once formed part of an underground railway station beneath the building.

Secundino Zuazo, the architect of the enormous Nuevos Ministerios, had designed the arcade in 1933. The lower-level tunnel had then been built in 1945 as an extension of the Madrid underground rail system. In the 1980s the arcade was partially transformed by Alejandro de la Sota into an exhibition hall.

The de-mapped tunnel was rediscovered while carrying out exploratory work during the feasibility stages of the project. This was a find that altered the designers' strategy, allowing them to excavate the building and reconnect the upper and lower levels of the space whilst also incorporating the long, thin channel within the project.

Concept

Two principal ideas organized the design and construction: first, and essential to any architectural intervention situated in a balanced and natural, or cultural environment, to modify the existing conditions only as absolutely necessary. In this way the space is activated, achieving a qualitative and substantial change while resolving the proposed program. Second. To give the space maximum flexibility so that it may accommodate the different possible uses – as a documentary archives, conference hall and exhibition space.[1]

A robust strategy was employed to remodel this building, one that on the one hand promulgated an almost surgical precision, with regards to any changes to the host, and on the other allowed the space to be reused as it was found.

The unusual dimensions of the host space reinforced this approach, with any new insertions being built to fit. The upper level was 29 metres (95 feet) long, 8.5 metres (28 feet) wide and 13.9 metres (45 feet) high.

The tunnel space in the basement also measured 8.5 metres (28 feet) wide but it was 4.7 metres (15 feet) high and 107 metres (351 feet) long. For much of its length it was located underneath the exhibition level. Therefore the strategy for reuse was based upon direct responses to the vagaries of the host building – an approach that resulted in the new elements being defined by the unusual scale and form of the existing building.

Top The long section expresses the length of the underground tunnel below the colonnade.

Above The basement plan. The gallery is to the left and the auditorium to the right.

Left The atmosphere of the space when in use is conveyed in this free-hand concept sketch by the designers.

Organization

The designers placed a main exhibition hall in the upper level of the space. The documentation centre and lecture hall were located in the subterranean basement tunnel. The unfortunate separation between the upper and lower levels was remedied by the removal of the ground-floor slab from the colonnaded upper hall. The removal of this floor instantly connected the centre with the rail terminus. However, the removal of the floor and the supporting vaults compromised the structural integrity of the building. To remedy this the designers inserted a new concrete channel into the basement. This was a structural element that would house the lecture hall and in turn brace the retaining walls of the space. The concrete channel was set away from the walls of the space in order to increase the autonomous appearance of the element, whilst allowing services such as lighting and electrics to be secreted behind it.

Entrance to the space was configured in two ways: the lecture hall can be accessed through a heavy steel door directly from the Paseo de la Castellana. This independent entrance can be used during a lecture or event. The main entrance to the centre is via the colonnade, which leads directly to the exhibition and archive space that then lead to the auditorium in the basement. The street-level entrance brings the visitor into the lecture space on a steel walkway overlooking the sunken auditorium. They descend to the basement via a steel stair that takes them past the projection booth and spaces for interpreters for the lectures.

Top left The removal of the floor slab of the upper level created a tall top-lit space for the auditorium.

Left The thick concrete wall not only reinforces the structure of the building; it also allows space behind it for the secretion of services such as electricity and lighting.

Top right The upper-storey windows of the colonnade can be blacked out with a large, heavy, black curtain pulled around the space.

Above The basement can be accessed from a street entrance that allows visitors to drop down into the room via a steel-framed structure containing stairs and spaces for projectionists, sound engineers and translators.

Detail

The interior of the building has been finished in a raw and uncompromising manner. Shuttered concrete was left exposed and contrasts with the marks and scratches caused by the process of hollowing out the existing building. No finishes or veneers or plastered surfaces were applied to the interior. Instead, the untreated surfaces of the space project an aesthetic of incompleteness, unifying old and new.

Any new parts inserted into the interior were treated in the same way. The auditorium space is contained in the concrete channel. The steel frame access and service element was made from untreated steel and glass. The exhibition space in the tunnel was formed from a concrete 'tray' inserted into the long, thin space. The markings of the power hammer, used to remove the dilapidated surfaces of the railway tunnel, add texture to the concrete. A new stair was fashioned from thin rods of untreated metal connected to flat steel-plate treads. In order to soften some of this toughness, and to dampen the acoustic issues prevalent in such a space, a heavy black curtain can be drawn around the auditorium, blacking out the space for any projections. Black Arne Jacobsen chairs are lined up ready for an audience, and artificial lighting takes the form of enormous glazed spheres, hung enigmatically in the space.

1 Aparicio + Fernández Elorza, *Architecture + Urbanism*, February 2006, p.60

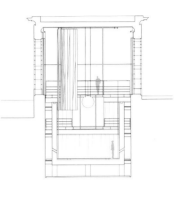

Above The detail of the long section shows the concrete channel and curtain, along with the platform lift that facilitates access to the auditorium.

Right The new auditorium is built to fit the existing channel of space.

Above right The U-shaped concrete channel sits into the basement, bracing the walls of the space.

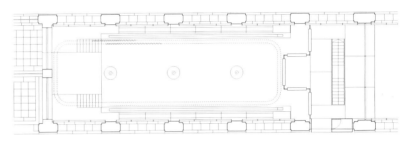

Right The roughly textured walls and the new steel staircase contrast with the polished-concrete floor of the basement.

PROJECT **Fleet Library**

DESIGNERS Monica Ponce de Leon and Nader Tehrani (Office dA)

LOCATION Providence, USA

DATE 2006

Top The grandly scaled banking hall with its barrel-vaulted ceiling has become the host space for the elements of the new library.

Above The host building formed an elaborate backdrop for the housing of over 250 scholars accessing 100,000 new books and periodicals.

Context

Founded in 1878, the Rhode Island School of Design's Fleet Library is one of the oldest art college libraries in the USA. Following the acquisition of the Rhode Island Hospital Trust Bank, the RISD commissioned Office dA to create a new home for the library. The listed host building was designed by York and Sawyer in 1917. It contained a grand barrel-vaulted main hall measuring 55 x 35 metres (180 x 114 feet), topped by an elegant vaulted coffered ceiling. The new library formed part of a development for the university that also included nine storeys of new dormitories occupying the old office spaces above the hall. These were accessed via lifts that also served the library, forging an intimate link between both spaces.

Concept

We wanted to maintain the scale of the banking hall, so we decided to install two objects as if they were informal elements in an ancient ruin.[1]

The designers were commissioned to reuse the existing building in order to house a new and expanded library programme. This included accommodating almost 100,000 books and 400 periodical titles in open shelves, along with space for 250 scholars to read and work. As well as this the library needed the usual multimedia spaces for accessing the collection and administrative offices to support the library in its general day-to-day management.

The existing building was on the National Register of Historic Places, so the designers decided that the new interior would not impact heavily upon the old. This strategy meant that if required, in the future, any new installation could be taken down and deployed elsewhere. Office dA decided to treat the host building as an elaborate backdrop for two new pavilions that were to be installed in the main hall. The pavilions were designed to augment the hall with a new layer of occupation, one that would add a modern resonance to the space. Both pavilions were designed to have a temporary appearance, a quality that would contrast with the more permanent setting of the highly decorative Italianate surroundings. Because of the proximity of the new student accommodation above, the designers also decided to treat the hall as an extension of the dormitories, and create an informal social hub or 'living room' in the library. A strategy that, it was hoped, would entice any reluctant scholars into the space.

Left Two new pavilions containing service, administrative and study spaces were installed in the hall. An informal 'lounge' was created between them which, it was hoped, would attract students from the halls of residence above the library.

Above The two-storey main study pavilion with its 'terrace' of tables and chairs on the upper level.

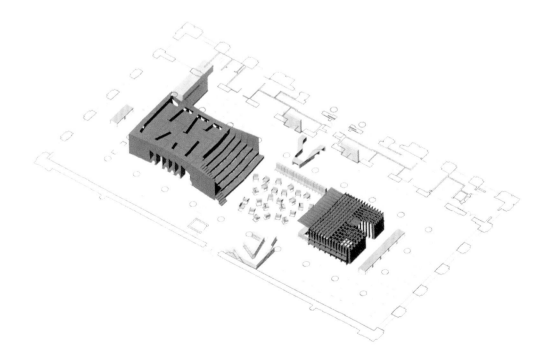

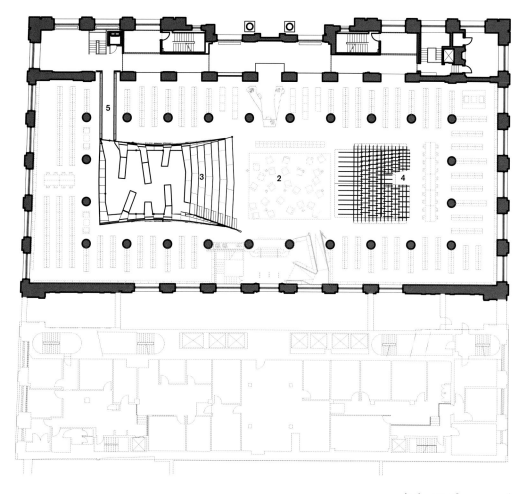

Left First-floor plan. The top of the study pavilion has a bridge linking it to the mezzanine level of the library.

Below left Ground-floor plan. The entrance is via the main corridor or the lifts linking the halls of residence above. The pavilions and central 'lounge' are installed in the main hall. Shelves of books are arranged in a linear fashion around the columns. Quiet spaces are placed at the edges of the large hall.

1 Entrance
2 'Lounge'
3 Study pavilion
4 Help desk
5 Bridge to upper level

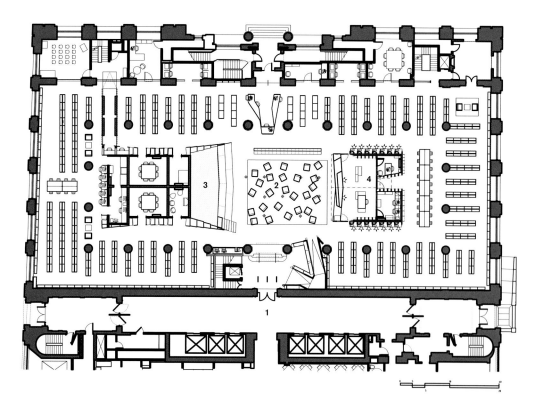

Organization

The main entrance to the library was placed directly opposite the bank of lifts servicing the dorms. This reinforced the connection between the students' home and study areas. The designers accepted the axial organization of the hall and placed the two pavilions centrally at either end of the space. Positioned in between the pavilions, and accessed directly from the lifts, is an informal 'lounge', consisting of low chairs, casual tables and standard lamps, arranged upon a colourful 'carpet' of light brown cork flooring. This comfortable and informal area is the extension of the living accommodation, and is the first space that the student enters. It contrasts deliberately with the formal language of the hall.

The new programmatic requirements of the library ensured that the impressive scale and height of the banking hall had to be fully utilized. Therefore the main study pavilion was designed to maximize its footprint. The double-height structure has an upper level that is accessed by a stair combined with a rake of seating, providing an auditorium for informal gatherings or lectures. Arranged on the ground floor underneath the 'terrace' are private meeting rooms that are acoustically sealed by the pavilion walls. The top level of the pavilion is a study area 'terrace' that also connects to a bridge leading to an upper existing landing of library provision and study spaces. These provide a place for retreat if a student becomes distracted by the grandeur of the hall. The lending and issues desk is contained in a one-storey pavilion, the edges of which contain computer terminals housed within a series of carousels.

Detail

The fabric of the existing building was restored back to its former glory. The marble columns and ceiling were cleaned and repainted in line with the original colour scheme. Budget constraints on the project led to the choice of cheap yet efficient materials. MDF was chosen for its malleability, sustainability and cost effectiveness. The pavilions were constructed from a steel frame and clad in CNC-routed MDF panels. The panels that form the flanks of the study pavilion were cut to accept study booths, whilst the issue desk pavilion was fabricated to house niches for computer terminals. The names of famous authors and thinkers are milled out of the panels along with letters that vary in size – this keeps the pavilion walls from looking overly monumental. Brown cork flooring is used in various 'aggregated' forms and with colours to outline the static spaces and the routes through the interior. This material was chosen to dampen the vast echoing room; its acoustic properties are also supplemented by its resilience and sustainability.

1 Monica Ponce de Leon, Office dA, quoted in *Architectural Record*, June 2007, p.200

Above The help desk in the main administrative pavilion.

Below left A stair that doubled as a rake of seating where an audience could listen to a lecture gives access to the upper level of the study pavilion.

Below centre Students can retreat from the grandeur of the hall into various spaces such as the booths set into the sides of the study pavilion.

Below right The mezzanine area of the hall is accessed via a bridge connected to the top of the study pavilion. Cork flooring is inscribed into the floor to denote the connection between new and old.

PROJECT # CaixaForum

DESIGNERS Herzog & de Meuron;
Patrick Blanc
(vertical garden)

LOCATION Madrid, Spain

DATE 2008

Above The expressive brushed-steel staircase that links the ground floor to the first-floor entrance/reception and ticket counter.

Left The removal of the roof and ground floor, as well as the closing of the existing windows, has heightened the drama of the building as well as increasing its usable floor space and its relationship to the public square.

Context

La Caixa, the philanthropic Spanish savings bank, owns and operates Social and Cultural Outreach Projects, dedicated to programmes in art, music, theatre and literature. Similar to its counterpart in Barcelona, the new CaixaForum in Madrid was realized by the inventive reuse of an existing building – a disused power station in the heart of Madrid. The designers managed to increase the 2,000 square metres (21,500 square feet) of the original building by five times in order to house the new gallery space and its associated functions.

The Central Eléctrica de Mediodía power station was designed by Jesús Carrasco-Muñoz Encina and built in 1900. It was connected to the Paseo del Prado – a prestigious thoroughfare linking the Prado, Thyssen-Bornemisza and Reina Sofia Museums – by a petrol station.

Concept

To become a public building we needed to create public space.[1]

The CaixaForum building was realized with a two-pronged strategy: recontextualize the urban scale of the building and develop the volumetric capacity to contain the necessary spaces to enable the art gallery to function efficiently.

A condition of accepting the commission to design the new forum was that La Caixa also purchased the adjacent petrol station. Its subsequent demolition allowed the designers to create a new public square, one that connected the site to its prestigious neighbours on the Paseo del Prado and which, in turn, linked it to a new public audience. In order to increase its visibility, the gable end of a neighbouring building (forming the side wall of the square) was clad in a vertical garden. The 2,000 plants from 250 species were a direct quote from and a visual link to the botanical garden across the road.

The huge volumetric growth was gained by robustly gutting the power station. The granite plinth upon which it sat was surgically removed, allowing the new public square to flow seamlessly under and into the building. This created a new square that went from the street into the heart of the space.

The brick skin of the old building, complete with windows sills and architraves, suggested an interior that was never there; the large open space had contained huge turbines that powered this side of Madrid. Herzog & de Meuron took the illusory façade one step further by bricking up the windows and topping and tailing the exterior, reducing the skin to a floating masonry curtain. The roof of the building was whipped off and replaced with a new rusting steel skin, one that was based upon a silhouette of the neighbouring skyline.

Above The first-floor reception space contains the ticket desk and bookshop and is a riot of lighting, brushed-steel flooring and exposed structure. Its light-filled qualities contrast with the relative gloom of the lower-floor entrance square.

Above right The new square links the building to the Paseo del Prado and is emphasized by a huge green vertical garden wall, covering the gable end of a neighbouring building.

Right The removal of the lower plinth of the building has created a subterranean public space that flows from the square and then into the city.

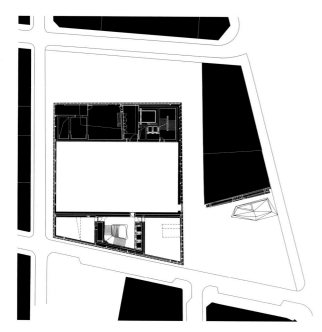

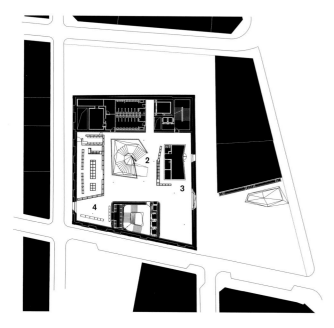

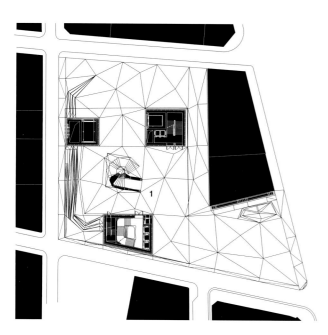

Organization

The robust reworking of the site and building allowed the designers to distribute the programme rationally in two ways. Spaces for events (lectures and so on) and services (car parking, mechanical plant) were placed under the new square and in the basement. The new floor levels inserted into the building above the ground level housed the entrance, galleries, restaurant and offices. The ground floor of the site was designated a public space, one that separated above and below and had provision for open-air shows and a possible café. Vertical circulation was organized into two expressive staircases. The most striking of these is accessed from deep under the floating building and consists of a dramatic, curved, brushed folded-steel stair that connects both the basement and first floor to the ground floor. The main stair is a sculptural concrete structure that links all floors throughout the building.

Two new openings were sliced into the façade. They correspond to the first-floor lobby and second-floor multi-purpose room. The bricked-up façade increases the enigmatic character of the building whilst ensuring that the rest of the gallery spaces are easy to control environmentally. The floating appearance of the building was achieved by making a concrete lining against the inside of the bricks. This is connected via diagonal trusses, some of which span 33 metres (108 feet), to the three vertical circulation cores of the building.

Detail

A robust strategy for the new materials complemented the tough character of the existing building. The heavy new roofscape of the building was clad in huge sheets of perforated steel. Rather than use Corten, a pre-rusted and therefore pre-weathered sheet steel, the designers wanted the rusting of the material to carry on, literally allowing the reddish rainwater to dribble on to and weather the masonry below. Inside the roof is the café, from which the view out of the building is veiled by the random patterns of the steel cladding. At the same time, sunlight is filtered through the gauze of the metal sheets.

The light, shiny, reflective first-floor lobby and the metallic access stair counterpoint the dark and heavy subterranean entry square. The first-floor lobby is a riot of criss-crossing fluorescent lamps, stainless steel floors and exposed structural elements; this playful space offsets the brooding darkness of the space below. The folded-steel stair is a continuation of the faceted steel soffit of the lower-level 'cave'. Walnut cabinetry hung on ceiling cables and suspended in the space forms the ticket desk and shop. The galleries are large, high-ceilinged neutral spaces with white walls, oak floors and adjustable lighting. These can be adapted to suit any type of exhibition configuration.

1 Harry Gugger, Herzog & de Meuron, quoted in *Icon*, April 2008

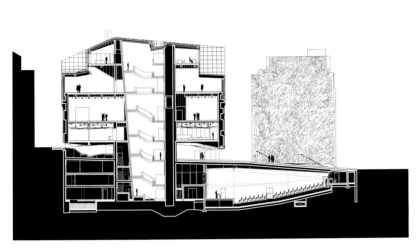

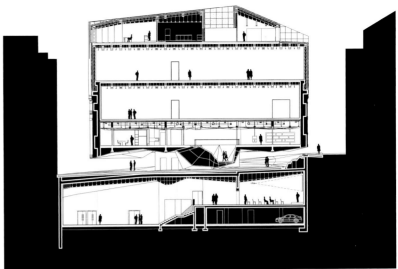

Top left The main stair gives visitors access to the various floors, including the lower-level auditoriums.

Left Each room of the gallery can be reconfigured in a variety of ways to house different scales of exhibition.

Above left The main concrete stair linking all floors of the building.

Above Dappled light is reflected into the café through the perforated-steel sheets of the roof extension. The apertures cut into each panel edit the view out of the space.

Top right The public route from the street continues under the building and right into the heart of the space, from where the new stair leads to the light-filled first floor.

Further reading

GENERAL

Alfoldy, Sandra, and Helland, Janice, *Craft, Space and Interior Design 1855–2005* (Farnham, Surrey: Ashgate, 2008)

Benjamin, Walter, *The Arcades Project* (Cambridge, Massachusetts: Harvard University Press, 2002)

Bourdieu, Pierre, *Distinction: A social critique of taste*, (Cambridge, Massachusetts: Harvard University Press, 1984)

Bourriaud, Nicolas, *Postproduction. Culture as Screenplay: How Art Reprograms the World* (New York: Lukas and Sternberg, 2010)

Breitling, Stefan, and Cramer, Johannes, *Architecture in Existing Fabric* (Basel: Birkhäuser, 2007)

Brooker, Graeme, and Stone, Sally, *Rereadings. Interior Architecture and the Principles of Remodelling Existing Buildings* (London: RIBA Enterprises, 2004)

Brooker, Graeme, and Stone, Sally. *From Organisation to Decoration: A Reader For Interiors* (London: Routledge 2012)

Casson, Hugh, *Inscape* (Oxford: Architectural Press, 1968)

Chang, Chuihua Judy, Inaba, Jeffrey, Koolhas, Rem, and Leong, Sze Tsung (eds.), *Harvard School Guide to Shopping* (Cologne: Taschen, 2001)

Corbusier, Le, *Vers Une Architecture* (first published 1923)

Debord, Guy, *The Society of the Spectacle*, no. 168 (Detroit, Michigan: Black & Red, 1983)

Duffy, Frank, *The Responsive Office: People and Change* (Streatley-on-Thames, Berkshire: Steelcase–Polymath, 1990)

Duffy, Frank, *The New Office* (London: Conran Octopus, 1997)

Edwards, Clive, *Interior Design: A critical introduction* (London: Berg, 2010)

Forty, Adrian, *Objects of Desire, Design and Society Since 1750* (London: Thames and Hudson, 1986)

Harvey, David, *The Condition of Postmodernity* (Oxford: Blackwell, 1990)

Hollein, Hans, and Cooke, Catherine, *Vienna Dream and Reality 1870–1930* (New York: St Martin's Press, 1986)

Hughes, Philip, *Exhibition Design* (London: Laurence King, 2010)

Jenkins Keith, *Re-Thinking History* (London: Routledge, 1991)

Kiesler, Friedrich, *Designer* (Ostfildern: Hatje Cantz, 2005)

Kracauer, Siegfried, *The Mass Ornament. Weimar Essays* (Cambridge, Massachusetts: Harvard University Press, 1995)

Kroloff, Reed, *Architecture by the Numbers: Winka Dubbledam and the Mathematics of Performance Design* (New York: Princeton Architectural Press, 2006)

Kurtich, John, and Eakin, Garret, *Interior Architecture* (New York: Van Nostrand Reinhold, 1996)

Littlefield, David, and Lewes, Saskia, *Architectural Voices. Listening to Old Buildings* (Hoboken, New Jersey: Wiley, 2007)

Lorenc, Jan, Skolnick, Lee, and Berger, Craig, *What is exhibition design?* (Hove: Rotovision, 2007)

Onions, C.T., *The Shorter Oxford English Dictionary – On Historical Principles*, third edition (Oxford: Oxford University Press, 1972)

Powell, Kenneth, *Architecture Reborn. Converting Old Buildings for New Uses* (London: Laurence King, 1999)

Rice, Charles, *The Emergence of the Interior* (London: Routledge, 2007)

Robert, Philippe, *Adaptations: New Uses For Old Buildings* (New York: Princeton Architectural Press, 1989)

Rojek, Chris, *Capitalism and Leisure Theory* (London: Tavistock Publications, 1985)

Salcedo Doris, *Doris Salcedo* (London: Phaidon, 2000)

Schittich, Christian, *Creative Conversions. Building in Existing Fabric. Architecture in Detail* (Basel: Birkhäuser, 2003)

Scott, Fred, *On Altering Architecture* (London: Routledge, 2008)

Short, Robert, *Dada And Surrealism* (London: Laurence King, 1994)

Sparke, P., Massey, A., Keeble, T., and Martin, B. (eds.), *Designing the Modern Interior: From the Victorians to Today* (London: Berg, 2009)

Woodward, Christopher, *Cafés and Bars. The Architecture of Public Display* (London: Routledge, 2007)

HOME

Ambaaz, Emilio, *Italy the New Domestic Landscape. Achievements and Problems of Italian Design*, exhibition catalogue (New York: Museum of Modern Art, 1972)

Benton, Tim, *The Villas of Le Corbusier 1920–1930* (London: Yale University Press, 1987)

Bourriaud, Nicolas, *Postproduction. Culture as Screenplay: How Art Reprograms the World* (New York: Lukas & Sternberg, 2002)

Brino, Giovanni, *Carlo Mollino: Architecture as Biography* (London: Thames and Hudson, 2005)

Cohen, Jean-Louis, *Le Corbusier Le Grand* (London: Phaidon, 2008)

Colomina, Beatriz, *Sexuality and Space* (New York: Princeton Architectural Press, 1999)

De Alba, Roberto, *Paul Rudolph The Late Work* (New York: Princeton Architectural Press, 2003)

Evans, David, *Appropriation* (Cambridge, Massachusetts: MIT Press, 2009)

Ferrari, Fulvio and Napoleone, *The Furniture of Carlo Mollino* (London: Phaidon, 2006)

Ferrari, Fulvio and Napoleone, *Carlo Mollino–Arabesques* (Milan: Electa, 2007)

Frampton, Kenneth, and Vellay, Marc, *Pierre Chareau – Architect and Craftsman* (London: Thames and Hudson, 1985)

Kalkin, Adam, *Architecture and Hygiene* (London: Batsford, 2002)

Kries, Mateo, and Von Vegesack, Alexander (eds.), *Joe Colombo – inventing the future* (Weil am Rhein: Vitra, 2005)

McLean, Will, Quik Build, *Adam Kalkin's ABC of Container Architecture* (London: Bibliotheque McLean, 2008)

Morris, Alison, *John Pawson: Plain Space* (London: Phaidon, 2010)

Ranalli, George, *Buildings and projects* (New York: Princeton Architectural Press, 1988)

Sudjic, Deyan, *John Pawson Works* (London: Phaidon, 2005)

Wood, Ghislaine, *Surreal Things: Surrealism and Design* (London: V&A Publications, 2007)

WORK

Breitling, Stefan, and Cramer, Johannes, *Architecture in Existing Fabric. Planning, Designing, Building* (Basel: Birkhäuser, 2007)

Duffy, Francis, *The New Office* (London: Conran Octopus, 1997)

Futagawa, Yukio, *Steven Holl* (New York: GA Document Extra, 1996)

Garofalo, Francesco, *Steven Holl* (London: Thames and Hudson, 2003)

Holl, Steven, *Anchoring* (New York: Princeton Architectural Press, 1989)

Hudson, Jennifer, *Interior Architecture: From Brief to Build* (London: Laurence King, 2010)

Hudson, Jennifer, *Interior Architecture Now* (London: Laurence King, 2007)

Myerson, Jeremy, and Ross, Philip, *Space To Work. New Office Design* (London: Laurence King, 2006)

Myerson, Jeremy, and Ross, Philip, *The Twenty-first Century Office* (London: Laurence King, 2003)

Nicholson, Ben, *Appliance House* (Cambridge, Massachusetts, MIT Press, 1990)

Powell, Kenneth, *Architecture Reborn. Converting Old Buildings for New Uses* (London: Laurence King, 1999)

Robert, Philippe, *Adaptations: New Uses For Old Buildings* (New York: Princeton Architectural Press, 1989)

Tagliabue, Benedetta, *EMBT Work in Progress* (Barcelona: COAC, 2005)

RETAIL

Barthes, Roland, *Empire of Signs* (originally published in 1970)

Beltramini, Guido (ed.), *Carlo Scarpa: Architecture Atlas* (Vicenza: Centro Internazionale di Studi di Architettura Andrea Palladio, 2006)

Bock, Ralf, *Adolf Loos: Works and Projects* (Milan: Skira 2007)

Brooker, Graeme, and Stone, Sally, *Context and Environment* (London: AVA Academia, 2008)

Chung, Chuihua Judy, Inaba, Jeffrey, Koolhas, Rem, and Leong, Sze Tsung, *The Harvard Design School Guide to Shopping/Harvard Design School Project on the City 2* (Cologne: Taschen, 2002)

Dal Co, Francesco, and Mazzariol, Giuseppe (eds.), *Carlo Scarpa: The Complete Works* (New York: Rizzoli, 1985)

Fitoussi, Brigitte, *Showrooms* (New York: Princeton Architectural Press, 1988)

Gravagnuolo, Benedetto, *Adolf Loos* (London: Art Data, 1982)

Gruneberg, Christoph, and Hollein, Max, *Shopping – A Century of Art and Consumer Culture* (Ostfildern: Hatje Cantz Publishers, 2002)

Jencks, Charles, *Architecture Today* (San Francisco: Harry Abrams, 1988)

Los, Sergio, *Carlo Scarpa* (Cologne: Taschen, 1994)

Los, Sergio, *Carlo Scarpa: An Architectural Guide* (Verona: Arsenale Editrice, 1995)

Manuelli, Sarah, *Design For Shopping: New Retail Interiors* (London: Laurence King, 2006)

Olsberg, Nicholas, *Carlo Scarpa: Intervening With History* (New York: Monacelli Press, 1999)

Opel, Adolf (ed.), *Ornament and Crime – Selected Essays* (Riverside, California: Ariadne Press, 1998)

Pettena, Gianni, *Hans Hollein – Works 1960–1988* (London: IDEA Books, 1988)

Patteeuw, Veronique, *Fresh Facts: The Best New Buildings by Young Architects in the Netherlands* (Rotterdam: NAi Publishers, 2002)

Ramakers, Renny, *Less More: DROOG Design in Context* (Rotterdam: 010 Publishers, 2002)

Ramakers, Renny, and Bakker, Gijs (eds.), *DROOG Design: Spirit of the Nineties* (Rotterdam: 010 Publishers, 1998)

Saito, Yutaka, *Carlo Scarpa* (Tokyo: TOTO Shuppan, 1997)

Stewart, Janet, *Fashioning Vienna: Adolf Loos' Cultural Criticism.* (London: Routledge, 2000)

Tagliabue, Benedetta, *EMBT Work in Progress* (Barcelona: COAC, 2005)

Vernet, David, and de Wit, Leontine, *Boutiques and Other Retail Spaces – The Architecture of Seduction* (London: Routledge, 2007)

DISPLAY

Anderson, Maxwell, *L. Scanning: The Aberrant Architectures of Diller and Scofidio* (New York: Whitney Museum of American Art, 2003)]

Beltramini, Guido (ed.), *Carlo Scarpa: Architecture Atlas* (Vicenza: Centro Internazionale di Studi di Architettura Andrea Palladio, 2006)

Bezombes, Dominique, *La Grande Galerie du Muséum National d'Histoire Naturelle* (Paris: Les Editions du Moniteur, 1994)

Dal Co, Francesco, and Mazzariol, Giuseppe (eds.), *Carlo Scarpa: The Complete Works* (New York: Rizzoli, 1985)

Dernie, David, *Exhibition Design* (London: Laurence King, 2006)

Diller, Richard, and Scofidio, Elizabeth, *Flesh–Architectural Probes* (New York: Princeton Architectural Press, 1994)

Fehn, Sverre, *The Poetry of the Straight Line* (Helsinki: Museum of Finnish Architecture, 1992)

Huber, Antonella, *The Italian Museum: The Conversion of Historic Spaces into Exhibition Spaces* (Milan: Edizioni Lybra, 1997)

Hughes, Philip, *Exhibition Design* (London: Laurence King, 2010)

Lepik, Andres, *OM Ungers. Cosmos of Architecture* (Ostfildern: Hatje Cantz, 2006)

Molinari, Luca, *Diller + Scofidio + Renfro. The Ciliary Function. Works and Projects 1979–2007* (Milan: Skira, 2007)

Norberg-Schultz, Christan, and Postiglione, Gennaro, *Sverre Fehn – Works, Projects, Writings 1949–1996* (New York: Monacelli Press, 1998)

Ungers, OM, and Vieths, S.,*The Dialectic City*, (Milan: Skira, 1997)

Weston, Richard, *Plans, Sections and Elevations. Key Buildings of the Twentieth Century* (London: Laurence King, 2004)

LEISURE

Almaas, Ingerid Helsing, *Vienna: Objects and Rituals. Architecture in Context* (Cologne: Ellipsis/Konemann, 1997)

Bangert, Albrecht, and Riewoldt, Otto, *New Hotel Design* (London: Laurence King, 1993)

Billcliffe, Roger, *Charles Rennie Macintosh. The Complete Furniture, Drawings and Interior Designs* (Cambridge: Lutterworth Press,1979)

Brooker, Graeme, and Stone, Sally, *Context and Environment: Site & Ideas* (London: AVA Publishing, 2008)

Bock, Ralf, *Adolf Loos: Works and Projects* (Milan: Skira 2007)

Crawford, Alan, *Charles Rennie Mackintosh* (London: Thames and Hudson, 1995)

Fitoussi, Brigitte, *Hotel* (Paris: Les Editions du Moniteur, 1992)

Grafe, Christoph, and Bollerey, Franziska, *Cafés and Bars: The Architecture of Public Display* (London: Routledge, 2007)

Gravagnuolo, Benedetto, *Adolf Loos* (London: Art Data 1982)

McDermott, Catherine (ed)., *Plans and Elevations: Ben Kelly Design* (London: Phaidon, 1990)

Opel, Adolf (ed.), *Ornament and Crime – Selected Essays* (Riverside, California: Ariadne Press, 1998)

Risselda, Max (ed.), *Raumplan Versus Plan Libre: Adolf Loos and Le Corbusier 1919–1930* (New York: Rizzoli, 1988)

Pevsner, Nikolaus, *Pioneers of Modern Design: From William Morris to Walter Gropius* (Harmondsworth: Penguin, 1984)

Savage, Jon, *The Haçienda Must Be Built* (London: International Music Publications, 1992)

Index

Picture credits

Specified drawings are supplied courtesy of Josephine Howes and Lizzie Munro. All other architectural drawings are supplied courtesy of the respective architects and remain the © copyright of the architects, unless otherwise specified. These drawings are for private reference and not for third-party reproduction.

All reasonable attempts have been made to clear copyright and attribute the image credits correctly, but should there be any inadvertent omission, or error, the publisher will insert the appropriate acknowledgement in subsequent printings of the book.

Front cover and endpapers: Olivetti Showroom by Carlo Scarpa, FAI. ©2012. Mark E. Smith/Scala, Florence
Back cover: American Bar by Adolf Loos. AKG-images/ Erich Lessing
6: Courtesy of COUSSÉE & GORIS Architecten: photographer Wim Van Nueten
7: Practice Architecture
8tl: Graeme Brooker
8tr: Surface Architects
9t: Lehrer Architects / Benny Chan/Photoworks
9b: Alberto Ferrero
10: © Associazione Archivio Storico Olivetti, Ivrea, Italy / Mario Giacomelli
11: Allan Wexler
12: Nigel Dickinson / Alamy
13tl: AKG Images / Ullstein Bild
13tr: Courtesy Toyo Ito & Associates, Architects
13b: John McCann / RIBA Library Photographs Collection
14tl: Estate of Gordon Matta-Clark on deposit at the Canadian Centre for Architecture, Montreal / © 2012 Estate of Gordon Matta-Clark / Artists Rights Society (ARS), New York, DACS, London
14tr: Cornbread Works / www.cornbreadworks.nl / Zecc Architects / www.zecc.nl
15: © Paul Warchol Photography
16t: © Jordi Sarra Arau
16b: © Michael Carapetian. Photographer
17: By kind permission of Professor Kenneth Frampton
18t: By kind permission of Professor Kenneth Frampton
18bl+br: © Jordi Sarra Arau
19t+b: © Jordi Sarra Arau
20tc+tr: © Michael Carapetian. Photographer
20br: © Jordi Sarra Arau
21t: © Michael Carapetian. Photographer
21br: By kind permission of Professor Kenneth Frampton
22t: L2-5-22-001 © FLC / ADAGP, Paris and DACS, London 2012
22b: L2-510-001 © FLC / ADAGP, Paris and DACS, London 2012
23tl: 33406 © FLC / ADAGP, Paris and DACS, London 2012
23tr: 17439 © FLC / ADAGP, Paris and DACS, London 2012
24t: 17438 © FLC / ADAGP, Paris and DACS, London 2012
24b: 17441 © FLC / ADAGP, Paris and DACS, London 2012
25tc: L2-5-33-001 © FLC / ADAGP, Paris and DACS, London 2012
25tr: L2-5-32-001 © FLC / ADAGP, Paris and DACS, London 2012
25cr: L2-5-18-001 © FLC / ADAGP, Paris and DACS, London 2012
25br: L2-5-16-001 © FLC / ADAGP, Paris and DACS, London 2012
26t: Courtesy Museo Casa Mollino
26b: Drawn by Lizzie Munro
27–9: Courtesy Museo Casa Mollino
30–3: Studio Joe Colombo, Milan
34t+b: Nick Wheeler / Architectural Digest
35t+b: George Ranalli Architects
36: Drawings: George Ranalli Architects
36cr+br: George Ranalli

37tl+tr+b: George Cserna
38t+b: Peter Aaron / OTTO
39c: LC-USZ62-123771 Paul Rudolph Archive/Library of Congress, Prints & Photographs Division
39b: LC-USZ62-123770 Paul Rudolph Archive/Library of Congress, Prints & Photographs Division
40tl: LC-USZ62-123773 Paul Rudolph Archive/Library of Congress, Prints & Photographs Division
40cl: LC-USZ62-123774 Paul Rudolph Archive/Library of Congress, Prints & Photographs Division
40bl: LC-USZ62-123775 Paul Rudolph Archive/Library of Congress, Prints & Photographs Division
41tc+tr+br+bc: Peter Aaron / OTTO
42t+b: © Richard Glover / VIEW
43: © John Pawson
44: Drawings: © John Pawson
44b: © Richard Glover / VIEW
45t+c+b: © Richard Glover / VIEW
46–49t: Peter Aaron / Esto
49b: Courtesy of Adam Kalkin
50t+b: Emma Cross
51t: Courtesy of Multiplicity
51b: Drawn by Josephine Howes
52: Multiplicity
53tl+b: Emma Cross
53tr: Sonal Dave architect ©Multiplicity
53tc+c: Tim O'Sullivan architect ©Multiplicity
54: Frank Lloyd Wright (1867–1959): Larkin Company Administration Building. Interior court view. 1905. Scottsdale (AZ), The Frank Lloyd Wright Foundation. © 2012. The Frank Lloyd Wright Fdn, AZ / Art Resource, NY/Scala, Florence. © ARS, NY and DACS, London 2012.
55tl: Paul Tolenaar for ReUrba 2 courtesy of Matthew Lloyd Architects
55cl: © Gerald Zugmann / www.zugmann.com
55tr: © Deidi von Schaewen / www.deidivonschaewen.com
56tl: Courtesy of FAT
p56tr: Hans Jürgen Landes / courtesy Behnisch Architekten – Stefan Behnisch, Martin Haas, David Cook
57: Fielden Clegg Bradley studios
58-60: Quickborner Team, Hamburg
62t+b: Ferran Freixa
63t: Miralles Tagliabue EMBT
63b: Ferran Freixa
64: Miralles Tagliabue EMBT
65tl+tr: Ferran Freixa
66t+b: © Richard Davies
67tl+tr+cr+cl: © Powell-Tuck, Connor & Orefelt
66br: © Richard Davies
68tl+tr: © Powell-Tuck, Connor & Orefelt
69tl+tr+cr+cl: © Richard Davies
70tl+tr: © Paul Warchol Photography
71–2: © Steven Holl Architects
73bl+br: © Paul Warchol Photography
74t+b: Courtesy Brooks + Scarpa / © Marvin Rand
75: Drawn by Josephine Howes
76–7: Courtesy Brooks + Scarpa / © Marvin Rand
78t+b: © Duccio Malagamba
79tl+tr: © Duccio Malagamba
79cr+br: Miralles Tagliabue EMBT
80: Drawn by Josephine Howes
81: © Duccio Malagamba
82t: Klein Dytham Architecture
82b: Drawn by Lizzie Munro
83: Klein Dytham Architecture
84tr+cr: Klein Dytham Architecture
84b: Klein Dytham Architecture
85tl+tr+cr+cl: Klein Dytham Architecture
85b: Klein Dytham Architecture
86: © Kilian O'Sullivan / VIEW
86c: SURFACE Architects
86bc: SURFACE Architects
87tl: SURFACE Architects
87tr: © Kilian O'Sullivan / VIEW

87br: SURFACE Architects
88: SURFACE Architects
89tc+tr: © Kilian O'Sullivan / VIEW
89bc: SURFACE Architects
90: TopFoto
91tr+cr: AKG-Images
91br: © 2012 Austrian Frederick and Lillian Kiesler Private Foundation, Vienna
92tl: John Maltby / RIBA Library Photographs Collection
92tr: © Peter Cook / VIEW
93t: Amin Linke / amin@aminlinke.com / © OMA/ DACS 2012
93cr: David Grandorge / courtesy of 6a Architects
g93br: Comme des Garçons
94t: Albertina, Vienna / www.albertina.at
94b: ORCH Chemollo / RIBA Library Photographs Collection
95tr: ORCH Chemollo / RIBA Library Photographs Collection
96: Drawn by Lizzie Munro
97tl+tc: Albertina, Vienna / www.albertina.at
97bl+bc: ORCH Chemollo / RIBA Library Photographs Collection
98t+b: © Associazione Archivio Storico Olivetti, Ivrea, Italy / Mario Giacomelli
99tl+tc: Drawn by Josephine Howes
99br: © Associazione Archivio Storico Olivetti, Ivrea, Italy
100cl: © Associazione Archivio Storico Olivetti, Ivrea, Italy / Ugo Mulas
100br: © Mark E. Smith Photography
101t+b: © Associazione Archivio Storico Olivetti, Ivrea, Italy / Paolo Monti
102t+b: Atelier Hans Hollein / Franz Hubmann
103tl+tr+cl: Atelier Hans Hollein
104t: Atelier Hans Hollein
104bl+br: Atelier Hans Hollein / Franz Hubmann
105bl+br: Atelier Hans Hollein / Franz Hubmann
106t+b: © Hiroyuki Hirai
107t+b: Kuramata Design Office
108-9: © Hiroyuki Hirai
110: DROOG
111t: Drawn by Lizzie Munro
111b: DROOG
112–13: DROOG
114–17: Courtesy of William Russell/Pentagram
118t+b: © Duccio Malagamba
119: Miralles Tagliabue EMBT
120bc+br: Miralles Tagliabue EMBT / Alex Gaultier
121tl: Miralles Tagliabue EMBT / Alex Gaultier
121tr: © Inigo Bujedo Aguirre / VIEW
121bl: © Duccio Malagamba
122t: Comme des Garçons
122b: © Ed Reeve / VIEW
123t: Comme des Garçons
123b: © Ed Reeve / VIEW
124–5: Comme des Garçons
126t+b: Roos Aldershoff
127: Merkx + Girod
128cr+br: Roos Aldershoff
128c+bl: Merkx + Girod
129: Roos Aldershoff
130: INTERFOTO / Alamy
131tl: Installation view of the exhibition 'Machine Art' (MoMA 1934). New York, Museum of Modern Art (MoMA). Photo by Wurts Brothers; IN34.2 ©2012. Digital image. The Museum of Modern Art, New York/ Scala, Florence
131tr: © 2012 Austrian Frederick and Lillian Kiesler Private Foundation, Vienna
132tl: © Collection Artedia / VIEW
132bc: Kurt Schwitters Archives at the Sprengel Museum Hannover / photographer: Wilhelm Redemann, Hannover / repro: Michael Herling / Aline Gwose, Sprengel Museum, Hannover © DACS, London 2012
132bl: © Fondazione Franco Albini
133b: Atelier Hans Hollein / Georg Riha

134t: Courtesy of Ken Christian
134b: Morley von Sternberg
135t: LAND Design Studio
136t: © Massimo Listri / CORBIS
136c: Archivio Carlo Scarpa / Museo di Castelvecchio / Comune di Verona
136bc: Vaclav Sedy © CISA – A. Palladio
137tl+cl+tr: Archivio Carlo Scarpa / Museo di Castelvecchio / Comune di Verona
138tl: © Alessandra Chemollo
138tc+tr: Archivio Carlo Scarpa / Museo di Castelvecchio / Comune di Verona
138bl: Vaclav Sedy © CISA – A. Palladio
138bc: © Luca Campigotto
139cl+cr: Archivio Carlo Scarpa / Museo di Castelvecchio / Comune di Verona
139bl: Stefan Buzas © CISA – A. Palladio
139bc: © Luca Campigotto
140t: The National Museum of Art, Architecture and Design, Oslo, Norway
140b: Graeme Brooker
141–2: The National Museum of Art, Architecture and Design, Oslo, Norway
143cl: The National Museum of Art, Architecture and Design, Oslo, Norway
143cr+br+bc: Graeme Brooker
144t: © Dieter Leistner / ARTUR / VIEW
144b: © Barbara Staubach / ARTUR / VIEW
145tr+bc+bl: Courtesy Deutsches Architekturmuseum (DAM), Frankfurt am Main
146tl: Courtesy Deutsches Architekturmuseum (DAM), Frankfurt am Main
146cl: © Dieter Leistner / ARTUR / VIEW
147t+b: © Dieter Leistner / ARTUR / VIEW
148t: © Collection Artedia / VIEW
148b: © Stephane Couturier / Artedia / VIEW
149t+b: © Stephane Couturier / Artedia / VIEW
150: Drawn by Josephine Howes / project materials courtesy Yvette Langrand
151cr: Jean Simounet
151bl+br: © Stephane Couturier / Artedia / VIEW
152t: © Mario Carrieri
152b: CuboImages srl / Alamy
153tr+br: Courtesy Canali Associati s.r.l
153bl: © Mario Carrieri
154t: Courtesy Canali Associati s.r.l
154cl+cr: © Mario Carrieri
155tl+tc+c: © Mario Carrieri
155cl+c: Courtesy Canali Associati s.r.l
156–9: Project credits: Paul Chemetov & Borja Huidobro © ADAGP, Paris and DACS, London 2012
156t: © Collection Artedia / VIEW
156br: AUA Paul Chemetov / www.paulchemetov.com / © ADAGP, Paris and DACS, London 2012
157: Drawn by Lizzie Munro
158tl: © Collection Artedia / VIEW
158cl: AUA Paul Chemetov / www.paulchemetov.com / © ADAGP, Paris and DACS, London 2012
159tl+tr+br+bl: © Artedia / VIEW
160t+b: © Seth Taras for Casson Mann
161tr+cr: © Casson Mann
161b: © Casson Mann
162: © Casson Mann
163tl+tr: © Seth Taras for Casson Mann
164t: Land Design Studio (photo: Nick Wood)
164b: © Philip Bier / VIEW
165t+c: LAND Design Studio
165b: AEG
166–7: LAND Design Studio
168: AKG-Images / Imagno
169tl: Image supplied courtesy Special Collections and Archives, University of Liverpool / © DACS 2012
169tr: Art & Architecture Collection, Miriam and Ira D. Wallach Division of Art, Prints and Photographs, The New York Public Library, Astor, Lenox and Tilden Foundations / ID 1555769. © DACS 2012

170tl+tr: Nigel Coates
170b: Graeme Brooker
17tl: © Dennis Gilbert / VIEW
171tr: Anoushka Hempel Design
172t: © The Hunterian, University of Glasgow 2012
172b: T&R Annan & Sons Ltd
173t: © The Hunterian, University of Glasgow 2012
173cr: Architectural Press Archive / RIBA Library Photographs Collection
174cl+bl: T&R Annan & Sons Ltd
175: Images Courtesy of Glasgow City Council: Archives
176t: AKG-Images / Erich Lessing
176b: AKG-Images / János Kalmár
177t: AKG-Images / Erich Lessing
178: Drawn by Lizzie Munro
179t: Albertina, Vienna / www.albertina.at
180: © Ben Kelly
181–2: © Ben Kelly Design
183: © Ben Kelly
184t: © Richard Bryant / ARCAID
184b: Starck Network / www.starck.com
185tl: © Richard Bryant / ARCAID
185r: Drawn by Lizzie Munro
186: © Tim Street-Porter / www.timstreetporter.com
187tl: © Richard Bryant / ARCAID
187tr: © Tim Street-Porter / www.timstreetporter.com
188t: © Harald Schönfellinger
188b: © Paolo Utimpergher / www.utimpergher.it
189: Drawings supplied courtesy Hermann Czech Architect
190tl+tr+br: © Paolo Utimpergher / www.utimpergher.it
191bl: © Paolo Utimpergher / www.utimpergher.it
191cr: © James Morris / VIEW
192t+b: © Jakob + MacFarlane / N. Borel Photography
193tr+cr: © Jakob + MacFarlane
193br: © Jakob + MacFarlane / N. Borel Photography
194t: © Jakob + MacFarlane
194cl: © Collection Artedia / VIEW
194bl: © Jakob + MacFarlane
195t: © Jakob + MacFarlane
195bl+br: © Jakob + MacFarlane / N. Borel Photography
195bc: © Collection Artedia / VIEW
196t+b: © Michael Moran
197t+b: Courtesy of Diller Scofidio + Renfro
198t: Drawn by Josephine Howes
198b–9: © Michael Moran
200–3: RARE Architecture
204–5: Derryck Menere / info@derryckmenere.com /Neri&Hu
206l: Neri&Hu
206tr–7bl+r: Derryck Menere / info@derryckmenere.com/Neri&Hu
207tl: Tuomas Uusheimo
208: Neri&Hu
209bl: Neri&Hu
209tr: Tuomas Uusheimo
209cr+br: Derryck Menere / info@derryckmenere.com/Neri&Hu
210: Graeme Brooker
211tl: Velvet and Silk Café by Ludwig Mies van der Rohe (1886–1969) and Lily Reich (1885–1947). Women's Fashion exhibition, Berlin, 1927. New York, Museum of Modern Art (MoMA). Mies van der Rohe Archive, gift of the architect. Acc. N.L139.©2012 Digital image Mies van der Rohe/Gift of the Architect/ MoMA/Scala / © DACS 2012
211tr: © Mark E. Smith Photography
211br: © Richard Glover / VIEW
212tl+tr: Morley von Sternberg
212b: Philip Vile
213tl+tr: © Peter Cook / VIEW
214tl: The Glasgow School of Art
214tr+bc: © Crown Copyright: RCAHMS. Licensor www.rcahms.gov.uk

215t: © The Hunterian, University of Glasgow 2012
216tl: Nicholas Breach / RIBA Library Photographs Collection
216tr: Edwin Smith / RIBA Library Photographs Collection
217t+br: The Glasgow School of Art
218t+b: Supplied courtesy Levitt Bernstein
219tl+tr: © Andrew Holmes
220tl+tc: Supplied courtesy Levitt Bernstein
220b: © Levitt Bernstein
221tl: © Levitt Bernstein
221tr: © Matthew Weinreb / www.thearchitecturalphotographer.com
222t: © Christian Richters
222c: © Mecanoo Architects
223tr+cr: Drawn by Josephine Howes
223c+br+bc: © Mecanoo Architects
224tl+cl: © Mecanoo Architects
224bl: © Christian Richters
225l: © Mecanoo Architects
225tr+cr+br+bl:© Christian Richters
226tl+tr+c: © Ulrich Schwarz / www.architektur-fotografie.net
226b: Klaus Block
227tr+c: © Ulrich Schwarz / www.architektur-fotografie.net
227cr: Klaus Block
228l: Klaus Block
228br: Drawn by Lizzie Munro
229tr+c+cr+br: © Ulrich Schwarz / www.architektur-fotografie.net
230–5: Mendaro Corsini Arquitectos
236–7: Courtesy Chartier-Corbasson Architects
238: Drawn by Lizzie Munro
239: Courtesy Chartier-Corbasson Architects
240t+b: © Roland Halbe
241t+br: Aparicio + Fernández Elorza
242tl+tc+c+bl: © Roland Halbe
243tc+tr+cr: Aparicio + Fernández Elorza
243br: © Roland Halbe
244t+c: John Horner
245tr: John Horner
245bl: Office dA
246tl+bl: Office dA
247tr+br+bc+bl: John Horner
248-9: © Duccio Malagamba / Herzog & de Meuron
250: © 2012, Herzog & de Meuron Basel
251tl+tr: © 2012, Herzog & de Meuron Basel
251cl+cr+bl: © Duccio Malagamba / Herzog & de Meuron

Author's acknowledgements

This book would not have been possible without the assistance and support of a number of people. At the University of Brighton I would like to thank Professor Anne Boddington and Dr Catherine Harper (now Dean of the University of East London) for supporting my sabbatical in order to undertake the majority of the work on this book. Philip Cooper and Liz Faber at Laurence King deserve many thanks for their perseverance and support throughout the project, along with my appreciation of their perennial good humour and readiness to apply a moderate twist of the arm when needed.

A huge debt of gratitude is owed to Sophia Gibb for her picture research and her remarkable detective work, unearthing some rare images of projects and locating the sometimes even more elusive photographers and designers responsible for them. Many thanks also to Henrietta Heald and Vanessa Green for their good-natured questioning and occasional mild persuasion during the exemplary editorial and design work, and to Kim Sinclair for her production work. I would like to offer thanks to all the designers, photographers and archivists who have supplied their work for publication, especially VIEW pictures and Yvette Langrand, who so kindly went out of her way to supply information on the Picasso Museum in Paris and the work of Roland Simounet.

I would like to express my gratitude to my 'Wunderkammer' unit students in Brighton, and in particular Josephine Howes and Lizzie Munro for their excellent contribution to the project in the form of a great set of drawings. I would also like to thank all my past students in Cardiff and Manchester, as well as my current ones in Brighton, who have sat through my '10 Rooms' lecture series. The series contained the origins of Key Interiors Since 1900 and these students in one way or other, including those asleep at the back, offered their feedback on the ideas contained in this book.

Finally, thanks to Claire for her patience and resilience, along with some timely critical interjections during the course of the project.